Education
& the Taming
of Power

Other books by Sidney Hook

Academic Freedom and Academic Anarchy
Religion in a Free Society
The Paradoxes of Freedom
The Quest for Being
Political Power and Personal Freedom
Common Sense and the Fifth Amendment
The Ambiguous Legacy: Marx and the Marxists
Heresy, Yes—Conspiracy, No
Education for Modern Man
The Here in History: A Study in Limitation and Possibility
Reason, Social Myths and Democracy
John Dewey: An Intellectual Portrait
From Hegel to Marx
Toward the Understanding of Karl Marx
The Metaphysics of Pragmatism

Education
& the Taming
of Power

Sidney Hook

Open Court Publishing Company
La Salle, Illinois
1973

In homage

To those who have suffered without yielding in the cause of scholarship and academic freedom at home and abroad at the hands of political tyrants, cowardly administrators, colleagues and student mobs.

Contents

Preface

There is a familiar yet profound irony in the history of ideas and outstanding personalities. The heresies and hereties of one period often become the orthodoxes and Establishment figures of another. In the case of John Dewey and his educational ideas, however, there is more paradox than irony. During most of his life his ideas in education were the object of fierce and unjust attack by leading politicians, churchmen, civil and military bureaucrats and corporation executives. This was especially true in the decades before the Second World War when Dewey's ideas had comparatively little influence on the organized school systems of the country. Nonetheless all their faults and limitations were laid at his door. Subsequently some of Dewey's ideas did acquire influence but it was reflected more in the language of educators than in the actual practices of the schools. At the time of his death he was still a strong critic of American education.

In recent years, however, movements of "radical" school reform have developed which have been widely but mistakenly interpreted as either inspired by the ideas of John Dewey or as their natural fruition. If my exposition of his educational philosophy is sound, it will be seen that it is as firmly opposed to these newer movements, even when they invoke his name and words, at to many of the existing educational practices against which they are directed.

John Dewey always warned against the use of labels to characterize complex positions. Today terms like "conservative," "liberal," "radical," "progressive," "right," "left" and their cognate expressions are used so confusingly that, unless precisely defined in relation to specific issues, they are more often obstacles than aids to communication. This is true not only in politics but in education where there is even a greater need for clarity.

The essays collected here reflect the history of American education during the third of a century over which they were written. They focus on recurrent problems and the pendular swings in educational opinion on how they should be solved, on what we should educate for and why. Although some minor changes have been made in the texts in the interests of topical relevance and comprehensibility, and to avoid needless duplication, I have let the essays stand largely as originally published. Despite pruning there still remains an element of inescapable repetition for which I beg the reader's indulgence. Perhaps some mitigation can be found in the fact that my views run against the main currents of educational thought today on many campuses.

Sidney Hook

South Wardsboro, Vermont
July 1973

Acknowledgments

I wish to thank the editors of the periodicals referred to below for permission to reprint as chapters of this book material that previously appeared in their pages.

2   *Harvard Educational Review*, Vol. XXVI, no. 2, Spring 1956
3   *Journal of Philosophy*, Vol. LVI, no. 26, 1959
6   *Papers on Educational Reform*, Vol. II, 1971
7   *Daedalus*, Winter, 1959
8   *The Humanist*, March-April 1969
10 *Encounter*, January 1972
11 *Harvard Educational Review*,Vol. XXXVI, no. 4, Fall 1966
13 *Journal of Medical Education*, Vol. XXXVII, no. 12, 1962
17 *Journal of Higher Education*, Vol. X, no. 1, 1939
18 *School and Society*, July 1956

Part I:

Studies in the Educational Philosophy of John Dewey

1

The Challenge

The time for plain speaking about American education in our day is long past due. A hoax is being perpetrated on the American public in the name of educational "reform," "innovation," and "freedom." The slogan of the marketplace, "the consumer is king," has become axiomatic in influential educational circles that have proclaimed their fundamental hostility to the free enterprise economy in all its forms. From Adam Smith to Friedrich Hayek the theorists of the free market have stressed the indefeasible right of the consumer to buy or sell what he wants without dictation from king or priest or commissar.

Whatever can be said for the slogan, "the consumer is king," as a descriptive or normative concept in understanding and regulating economic affairs, it is a confused and confusing directive for the education of the young. For it is only when students achieve some maturity and an awareness of their educational needs and capacities that they are in a position to make intelligent educational choices.

The ability to make these informed choices is largely a function of the education they have already received, an education that does not depend upon their own untutored decisions, but rather on an adequate exposure to, and exploration of, the great traditions, organized subject matters and disciplines, and the dominant values of civilization. The normal time for autonomous educational decisions is during the mid-college period, after most of a student's general education has been completed.

The disregard of this and related considerations has resulted in a state of affairs in which American students are receiving more schooling than education. The recommendation of some irresponsible educators that therefore it would be well to forgo schooling altogether is comparable to the recommendation to a person suffering from an unhealthy diet that he forgo eating or that he eat anything he pleases. A healthy and mature person may certainly thrive by eating anything he pleases, and a mature well-educated person does not require, and may not even desire, schooling. But just as the obvious, common-sensical remedy for a diet that results in undernourishment is one that is more nourishing, so the remedy for schooling that fails to educate properly is improved schooling.

Until the student has reached a point of maturity where he can undertake his own education with self-knowledge and confidence, the education he receives through schooling must be based on his objective needs. What a young person wants is not always a reliable sign of what he educationally needs. Every experienced teacher will testify to the truth of this proposition. Good teaching consists in stirring and motivating the student to want what he educationally needs—not by coercion or extrinsic rewards, but by the arts of guidance and by evoking an interest in the problem or task to be learned. To a very large extent good teaching consists in the education of wants, desires, and tastes. Unfortunately, the proposition that student wants are not unfailing signs of needs is denied by many of the educational fads and fashions of our time. The consequence is that any learning that does not appear as a by-product of fun or games or is not acquired by the spontaneous outreaching of the student for new experience is denounced as a tyrannical imposition of the values, tastes, and judgments of an older generation upon the captive young. Examples abound on every hand. One educator, in describing a highly touted curricular innovation at his university, proudly stresses the fact that the selection of courses for students was not guided by what was educationally "good for them." He informs us that "serious consideration was given to what the students might *like* to take instead of what would be 'good for them.' "[1] If we ask why the offerings to students could not be made after serious consideration was given to what was educationally good for them, the only intelligible, if not intelligent, answer is that what students *liked* was obviously the best index to what was good for them.

If we believe on the basis of objective evidence that not all things or experiences are good for educational growth, that some things and experiences are educationally better than others, that what we like to do we often regret having done, that the desired is not synonymous with the desirable, then we cannot accept the assumption that what a student likes is what he should get. To be sure, his likes should *always* be considered—but with an eye to strengthening them or correcting them in the light of his educational needs.

It is to this questionable premise—that students' likes are the best indication of their educational needs—that most of the weaknesses and absurdities in the curriculums of our liberal arts colleges can be traced. The unparalleled extension of the elective system to a point where requirements have been abolished not only for specific courses but for general areas of study is another disastrous consequence of this allegedly progressive view. The over-all result is that today one can take little for granted regarding the typical college graduate's knowledge of the past or present, his intellectual skills, and his cultural sensibilities. Granted that there has never been any equivalence between diplomas or degrees awarded by different liberal arts colleges with different faculties and student bodies. But in the past there was something common in the education of college men and women. It may not have been of a very high level and individuals shared it in varying degrees. But it was there.

[1]*New York Times*, August 13, 1972.

Our overriding problem today, in the era of universal access to higher education, is to establish or re-establish a viable common core curriculum for general liberal arts education, and to gear the curriculum of the elementary and secondary school to it. Special educational provisions can be made for those unable to profit from this course of study, but even in their case an orientation toward liberal education should as far as possible be preserved. Those to whom this will appear merely as a return to the educational system of the past are in error. By and large the educational offering of the past was an eclectic overlay on a decayed classical curriculum modified in piecemeal fashion to meet industrial and commercial needs. It was not inspired by any coherent philosophy of education. It grew without planning.

The argument for a general liberal arts education is reasonable and persuasive in the light of the alternatives that have developed. There are common educational needs men and women have that must be met if they wish to feel at home in the modern world. This requires exposure to, and competence in, some bodies of knowledge, the acquisition of certain skills in communication, argument, and evaluation of evidence, and familiarity with the problems, values, and traditions of contemporary society. All this is reinforced by the necessity of developing an intelligent electorate.

The details of such a curriculum will be considered in subsequent chapters; a few remarks here may obviate initial misunderstanding. General education does not constitute the whole of a student's education. There should always be an opportunity for the student at the appropriate time to select courses that relate to those individual needs and powers that are not common but unique to him or her. Nor should the substance of liberal education consist of fixed courses but of subject matters, intellectual skills, and fields of interest. What is constant should be their educational *function*; their specific content and organization should be historical *variables*. For example, fifty years ago a study of contemporary civilizations and their value conflicts would have included only peripheral references to the Orient; today the Orient would be given an inescapable, if not central, emphasis.

4

We may legitimately inquire about the fate of general liberal arts curriculums established in many prestigious American colleges following World War II, which gradually have been eroded by more recent innovative tendencies. By and large these general education curriculums were a move in the right direction. Why, then, did they fail? For a number of reasons.

In most institutions general education curriculums fell victim to the impatience of superior-endowed students desirous of embarking upon specialized careers who, often abetted by the departments of their specialties, sought exemption from their required courses. Instead of exploring the possibility of discriminatory exemption based on intelligent guidance and demonstrated capacity, the question was posed in terms of the retention or abolition of the courses in question. To a large extent the dissatisfaction of these superior students reflected the failure of the teaching in these courses to make the problems and material studied stimulating and intellectually challenging. Because the greatest educational honors and rewards went to publication and research rather than to creative teaching, the general education courses were turned over to young and inexperienced teachers, fresh from their immersion in narrow and highly technical doctoral research projects, by whom the assignment was often regarded as a chore.

Not long after this tendency developed, the colleges were swamped with large numbers of students who previously had been considered unable to profit by any schooling beyond the secondary level. The educational aftermath of the "civil rights revolution" in the early 1960s was a national movement to open the doors of our colleges to members of minority groups, few of whom would have qualified by the criteria of scholastic achievement that had been accepted until then. The convergence of pressures—from the specially gifted students who felt that general education courses hindered their professional futures, and from the disadvantaged and poorly qualified students for whom these courses seemed at least initially beyond reach—set up a strong tide of negative critical opinion. There was surprisingly little resistance, even from those

5

who were convinced of the educational validity of general liberal education, to demands for the abandonment of curricular requirements—especially when these demands became intertwined with political issues that emerged in stormy fashion on American campuses.

More and more, students, with the encouragement of some faculty members, demanded "to do their own thing" not after their introduction to the organized disciplines of the required curriculum but at the very outset of their college careers. The extent to which this has gone is revealed in a discussion among three teachers, all extremely sympathetic to students whose revolutionary attitude toward society extends toward the schools.[2] It goes without saying that their students reject the "traditional" college curriculums and teaching techniques of the 1950s and 1960s. The teachers report with manifest approval that their students, in the words of one of the participants, "don't have the sort of *guilt* thing that we have about really having to master a thing. The whole idea of mastery is dead." Interest in, and capacity for, consecutive thinking is equated with conservative politics. The important thing to encourage at the very outset, according to these teachers responsive to the mood of their students, is "a deep, personal, affective sort of commitment," not to the intellectual problems and fields that every good teacher can uncover in the course of instruction, but to anything whatsoever, whether it be "folk-lore or Jungian stuff and so on." What is decisive in the search for legitimate subject matter to study is not what the best-trained minds in the arts and sciences regard as meaningful, and contributory to educational growth and mastery, but what matters to "the people" outside the academy.

This points to another factor that has contributed to the erosion of general liberal arts education. It is the view that such a curriculum is wedded to the political values of the Establishment and power-elite of the Western world, and that it is impossible to study critically the values embodied in the Western traditions and the manifold challenges to them, without proselytizing for them. Since it is unrealistic to expect a general education curriculum to be

[2]*Change*, April 1972.

openly organized from the point of view of revolutionary politics, the best strategy is to fragment the curricular offerings into individualized and specialized courses that can more readily be filled with revolutionary content or oriented in that direction. It soon became apparent that the critics of general liberal education from this quarter of the ideological compass were not objecting to indoctrination at all, but only to the wrong kind of indoctrination.

Where the very concept of objectivity is called into question, truth is sacrificed with an easy conscience. An unprejudiced survey of the general liberal education curriculum, so vehemently downgraded, discloses that it includes a study of the great revolutionary classics, movements, and events of the modern world. If its teaching entailed a propagandistic approach to, and indoctrination in, bourgeois values, it would be hard to explain the emergence of student radical leadership, most of which was nurtured on this curriculum. Indeed, some of these students claimed, for polemical purposes that make it hard to determine their degree of sincerity, that the sources of their idealism were the ideals and ideologies to which they had been exposed. But the main burden of their complaint was that the American system of higher education was itself a politicalized institution, embattled in defense of the *status quo*, and that this was reflected in its academic requirements. Except on an arbitrary reading of the term "political," which would make it practically equivalent to any exercise of choice, the charge was demonstrably false. It is significant that it was made originally as a retort to criticisms by scholars of the demands made by activist students and their faculty allies that the university as a corporate body abandon its traditional neutrality and take public positions on controversial political issues like Viet Nam and related matters.

Naturally, as the inroads against the general education curriculum developed, a quest for theoretical justifications began. These were purely *ex post facto* in the sense that after yielding to demands of students for the fragmentation of studies, rationalizations were sought to make the curricular modifications more palatable. Some of them were drawn from John Dewey's philosophy of education, and particularly from his emphasis upon

7

participation in the functioning of healthy, democratic institutions. The extent to which Dewey's ideas have been misunderstood and traduced is the theme of some of the chapters in this book.

In addition appeal was made to the educational value of raw experience unrefined by reason. And not only to raw experience but to its particularity. The latter was interpreted in such a way that from the truism that no person could *have* another person's experience the conclusion was reached that he could never understand it. When this was applied to groups and to the justification of "black studies" from a nationalist perspective, the result was educationally disastrous. It was denied that particular group experiences could be understood as expressions of the human experience under specific historical conditions. Some groups were excluded on epistemological grounds from learning or understanding the experience of others. Some militant protesters against white racialism contended that "black studies" could be properly taught only by blacks. Some even went so far as to claim that if white students were to study the black experience its essential elements would be opaque to them. Even sensitive persons who should have repudiated this kind of nonsense took positions, on confused and compassionate grounds, that encouraged it.

Knowing or understanding is a mode of experience, but experiencing is not a mode of knowing or understanding. "There is something about events and objects that only experience can give . . ." writes M. Bloomfield.[3] What is this something that only experience can give? Obviously only the experience of them. But then he goes on to say that it can give us much more—"no one but a black man can understand certain aspects of the black experience." Now this is written by a man who is not black. How, then, even if it were true, could *he* know it without palpably contradicting himself? In an effort to balance his view he confuses it further. He adds: "Yet there is something about the black experience that only someone who can get out of it and look at it from the outside can understand." Since "to get out of" the black experience one must have had the experience of being black, how can

[3]*Daedalus*, Spring 1970, p. 258.

any white man understand this "something"? The claim refutes itself.

There were scholars in the not too distant past who denied that anyone but a Christian could properly teach a course in Western Christian civilization. At one time this was a rationalization for excluding Jews from teaching at some prestigious universities in departments where such courses were being offered. And not long ago it was argued that only Communists or members of the Communist Party could properly teach courses in the theory and practice of Communism—argued sometimes by the very persons who insisted that members of Fascist organizations could not, in virtue of being Fascists, teach the theory and practice of Fascism properly. It is a sad commentary on our times that one of the typical racist arguments used in the past to bar blacks from careers of study in which the historical experience of non-blacks was central should be employed by some who regard themselves as "progressive."

A genuinely liberal general education studies the human experience in its different racial, national, and sexual modes. There are truths about races, nations, classes, men, and women, but there are no racial, national, class, or sexual truths. There is no truth about the experience of a human being that another human being with intelligence, imagination, and sympathy cannot grasp. If Tolstoy can portray the emotions of a woman in love more truthfully, according to women, than novelists of their own sex, then a theory of knowledge that contests this fact or makes it problematic must be declared inadequate.

It is not an expression of intellectual imperialism or paternalism to deny that there are racial or national or class truths or to seek criteria of evidence that, allowing for differences of subject matter, are invariant and universal. There are different patterns of morality but if we are seeking to define morality or the moral point of view it is not parochial to isolate what is central to it. Similarly, it is possible to recognize that there is an ethos of civilized discourse, that there are certain amenities and civilities of the intellectual life, without being a snob or a stand-patter.

Never have academic manners and morals sunk so low as in recent years. They seem more appropriate to protagonists in class struggles facing each other across barricades than to a community of scholars, of teachers and learners. Intellectual sophistication consists apparently in interpreting outbursts of violence and disruption as new forms of vitality that enrich the perspective of pluralism. One scholar sympathetic to new forms of cultural excellence decries what he calls the "paternalistic and psychological imperialist roles" of the humanist and condemns the humanistic view that "the elaborate, elegaic appraisals of individual choice are at the center of all serious and civilized morality."[4] This is overwritten poppycock. Why should any intelligent person, humanist or not, believe that appraisals or evaluations of individual choices should be "elaborate and elegaic"? What the writer is really saying is that he does not agree with the view that individual choice is at the center of civilized or reflective morality. For this may lead us to condemn certain kinds of behavior as uncivilized, a condemnation that to him represents the vice of an imperialistic humanism. He gives an illustration of this humanistic vice by reporting a condemnation of a student who reacts against what he reads in Henry James with such intense hatred that "for symbolic emphasis [he] rips up his neat paperback text of *The Ambassadors* and throws it out of the seminar window." Of the indignant reaction of the humanist to this piece of intellectual barbarism, he writes: "We have no right to confiscate [condemn?] emergent forms of intellectual vitality in the way we incline to."

Why not? Shall we wait until this emergent form of vitality develops to a point where the teacher, too, is hurled after the book, until the defenestration of "reactionary" professors spreads from West Germany to the United States? What a miserable evasion of moral responsibility! It is not the angry student's judgment we are condemning—that we should discuss—but his uncivilized action. As well say that the Nazis who burned the books of Heine "for symbolic emphasis" were giving vent to an "emergent form of intellectual vitality."

The presupposition of the series of essays that constitute this book is that all reforms and modifications proposed for higher

R.J. Kaufmann, *Daedalus*, Summer 1969, p. 707.

education in the United States—some of them very desirable, *e.g.*, prolonging the academic time-table for some students and contracting it for others depending on their interests and capacities—are extrinsic to *what* is learned and *how*, to the curricular fare offered and consumed. I nowhere argue in this book or anywhere else that an adequate education will increase one's earning power or social status. Even if true, that is irrelevant. To me all the legitimate justifications of education reduce themselves to its function in enabling human beings to become more sensitive, intelligent, humane, imaginative and reflective persons. Whether it will make them happier, I do not know. If it makes them wiser, that is all we have a right to expect.

The wisdom may be reflected in their political judgment. That was the hope of Jefferson and Dewey. It is true that countless individuals have bettered their economic position in consequence of their schooling. But it is far from true for all. It is unrealistic to expect economic and other injustices to be remedied *directly* through equal educational opportunities. For they may depend upon factors beyond the reach of mere schooling. Yet it is legitimate to rely upon the *indirect* effects of a good education in reducing social injustices through the growth of political insight and sophistication. Schools should not enlist themselves in behalf of *political* programs to reform society. They can, however, develop highly motivated, intelligent citizens to do so.

I am conscious of no change in my basic educational philosophy since the days when my Platonic realism dissolved in the classrooms and seminars of John Dewey. I am still gratified that my *Education for Modern Man* won his endorsement when it was first published as an application of his ideas to higher education. Although change is the law of all life and especially of human affairs, I do not believe, nor did he, that what is new is necessarily true and what is old false, but that the test of both is to be found in their consequences in human experience. Like Dewey I find that the term "pragmatism" has been so corrupted by its misunderstanders that I prefer "experimental" as a characterization of my philosophy—provided that we remember that we cannot doubt, or experiment with, all things at once, and that, unless we are

11

already in the possession of some truths, the results of any particular experiment can establish nothing. At the same time no accepted truth is beyond experimental challenge.

Nonetheless I would lack candor if I did not confess to a growing consciousness of one lacuna in Dewey's thought, and in mine, which here can only be mentioned but not adequately explored. I have followed Dewey in his impressive elaboration of the Socratic tradition that intelligence is the central virtue in the moral life of man. On the basis, however, of close observation of faculties both at home and abroad during the recent crises of the universities, I have concluded that although there is no substitute for intelligence, it is not the source or guarantee of moral courage, of the willingness to risk something in action in defense of the convictions tested and warranted by intelligent inquiry when they are disputed or threatened by the new barbarians. Possessing moral courage himself, Dewey took it for granted that others had it. Again and again in recent years I have encountered intelligent persons who have been too fearful to condemn publicly what they regarded as educational nonsense and outrage or to defend publicly what they regarded as true.

I am not satisfied that anyone today knows how moral courage is distributed, or how it can be developed. There is no evidence that there is a specific gene for it, although the absence of some genetic trait may inhibit its presence. Unless it is more widely distributed among those who have genuine knowledge and wisdom, power will fall into the hands of those who have great daring but are deficient in knowledge and wisdom. Although certain dialectical definitions of courage suggest that it entails true knowledge or wisdom, the converse is certainly not true. Anyone who has seen highly intelligent men and women vote against their better judgment or remain silently compliant out of fear—stark naked fear that "the campus will be torn apart"—or yield to educational demands previously deemed unreasonable lest their offices, classrooms, and laboratories be destroyed, will not accept any dialectical analysis that purports to explain away these grim facts of experience.

The history of education, like all history, is full of surprises. No one anticipated as recently as ten years ago the violent and chaotic developments in American education that began in Berkeley in 1964 and whose repercussions extended to countries which had been until then profoundly unconcerned with higher education in the United States. No radical reformer in his wildest prophecy anticipated the extent to which in a few years the basic pattern of study would be modified and the students recognized as legitimate authorities not only in regulating their social life but in determining their curricular requirements, and the standards by which they were to be judged, if judged at all. Objective factors, to be sure, like their completely praiseworthy participation in the civil rights movement, the assassination of Martin Luther King, the Viet Nam war served as catalytic and precipitating agents. But no one predicted the role they would play.

The complex and indeterminate nature of the future is one reason why I have not surrendered hope that the intellectual and moral responsibility of American educators will reassert itself and the quality of American education improve. It will never return to what it was. But what American education was in the past and what it is in the present do not exhaust the possible alternatives for the future. The surging tides of irrationalism that have spawned some of the shoddiest proposals for painless and guaranteed education that were ever heralded as reforms will recede as the shipwrecked careers and lives of their victims become visible. The tasks in both domestic and foreign affairs that the United States as a nation must undertake if a free, peaceful, and prosperous world is to emerge, despite current threats and tensions, may serve as a stimulus, as future crises develop, for a more intelligent approach to education. It may be that, when it becomes apparent that resistance to unreason and violence is not necessarily fatal and sometimes is fruitful, that defeat in a good cause is rarely as disastrous as failure to resist a bad one, then sufficient moral courage will be found in the academy to risk something in behalf of the findings of intelligent inquiry.

2

The Scope of Philosophy of Education

There is a great deal of nonsense talked about philosophy of education. This is particularly true of claims that a metaphysical or epistemological position has logical implications for educational theory and practice. Any two philosophers who share a common philosophical position, whether it be objective idealism or pragmatism—or even Thomism—may still disagree with each other about specific educational objectives and techniques. And educators who agree about the desirability of certain educational aims and methods may disagree profoundly in their world outlook.

The notion that the resolution of educational problems, whether it be the place of the project method or the role of vocational courses in a liberal arts curriculum, depends upon one's "theory of reality" is almost comical if it suggests that we cannot as educators achieve a sensible agreement about the first unless we agree about the second. If that were true, then since there is no likelihood that we will agree about theories of reality, our prospects of ever agreeing about educational matters would be remote indeed. Nonetheless there are many educational questions on which substantial agreement has been reached, for example, the impor-

15

tance of motivation, the use of visual aids in instruction, the integration of cognate subject matters by educators who are at odds with one another in their metaphysics and epistemology. The specific educational problems about which they differ, like, say, the different methods of teaching reading, they hope to settle as a rule through continued empirical inquiry. And as I understand empirical inquiry it includes investigation of value proposals in the light of our common value commitments and examination of the consequences of acting on the proposals.

But surely, it will be objected, *some* metaphysical or theological beliefs entail some educational corollaries, if only in the way of what should be taught. For example, does it not follow that if one believes in the existence of God, religion should be taught in the public schools? I do not see that it follows logically at all. As a matter of fact many religious people who do believe in God do not believe that religion should be taught in public schools. And it is perfectly conceivable that some who do *not* believe in the existence of God or in any religious doctrines should nonetheless believe it desirable that religion constitute part of the curriculum. A number of statesmen and their advisors known for their personal religious skepticism have held that it was desirable to give religious instruction in state schools in order to strengthen the foundations of peace and order.

The phrase "a philosophy of education" is an ambiguous expression that designates two related types of inquiry. We may ask questions like: (a) what role does education play in the organization of society and the transmission of culture? How are individual needs and interests affected by community traditions and institutions? Or—and this is the chief concern of a philosophy of education—we may ask questions like: (b) what are the *ends* of education? What kind of society can best further these ends? And having answered them tentatively we go on to inquire: what knowledge, skills, and techniques shall we impart, what habits and values and powers shall we encourage, in order to achieve these desirable interrelated personal and social ends?

It is apparent at once that the philosophy of education is primarily concerned with questions of value, with issues of ethics and social philosophy. Insofar as philosophy can be distinguished from science, where science is broadly regarded as ordered, grounded knowledge including its language and principles of organization, philosophy is the study of desirable ways of life. Its end is wisdom. It is in this sense that Dewey writes: "If we are willing to conceive education as the process of forming fundamental dispositions, intellectual and emotional, toward nature and fellow men, philosophy may even be defined as *the general theory of education.*"

The philosophy of education, more conventionally understood, is inquiry into the attitudes and dispositions that formal schooling should aim to develop in students. But does not this in turn depend upon metaphysics or epistemology? The answer seems to me to be clearly "no." No ethical statement can be deduced from a metaphysical one except where we are dealing with disguised value judgments in the form of metaphysical expressions. If our values depend upon our metaphysics or theologies we should be at one another's throats all the time. We are more convinced of the validity of our moral judgments, for example, that it is wrong to inflict pain upon another for the mere sport of it, than we are of *any* alleged metaphysical or theological justification of our ethical judgment. This does not commit us to ethical intuitionism. Although there are many statements of fact the disproving of which might affect the validity of our moral judgments, I cannot see what differential bearing statements like "Being Is One" or "Being Is Many" or "God Created the World," or their denials, have on such statements as "sharing is better than stealing," or "actions performed voluntarily are nobler than those done under compulsion."

The derivation of the ends or objectives of the educational process is no easy task. It involves detailed study of the biological, psychological, and historical nature of human beings, their culture and traditions and focal problems, in short of anything that is *relevant* to settling the questions: What is of worth in human life? What knowledge and power are necessary to discover it and to make it part of the texture of human experience?

But surely, it might be objected, does not the relation between progressive education and pragmatism show that the foregoing is

17

false? Is not progressive education specifically related to the pragmatic or experimental philosophy of Dewey, either as conclusion to premise, or as corollary to conclusion, or as a particular application of a general principle? To make any such affirmation is to fall into a profound missapprehension of the character of both progressive education and Dewey's philosophy. This misapprehension is very widespread and accounts for the fanatical and hasty criticism of modern or progressive education, not on the grounds of empirical evidence drawn from concrete educational experience, but on grounds of antecedent opposition to Dewey's naturalism and his theory of meaning, truth, and experience.

There is considerable historical evidence to show that Dewey reached his characteristic educational insights before he elaborated his characteristic philosophical views. Aside from the historical evidence, Dewey himself has often maintained that what is called progressive or modern education is the result of the verified findings of scientific psychology applied to the processes of learning and teaching, and of the introduction of democratic ideals and procedures wherever relevant in the classroom and school experience of the student. (Let us recall that even student self-government, commonplace as it is today, would have been incomprehensible to most educators at the turn of the century.) The refusal to follow the lead of scientific method in developing new approaches and techniques in learning, or to adopt democratic values in classroom experience, reflect moral differences, not metaphysical or epistemological ones. It is perfectly possible, however, to accept the findings of scientific psychology about the learning process and to believe in democracy in education and still reject the pragmatic philosophy as was the case with Felix Adler and Bertrand Russell, men as far apart from each other as each is from Dewey. Dewey would argue, however, that what they accepted on the plane of practical and moral experience made their characteristic philosophic doctrines implausible.

Dewey believes his theory of experience can more adequately account for the way in which we learn effectively than any other theory of experience, just as he believes his theory of inquiry does greater justice to the way in which human beings actually solve

18

their concrete problems than do conventional theories of meaning and truth. His theories of experience and inquiry come focally into play when difficulties arise in teaching and learning or when puzzles and paradoxes arise in investigation. In this sense, Dewey believes his philosophy is better grounded in the facts of scientific inquiry, of education, law, art, and practical experience, when these have satisfactory or prosperous issue, than are other philosophies. Dewey is convinced that "education is the laboratory in which philosophic distinctions become concrete and are tested" because it is pre-eminently the area in which moral attitudes are developed and understood in relation to knowledge of facts of different kinds and degrees of warrant. He invites philosophers to formulate their theories and distinctions in such a fashion that they can be squared with what actually happens in the serious activities of the school, court, marketplace, and scientific laboratory. Otherwise their theories may be consistent but incredible and their distinctions subtle and yet irrelevant.

To encourage philosophers as Mr. Broudy does "to derive [a philosophy of education] from some philosophic position such as Idealism, Realism, Thomism, Pragmatism, or Existentialism,"[1] is to encourage them to perpetrate garrulous absurdities. Philosophers would do better to test their philosophical positions by first familiarizing themselves with what takes place in the educational (legal, artistic, scientific, social) process. Similarly, when Mr. Price writes that "the epistemology of educators consists in an attempt to derive from an epistemological study of the method of knowledge a description of the procedures by which learning may be furthered, and a consequent recommendation that such courses be pursued in the schools,"[2] he has put the cart before the horse. Epistemology is bad enough in its confusions of logic and psychology: epistemology of education is worse. No one ever derived a single item of new knowledge about learning either from

[1] Harry S. Broudy, "How Philosophical Can Philosophy of Education Be?" *The Journal of Philosophy* LII (October 27, 1955), p. 617.
[2] Kingsley Price, "Is a Philosophy of Education Necessary?" *The Journal of Philosophy* LII (October 27, 1955), p.628.

epistemology or epistemology of education. What we know about reliable procedures by which learning may be furthered, we know through scientific or empirical psychology without benefit of epistemology or metaphysics. Similarly a recommendation that certain courses, whether of method or content, be pursued does not depend in the least upon epistemology but upon our conception of the ends of education and the best way to achieve them. We should look to education and psychology and other concrete fields in which knowledge is gained in order to see whether our theories of knowledge make sense. Philosophers should not presume to determine whether the specific results won in these fields make sense in the light of their abstract and general theories of knowledge. What is true of "the epistemology of education" is true also of "the metaphysics of education,"[3] only more so.

A philosophy of education, worthy of consideration, will not develop as a result of philosophers *applying* their philosophy to questions of education. It will develop when philosophers and educators, as well as other intelligent citizens, concern themselves with questions of education, explore their bearing on conflicting value commitments, and seek some comprehensive theory of human values to guide us in the resolution of conflicts.

[3]*Ibid.*, p. 631.

3

The Philosopher of Growth

One of the most endearing features of John Dewey's personality was his openness to ideas and suggestions whatever their source. At the very height of his philosophical career and even toward its very close, he was always sensitive to the possibility of new facets and dimensions of experience, to new problems and to new aspects of old problems. He was rarely satisfied with his own formulations. What he sent to the press was never a final version of his ideas but the latest draft of a position that was not yet completely thought out in his own mind and which he sincerely hoped would be developed by others. A few months after his 90th birthday had been celebrated, he remarked: "Only in the last two years have I come to see the real drift and hang of the various positions I have taken." And when death came, it interrupted him in the midst of a new interpretation of the history of modern philosophy. The world for him was more than we can ever say about it and he was convinced that every reflective mind could refract the many-colored scene of human activity in a distinctive and interesting way.

Some of John Dewey's theories in philosophy were revolutionary, so much so that his conception of thinking and of mind could only with difficulty be expressed in terms of the inherited incoherences of the traditional philosophical vocabulary. But his conception of philosophy was as old-fashioned as that of Socrates. Philosophy for him was a quest for wisdom, a survey of existence from the standpoint of value, a criticism of the methods by which we appraise the modes and values of experience. What the professional philosopher does—or should do—systematically, other men and women do episodically. He was therefore prepared to heed and follow up any intimation of truth, any insight or vision that lit up the human scene, in complete independence of its academic credentials. It was the authenticity of the experience which engaged his interest, and he had a rare feeling for it.

John Dewey's correspondence with Mrs. Frost differs only in volume and duration from the vast correspondence which he carried on with many others. There is hardly anyone who wrote to Dewey who did not receive a reply from him. This was not only because of his innate courtesy but in most cases because of the enkindling effect of what others said and thought upon him. He often told me that he was indebted for some of his seminal ideas to men and women who had tried to make sense of their own experience without the benefit of the technical idioms of the philosophical schools and traditions. If he had any partiality it was for those who wrestled with problems at first hand in the thick of life-situations. The fact that others, with whom he sometimes sought to share his discoveries, could not always see the glimmer of light in the dark and obscure passages of the manuscripts and letters he received, led to no alteration in his judgment, to no weakening of his confidence. For, judging all things by their fruits, he was convinced that anything that suggested fresh thought to him must be itself inherently or potentially thoughtful.

The same attitude which John Dewey displayed toward his correspondents he revealed during his long career as a teacher. Judged by the external trappings of the dynamic classroom teacher, John Dewey was among the worst teachers of the world. He was completely devoid of the histrionic arts which a good teacher, even when he follows Dewey's principles, must summon up to awaken interest or command attention, and which always facilitate communication between teacher and student when attention is lagging. It is not likely that he would ever have been chosen as a master teacher for television, especially at an hour when the audience is struggling to stay awake.   Nonetheless John Dewey was a great teacher for those students whose interest in ideas had already been aroused and who were struggling to articulate their philosophical insight. Dewey's reaction to his students' efforts to see and to say things freshly was not to refute but to encourage, to help ideas get stated. He was more patient with his students than they were with each other. In one of his letters he says that "delaying is one manifestation of the active potency of time"—and he charitably interpreted groping and obscure formulations as such delay. Teaching for him (when he wasn't lecturing) was a kind of intellectual collaboration. Students were helped to overcome their native self-doubt by an unexpected accession of unsuspected intellectual power that often provided the momentum to surmount what had seemed formidable obstacles. With the rarest of exceptions, this was Dewey's unfailing attitude even to those of his students who had come to Columbia University inoculated against his philosophy by previous teachers and who used his ideas as scratching posts for the development of their dialectical teeth and claws. Having been taught by Morris R. Cohen as an undergraduate to believe that pragmatism was a philosophy that made our wishes, which were real, into horses, which were imaginary, I constituted myself the official opposition for an entire year in one of Dewey's large lecture classes, to the annoyance not of Dewey but of my fellow students who objected to the constant interruption of their slumber. I became converted to pragmatism in the most unpragmatic way. With Dewey's encouragement I sat down to write what I thought would be the definitive refutation of pragmatism on the basis of Peirce's theory of leading principles. The argument carried me to conclusions I did not wish to reach—and protesting all the way, I went to Dewey himself, after Morris Cohen failed me, to tell me what was wrong in where I was coming out. This time, too, Dewey encouraged me but with a grin. He could find nothing wrong with the argument.

   There is no doubt that Dewey encouraged too many, and I

suspect that he sometimes realized this. But he knew what he was doing. He was more fearful of encouraging too few, of withering with chill winds of criticism or imperious demands for immediate clarity, insights struggling to be born, of inhibiting powers on the verge of development. Some of his professional colleagues felt there was enough error and nonsense in the world and that what could not stand up against the sharp sickle of criticism was hardly worth cultivating. Dewey's attitude was that one genuine insight or fruitful vision was worth the risk of many errors. It was not that he was tolerant of error. He believed, however, that in honest inquiry even errors could play a constructive function, that we could learn from them to devise "the means of invention and circumvention" which marks creative intelligence at work in the process of growth. What he prized above all was the quality of *becoming* in human beings.

All who knew John Dewey have at one time or another said that he lived his philosophy as well as taught it. In his living and in his teaching he regarded growth as the key educational and moral value. I am firmly convinced that when all the dust of controversy settles, John Dewey will be regarded as the philosopher of human growth in the age of modern science and technology, as the philosopher who saw man not as a creature with a fixed nature, whether conceived as a fallen soul or a soulless configuration of atoms, but as developing mind-body with an historical career, who, because he does something in and to the world, enjoys some degree of freedom, produces consequences never witnessed before, and leaves the world different from the world into which he was born.

The concept of growth, as John Dewey understood it, is not a simple one and some analysis is necessary to see its central position in his thought. As everyone knows, in his *Democracy and Education* Dewey maintained that there was no one end or goal in education to which everything else was subordinate. The closest to an all-inclusive educational end was the principle of growth itself conceived participially as the process of *growing*. This brought the retort that there are all sorts of growth in experience, some of them vicious, some even fatal to their subjects as well as, so to speak, to their objects, or victims. Unless growth has a direction, there is no genuine development. Unless we have antecedent knowledge of what is good, we do not know if the development is even desirable. We sometimes find ourselves wishing not only that something wouldn't grow but that it had not come to be.

Dewey used to reply to this that growth in education as in life develops the standards by which its direction and desirability are judged. There is growth and growth. There is the growth which generates obstacles to further growth, and the growth which creates the conditions for further growth. There is a growth which prevents and growth which encourages the processes of education. The important thing, said Dewey, is that "the conception of growth must find universal and not specialized limited application."

It is questionable whether this ever satisfied Dewey's critics. But it is obvious that for Dewey growth is an inclusive and not a single exclusive end. It embraces *all* the positive intellectual, emotional, and moral ends that appear in everybody's easy schedule of the good life and the good education—growth in skills and powers, knowledge and appreciation, value and thought. For Dewey, however, it is not enough to list these ends; they must be brought into living and relevant relation to the developing powers and habits and imagination of the individual person. We grow not by worshiping values, but by realizing them in our daily behavior. The pattern of realization is an individual thing even when the values are common. There are different rates of growth, different styles of growth; but when they maximize our powers to grow they are all ways by which we grow in maturity. We are mature to the extent that we form habits of reasonable expectation on the basis of what we know about the world, our fellows, and ourselves—to the extent that we can cope with an ever-changing environment, make sense of new experience, and escape both the petrifactions of routine and the blind outburst of impulse. The growth, consequently, which Dewey identifies with genuine and desirable education is a shorthand expression for the direction of change in a great variety of growths—intellectual, emotional, and moral. It excludes, therefore, the kinds of growth which interfere with or reverse the direction of change in this variety of growths—it excludes growths in prejudice, arbitrariness, hate, invidious prestige, power and status, and even that miscellany of knowledge which burdens a mind not in training for a quiz show. More important still, it becomes clear why in the interests of growth Dewey became a critic of specialized and narrow vocationalism, of merely professionalized education, and why he became the protagonist of a liberal and general education for *all*. The same analysis that has been made of growth as an educational end can be extended to Dewey's assertion that in ethics "Growth itself is the only 'moral' end." Dewey should not have said "only" but "central" or "most inclusive."

Dewey's concern with growth and the emphasis he gives it flowed in part from his post-Darwinian naturalism. Man is as authentic a part of nature as other things that have careers in time, but he is a part of nature which, to keep its very equilibrium and to remain alive, must enter actively into the processes that condition its very nature. Man must grow with the things which challenge him in this contingent and dangerous world or else he dies. Dewey had the courageous but not unqualified optimism of a man embattled in perpetual struggle for a *better* world. The effort and risk were worth making even against odds. His optimism was never on that stupendous cosmic scale of his supernaturalist critics who believed that man could find a final peace by a faith in or a leap to some transcendental source. Although the world can be made less contingent and less dangerous, it will never be a safe place for man because of the very differences his own growth, especially the growth of his knowledge, makes to the world. Dewey believed that in a world of rapid change man must find peace in action rather than withdrawal. Events have a way of breaking in the doors by which we would seek to escape them. To be serene in the very midst of affairs is the "top of sovereignty."

Because there are various kinds of growth and failures to grow, there are various kinds of death. In one of his letters to Mrs. Frost, Dewey writes of "that large class of people who live on the physical plane and who find such ease in their dogmas of habituation that for all practical purposes they are lifeless." Dewey would have said the same thing about those whose mental life is lived only in the after-glow of their memories, memories of past triumphs and achievements. They, too, have effectively ceased living. To live is to grow with the problems and challenges of the present, and whatever helps realize the processes of growth helps us to stay alive and intellectually young. "Keeping young," writes Dewey, "seems to be a function of using maturity as a source of new [experiences] and contacts."

There is another aspect of Dewey's concept of growth and another sense in which he intended the conception of growth to be given "a universal and not a specialized limited application." We tend to think of growth as primarily a biological or psychological category, but *human* growth cannot be understood without going beyond biology and psychology, whose terms are abstracted from the inclusive social and cultural matrix. The organism grows not only in and with its natural environment; it grows with other organisms in society. There are societies (perhaps it is better to say there are families, for as yet there is only a vision of such societies) in which growth is the ideal norm *for all*. It was because he took the growth of every individual person as his moral ideal that Dewey committed himself so wholeheartedly to democracy. Discussing the idea that the object of learning should be continued capacity for growth, he writes: "This idea cannot be applied to all the members of a society, except where the intercourse of man with man is natural, and except when there is adequate provision for the reconstruction of social habits and institutions by means of wide stimulation arising from equitably distributed interests. And this means a democratic society!" He links the ideas of growth and democracy more explicitly in a passage in which he says: "A society of free individuals in which all, through their own work, contribute to the liberation and enrichment of the lives of others is the only environment in which any individual can really grow normally to his full stature." This is an overstatement—for if it were true we should have to conclude that no individual has ever grown to his full stature. But its very overemphasis should indicate how important for Dewey, democracy is as a moral ideal. It indicates also that "the liberation and enrichment" of life is integral to the meaning of desirable growth. The phrase "the liberation and enrichment" of life signifies a great many values which when stated abstractly

27

sound platitudinous and preachy but which taken in the context of Dewey's philosophy of education, art, society, religion, and conduct are immensely suggestive. The "liberation and enrichment" of life consists in the experiences of happiness and delight, intellectual adventure, friendship and love, knowledge and art, of unity with the world and ourselves—and of many other things. But to aim at these values for all involves a program of profound social reconstruction.

Long before the discovery of nuclear energy and its vistas of tremendous power were even dreamed of, Dewey was convinced that modern science and technology had given man an unprecedented opportunity to reconstruct his social world. Man can no longer be reasonably considered as an object of historical forces but as a co-determiner of his own history. Granted the importance of natural resources, armed with science, men themselves become the most important of all natural resources—provided only that they have the desire and resolution to make use of their knowledge. Dewey maintained that once men set out to put knowledge and intelligence to use, the relevant test of all social institutions becomes their impact upon the quality of human life and experience. No more radical criterion can be envisaged, for it applies not only to the operation of the *status quo* but just as much to all proposals to modify it or revolutionize it.

One of the ironies of intellectual history is that despite Dewey's sharp indictment of industrial society in America and his criticism of the cult of the practical and useful, he himself has been charged with an easy acquiescence in the values of machine civilization, and of elaborating a philosophy of practice that lends itself to its justification. It is true that Dewey regarded the periodic complaints against the industrialization of culture as a romantic nostalgia for times that were not recoverable. But only a perverse misreading of what Dewey understood by "the useful" can account for the rest of the criticism. His meaning was made clear in his demand during the days of the depression: "Regiment *things* and free *human beings*." He believed the first could be achieved through scientific technology and the second by scientific social inquiry and the arts of democratic government. He dared our

28

age, which worships science almost superstitiously but ignores its rationale, and the social implications of its logic and ethics, to apply scientific method to the problem of making industry serve men, to the problem of liberating human energy and humanizing its expression, to the problem of organizing industrial relations in order to meet the imperatives of educational growth.

For Dewey, scientific method or planning in the interests of efficiency and production is one thing—and by far not enough. Here commodities, their quantity and rate of output, are king—and everything which bears upon the quality of life of the maker and the user of commodities is disregarded as irrelevant. Scientific method in the interests of the humanly useful is quite another thing for Dewey—and the only rational basis for social criticism. It is instructive to note, as the critics have *not* done, how Dewey defines the useful. "To be useful," he says, "is to fulfill need. The characteristic human need is for possession and appreciation of *the meanings* of things." From this point of view "the only thing essential to the idea of utility is its inherent place and bearing in experience." It remains only to relate that inherent place and bearing in experience to the needs of personal growth.

It cannot be emphasized too strongly that in an educational context growth is to be conceived in personal terms. The desirability of personal growth does not automatically carry over to growth in organization, growth in the economy, or technology, or population. Such growth may interfere with the quality of human growth. The educational decision, to the extent that it is a moral decision, must consider the impact of size, numbers, and complexity on the opportunities offered for individual personal growth. Under certain circumstances this may lead to contraction and decentralization rather than expansion.

In one of his early popular writings Dewey describes the lot of most members of industrial society in terms of a contrast between "living one's life" and "earning one's living." He implies that a society worthy of men would be one in which, as men earned their living, they would have opportunity for the growth and self-fulfillment which are required both for a sense of significance and a sense of enjoyment in life. This explains why Dewey placed such great emphasis on the importance of vocations—on life callings—and why he considered an education conducted without any reference to it a leisure-class pursuit. But for all of Dewey's optimistic expectations about the power of applied science, the effects it wrought were greater, if not better, than he had imagined. It is an open question whether all or even most work in modern industrial society can be made meaningful, whether it can engage the individual's interest and creative capacity so as to make possible that feeling of significant achievement which the good teacher or physician or skilled craftsman has. The prospective consequences of applied science, once the danger of war is lifted and full use can be made of nuclear energy, make problematic not so much the achievement of meaningful vocations as the meaningful use and enjoyment of leisure.

Far from undermining, this reinforces the importance Dewey gives to growth as the encompassing and justifying end of education. During his life Dewey was just as keen a critic of the leisure-time activities of our society as of its mechanical and industrial processes whose impress they reflected. To what extent, he asked, do the leisure-time activities of the great masses of individuals contribute to their intellectual and emotional growth, to a liberal and humane outlook on affairs, to a deeper sympathy for all suffering creatures, to a wider appreciation and more reflective judgment of values, beliefs, and conduct, to a richer and more diversified personal experience? Very imperfectly, is his answer. Life is certainly easier than it used to be; and as far as the burden of physical toil is concerned, it will be much easier in the future. But it is far from obvious that human lives will by that fact alone be more meaningful and satisfying than they used to be.

For these and other reasons Dewey's philosophy of growth possesses a continuing *actualité* not only to basic problems of education and public policy but to the whole of human experience. Dewey is the philosopher of human freedom in this our revolutionary age of modern science, whose faith in man is rooted in faith in the arts of intelligence. Alfred North Whitehead in assessing Dewey's influence once said that the magnitude of his achievement "is to be estimated by reference to the future"—a future in which Whitehead confidently asserted that "for many generations the North American Continent will be the living center of human civilization." Events since Whitehead wrote have made that prediction another illustration of how contingent the universe is. The living center of human civilization has shifted many times and in the future there may be more than one center. But we can with assurance predict that wherever that center is, if those who live in it are imbued with a passion for human freedom and an equality of concern for all persons to reach their maximum growth as human beings, it will find a guiding and coherent philosophy in the thought of John Dewey.

4

Modern Education & Its Critics

The growth of the educational enterprise in the United States has been accompanied by, among other things, a growth in the volume of criticism. This criticism has come from all quarters of the ideological compass. It has been directed against every aspect of American education. The cost of the physical plant; the organization of the schools; the training of teachers; the character of their instruction, whether given or received; the nature of the curriculum; the philosophy or the lack of philosophy behind it—all have been the target of vigorous attack.

To the extent that such criticisms make the community aware of educational problems and of the enormous stake all citizens have in the proper functioning of our schools, they should be welcomed even when they seem intemperate and ill-informed. For our hopes for more and better schools are more likely to be realized as a consequence of public criticism, adequately met, than of public indifference. After all, no matter how valid we believe our educational objectives to be, there is no reason for complacency when we survey the educational results. And if our very objectives are challenged, we are under a moral and intellectual obligation to offer a rational defense of them.

One thing we know in advance: Not all criticisms can be well founded, for many are incompatible with each other. On the other hand, it is unlikely that they will all be unjustified. Our very commitment to free inquiry in our schools should lead us to accept the results of such inquiry about any one, or all, of our educational commitments.

Now it is perfectly true that some attacks on modern education are not made in good faith. They are part of campaigns to capture or influence the schools for partisan goals or programs which are themselves to be exempt from critical exploration through the normal processes of education. Such attacks should be met and repelled, not by the educators attacked, but by their fellow citizens. But until it becomes patent that good faith *is* lacking, educators should be the first to consider the ostensible reasons offered for dissatisfaction with the schools, even if the ostensible reasons are not the real reasons. We must not forget that, in the last analysis, the relevant evidence for the truth or falsity of what a man says does not depend upon his ulterior motives in saying it.

Before considering some of the chief criticisms of American education, it would be well to keep firmly in view some of the chief accomplishments of American education. This is necessary, not only for a proper historical perspective, but also because some of those very achievements are the cause of current difficulties and misunderstanding.

1. The American school and educational system has been the prime agency of achieving a unified democratic nation out of diverse ethnic groups of varied national origins. This result has been obtained without the oppressive measures which usually marked the emergence of great states in the past, and without the forcible imposition of a uniform cultural pattern from one central source.

2. The American educational system has provided an educational ladder on which millions have climbed to a better social life. In the past man's vocations have been closer to what Santayana has called "natural society" than to "free society." That

is to say, they have been determined more by the accidents of kinship, association, and inherited social status than by free choice in accordance with talent and inclination. This is still the rule for most of mankind, but it is less so in the United States than in most countries of the world.

3. Despite its early denominational beginnings and despite the ever-recurrent tendency of religion to bring the glad tidings of salvation into the classroom, the American school system is predominately secular. Although it permits study of the materials of religion wherever they are culturally relevant, it has remained neutral in the great conflicts of religious faiths.

4. The American educational system has come nearest to achieving a classless school in the entire history of human society. *Morally*, this is its most glorious achievement. *Educationally*, it has created prodigious difficulties and theoretical confusions which we shall subsequently discuss. No judgment, no plan of reform for American education, is likely to be worth examining if it overlooks the significance of the fact that in a nation of 160 million more than 80% of the young men and women are receiving a high school education: that whereas in 1900 barely 700,000 students were enrolled in high school, in little more than one generation later, over 7,000,000 students were enrolled; that whereas in 1900 fewer than 250,000 students were enrolled in our institutions of higher learning, today over 2,300,000 are enrolled. That these absolute and relative increases do not hold for every group is, of course, true; but if Mr. Paul Hoffman is correct, even "the percentage of our Negro population at present enrolled in educational institutions above the high school level is greater than the percentage of Britons, French, and Czechs—to say nothing of the Russians—who are receiving comparable training."[1] Despite the tremendous inequalities and complexities which still exist, the direction of the development is quite clear.

5. Finally, notwithstanding the tendencies of human inertia, the activities of pressure groups and vested interests, the character

---

[1] *Oberlin Today*, Vol. II, No. 8 (Dec. 1953). This does not in any way imply, of course, that the characters of these institutions, or their educational quality, are comparable.

of American education has shown a susceptibility to change—disregarding for the moment the wisdom of some of the changes. It has never been doctrinaire and inflexible. It has shown itself hospitable to criticisms and receptive—perhaps too receptive—to needs, claims, and demands from industry and government. Even without external pressure or stimulus, it has initiated a wide variety of experiments. That this capacity to learn and change is a virtue must be granted even by the most hostile of its present-day critics. Otherwise there would be no point in *their* urging changes.

This brings me to my theme: modern education and its critics. There is a certain ambiguity in the phrase "modern education." Some critics mean by it "current education," not all of which should be regarded as modern. Or it may mean progressive or the new education, not all of which is current. But whatever their differences, all the critics I shall discuss find current education on every level objectionable to the extent that it reflects the theory and practice of the new education whose principles have been sketched in broad outline by John Dewey. Some of the critics find conventional education, present or past, objectionable too. But on the whole the burden of their criticism is that modern or new education is so inferior to what it has replaced that it hardly warrants the name of education. And since, despite these detractors, it is spreading, they regard it as the chief enemy of what by definition—by *their* definition—is called "true" education.

1

I propose here to consider some general criticisms of modern education and the assumptions behind them. And for occasions of this sort I shall proceed in an unprecedented way but one consistent with the principles of modern education. I shall take as points of concrete departure the recent writings of three widely heralded critics—Mr. Albert Lynd, Mr. Robert Hutchins, and Mr. Arthur Bestor—examining in each case some central points in their animadversions against modern education. After assessing the validity of their charges and the worth of their major recommendations, I shall conclude with some critical observations of my own.

To begin with we must distinguish between the substance and the manner of these criticisms. The manner is almost invariably rude and contemptuous. The title of Mr. Lynd's book is *Quackery in the Public Schools.*[2] Professional educators, especially professors of education, are the quacks, and the teachers, with some exceptions, their unwilling or willing victims. The former are pictured as "illiterate," unable to express themselves in effective English or to draw elementary logical inferences. They are "boondogglers," "copper-riveted bureaucrats," and engaged in a dual conspiracy—a *professional* conspiracy—to pile up needless requirements of education courses (educationally unprofitable to those who take them but financially profitable to those who give them), and a *political* conspiracy to evade the will of the community by imposing their own philosophy of man, God, and universe on the schools. Because John Dewey's educational theories have opened the door to these boondogglers and conspirators, writes Mr. Lynd, "I make no apology whatever for the inclusion of his name and doctrines in a volume concerned with 'quackery in the public school' " (p. 207).

One is tempted to ignore Mr. Lynd or to retort in kind. But he speaks for many who feel and believe as he does, and if we are interested in the truth we must reply to his arguments, not to his abuse. The trouble is that it is difficult to find a coherent argument. He uses the anecdotal method and confuses illustration with proof.[3]

Let us state his argument for him. His charge is that modern schools have by and large failed to fulfill their proper function. Their proper function is to teach students how to think, to develop their powers of observation, to make them aware of their cultural origins and continuity with the past, and to instill in them a devotion to the heritage of freedom. In the past these ends were

[2]Boston, 1953.

[3]Although fiercely indignant with modern educators for their unscholarly habits, he devotes the longest chapter of his book to a jeering commentary on the views of Mr. Kilpatrick—not all of whose ideas are accepted by many modern educators—without a single quotation from any of Mr. Kilpatrick's writings. Instead he contents himself with quoting some loose and ungrammatical sentences from a book by one of Mr. Kilpatrick's uncritical admirers.

37

achieved by "formal study in skills and abstract principles": in the elementary schools, through conscientious application to the three R's; in the high schools, through the conventional curriculum of mathematics, foreign languages, grammar, Latin, systematic history, and some sciences; in the colleges, through more of the same. The products of our schools today cannot think or observe properly. They are ignorant of history, and impatient of the intellectual and moral discipline necessary to freedom. All this is a consequence of the abandonment of the conventional curriculum. But the cause of the abandonment is the acceptance of the ideas of the new education whose fountainhead is Dewey. Therefore, to the extent that professional educators and teachers profess allegiance to these principles, they are opposed to "true" education; to the extent that our schools are operated on these principles, they cannot impart "true" education.

Nowhere does Lynd consider whether the ends of a proper education—which he fails to see are among the ends of modern education, too—were *in fact* realized by the traditional curriculum, or whether they were more *completely* realized by the traditional curriculum than by current curricula. He simply ignores all the failures of the past and all the successes of the present. By Mr. Lynd's anecdotal method one could make out a very damaging case of widespread failure in the past. But such a method establishes nothing.

Nor do his historical references establish much more. Examine—in the light of historical evidence—the typical, exaggerated claims by critics of this school that the classical curriculum has been the chief and continuing support of freedom in the Western world. After all, the European countries in which the educational curriculum was and still is the most conventional, in which the secondary schools give *all* students instruction in the classical disciplines, so dearly beloved of Mr. Lynd, were the countries which produced, often with the direct connivance or benevolent neutrality of their classically educated elite—Fascism, Vichyism, Nazism, and Bolshevism.[4]

[4]As a movement Bolshevism is the creation of middle-class intellectuals schooled in the classical curriculum of their day.

Now I am far from saying that there is a direct causal connection between the classical curriculum and these movements, although it is hard to imagine them engulfing a nation whose schools were thoroughly imbued with the spirit and methods of modern or progressive education. What I am saying is that the classical curriculum was certainly not a sufficient safeguard against the *emergence* of a new barbarism.

To Mr. Lynd the assumption of a causal relation between the classical training of a country's elite and the emergence of totalitarianism is a *post hoc, propter hoc* fallacy. And he is right, because the first can and has occurred without the second. But is it any less of a *post hoc, propter hoc* fallacy to assume that the decline in the ability to read, write, and think on any level—assuming that there has been such a decline—is due to a change in curriculum or to new methods of teaching certain subjects rather than to the fact that we are trying to educate a whole people, including those he calls "the slow-witted" and "dullards," instead of a selected group? Mr. Lynd must admit the possibility that, even by his standards, at least some of our students can read and write and think as well as the students of the past. Perhaps their number, in proportion to the entire population of school age and not merely to those in school, is just as great today as in the golden age of yesterday, when many were not in school because they were dropped as uneducable. Would it not then be a decided gain, a great gain, if we could teach something of worth to those whom Mr. Lynd's curriculum and methods could teach nothing? There are, of course, natural dullards. But there are others who are dullards in relation only to a specific curriculum or a specific method of teaching. By clinging to the conventional curriculum, Mr. Lynd has no way of distinguishing them.

In appraising the relative claims of the past and present systems of education, conclusions are difficult to establish. Unless we can evaluate the work of groups comparable in native ability, educational opportunity and social background, our results are scientifically worthless. But on an elementary level it seems possible to make not altogether unreliable studies of comparison between the performance of children in the three R's today and one or two generations ago. These comparisons do not show any conspicuous decline. Mr. Lynd refuses to accept the results because "there is at hand formidable evidence that many of the educationists in power today are not qualified to judge children's performance in the fundamentals" (p. 22). But Mr. Lynd regards himself as qualified to judge that graduates of our high schools are illiterate because he found one student, and his business friends found a few others, who couldn't compose a coherent letter.

In the light of this illustration of what a classically trained mind regards as probative evidence, it is not surprising that Mr. Lynd should caricature what actually goes on in the schools of the country, misinterpret Dewey's recommendation to relate subject matter to needs and interest into a recommendation to dispense altogether with subject matter, and misconceive what is said of "felt needs" as if it implied that needs do not exist unless they are felt.

But the main point I wish to make is not that Mr. Lynd has misread the works of modern educators or that his opposition to it flows from inaccurate empirical observations of the practices of modern education. It is rather that his opposition is *a priori*. It derives from his view that practices of modern education *must* be bad because they are logically bound up with Dewey's philosophy of pragmatism. He believes that if he accepts these practices as valid, such acceptance would logically imply the validity of Dewey's pragmatism. However, since he is convinced that pragmatism is false, he concludes without the necessity of any further examination that the educational theory and practice which allegedly imply it are also mistaken.

This is a profound error, but one so widespread that I wish to discuss it at some length. For it is this error which is responsible in part for the belief that educational issues are at bottom issues of theology and metaphysics.

Although there is an organic connection in Dewey's own thinking between his philosophical ideas and his educational proposals, they are not related as logical premise to logical conclusion. Dewey, of course, believed that the soundness of his proposals constituted some evidence that his philosophical method

40

was fruitful. But he never contended that before one could determine whether or not those proposals were sound, one antecedently had to accept pragmatism. Their soundness was to be a matter for independent investigation.

One of the great obstacles to an objective judgment of the claims of modern education is precisely the notion, as Mr. Lynd puts it, that "agreement with the basic philosophy of Mr. Dewey is the logical price of agreement with his educational theories" (p. 203).[5]

What, then, is this Deweyan basic philosophy? Says Mr. Lynd: "It excludes God, the soul, and all the props of traditional religion." But since Mr. Lynd is a firm believer in God, the soul, and all the props of traditional religion, he rejects out of hand Dewey's educational theories and the practices based on them. Believing what he does, he *must* hold progressive or modern education to be pernicious, no matter what the empirical results are. For the question is no longer empirical but metaphysical and theological. Mr. Lynd admits this on occasion. He tells us that he would still oppose progressive education "even if the strongest claims of the progressivists about their success with the three R's are true" (p. 205). If he understands his own words he is telling us something more. He is telling us that he would still oppose modern education even if *all* its claims were true.

It becomes necessary, then, to put the question in its proper light. For if it were true that modern education is logically bound up with certain beliefs about God, immortality of the soul, and transcendental moral law, we can have no more agreement about education than we can about theology.

Now as I understand it, and as Dewey often explained, progressive education is based on two generic principles. The first is that the verified results of scientific psychology should be brought to bear on the processes of learning. The second is that the values and ideals of democratic life should, as far as possible, be introduced at the appropriate levels in the student's own

---

[5]Elsewhere he says that they are only compatible, which is, of course, another kind of relationship. But Mr. Lynd is not concerned with logical niceties.

educational experience. Acceptance of either or both of these principles does not entail acceptance of Dewey's technical philosophy of instrumentalism. If it is true that there is no transference of training from one field to another; if it is true that effort is a function of interest; that interest follows perception of meaning; and that involvement, active or imaginative, in a problem multiplies and dramatizes opportunities to grasp meanings—why should these truths not be guides to teaching? If the end of education is the development of independent thinking, is not the psychology of how we learn and how we think of fundamental relevance in achieving this end?

But listen to Mr. Lynd: "If human behavior depends upon patterns of habit and impulse as Dewey believes," he complains, "then instruction by exhortation is largely useless." Well, *does* human behavior depend upon habit, impulse and, as Dewey would add, the redirective cues of intelligence? This is a psychological question. Not so, according to a whole school of critics. This is a metaphysical or theological question. And since Dewey denies that "a soul or self exists apart from its own experiences," Dewey's empirical psychology is unacceptable. But this is a *non-sequitur*. If the soul exists, embodied or disembodied, *apart* from its own experiences, nothing follows about how human beings learn *in* and *through* experience. The only item in an educational curriculum that would seem to follow from faith in the substantiality of the soul is instruction in the religious dogmas regarded as necessary for its salvation. Even this is not strictly necessary, for one can believe in the soul without believing that it must be saved, or believe that it must be saved without believing that its salvation is the business of the public schools.

This refusal to evaluate the fruits of modern education on the ground that they all stem from the poisoned roots of pragmatism is also manifested in the discussion concerning the place of democratic and moral experience in the schools. Mr. Lynd and others insist that the stress upon shared experience and democratic participation in setting some intermediate goals of learning, especially in the early years, is wrong because "Dewey insists that human nature itself is the only source of workable moral guides," instead of a "higher" reality, God or some transcendental ideal. Apparently the experience and results of democracy, as contrasted with its alternatives, cannot be assessed or taken as a guide to practice unless democracy is properly grounded in a "higher reality."

Here, too, the argument rests on a demonstrable error. Our whole American experience is testimony to the fact that cooperation and progress on the plane of democratic action is possible without a common belief in first or last things. The same is true for the entire spectrum of human values. We agree on values because of their quality and consequences in experience and yet disagree about their status in the universe. For example, kindness, veracity, conscientiousness recommend themselves to all of us in terms of immediate qualities and observable effects, without any necessity for a prior consensus on their alleged ultimate presuppositions. Do we not every day agree on hundreds of truths even though we may completely disagree about definitions of *the* truth?

It is because progressive educators *believe* in democracy, and not because they *disbelieve* in cosmic ultimates, that they wish to develop students capable of self-discipline, thoughtfulness, and willingness to examine other interests when a conflict of interests arises. And that is why they seek to introduce democratic processes into the child's experiences in the classroom. It is easy to caricature this into the statement that they believe everything should be decided by vote with the teacher either not voting or having only one vote. Their true meaning can be better understood by recalling the atmosphere of the conventional classroom not so long ago.[6] One can accept the injunction to encourage democratic participation and still recognize distinctions among the matters on which students should be consulted and permitted to decide, the matters on which they should only be consulted, and the matters which

[6]Their true meaning may be more apparent in the light of an incident that I can still vividly recall. Thirty-six years ago almost to a day, a group of Brooklyn high school students proposed, for the first time in those parts, a scheme of student self-government. They were denounced by educators and editorial writers as Red Guards and Black Guards (the colors of the school) intent upon establishing soviets in the educational institutions of the U.S. In those days students asked questions only when they were invited to ask them—which was not often.

they should be permitted only to question—but always freely to question. Any specific classroom procedure should be tested by its observable or anticipated effects as contrasted with the effects of alternative procedures, not in terms of its relation to a cosmic or higher reality.

No matter what "higher reality" is postulated it can be shown that mutually inconsistent programs of experience are compatible with it. This is as true for a program of studies in the school as for methods of teaching and a scheme of values. But if one cannot derive a program of studies from metaphysics and one refuses to follow the test of consequences—what can be done? There is no alternative but to fall back on tradition for one's curriculum—which Mr. Lynd not unexpectedly does.

As a rule the traditional curriculum means the curriculum on which the critic was brought up. But it is always described as the accumulated wisdom of the race. What is overlooked is that we not only inherit a tradition but create it, that tradition consists in large measure of departures from tradition, and that the wisdom of tradition establishes its wisdom by its continuing relevance to problems of the present. We cannot escape responsibility for *our* selections and decisions merely by transmitting from our ancestors what they themselves did not always inherit from their own. Merely to transmit tradition is not a counsel of wisdom but of timidity. Speaking of the conventional disciplines, Mr. Lynd says that "there is more wisdom in 'the subject matters' of mathematics, of literature, of history than in any teacher or body of teachers however wise." As one who strongly believes in subject matter and that modern education is not adequate unless it teaches subject matter, and that sometimes subject matter has not been sufficiently stressed, I regard this glorification of subject matter *qua* subject matter as absurd. It reverses the wisdom of Socrates, to whom all subjects and subject matters were merely points of educational departure. For Socrates taught that wisdom, begun with a consciousness of our ignorance, is insight into the nature and career of human values as they bear upon the predicaments of men. Subject matter is neither wise nor foolish; it contains only the *materials* for wisdom—as well as for use and enjoyment. That is

44

why neither history nor experience teaches by itself unless an instructed mind is willing to learn from it.

2

A second type of criticism goes further than that so far considered. It underlines current strictures against modern education but is not content with a return merely to the conventional models. It substitutes a comprehensive conception of education—new in form but perennial in essence—to guide the remoulding of our educational institutions. This conception, whose banner bearer is Mr. Hutchins, has been worked out in detail for liberal education of a specific kind—the only kind there is, we are assured—on the college level. The curriculum of the elementary and high schools is to be reorganized in such a way as to make this kind of liberal education possible for all students.

This view, whose most recent expression is found in *Conflicts in Education*[7] is frankly and proudly non-empirical. It makes great play with deductions from axiomatic first principles and proposes to do what I have tried to show cannot be done, *viz.*, validly to derive a desirable educational program from metaphysical premises.[8]

Here I wish only to analyze some of the leading assumptions behind his position. The first assumption concerns the ends of education and how they are derived. The second concerns the curricular means by which these ends are to be achieved. The third, and most important, concerns the claim that to deny the adequacy of Mr. Hutchins' curricular means involves a denial of the democratic philosophy itself.

That the *central* aim of education should be the development of man's power of thought is, so far as I know, denied by nobody—provided we do not identify power of thought with a specific intellectual skill. But, whereas most educators justify the emphasis on thought because of its key role in the organization of

[7]New York, 1953.
[8]In my *Education for Modern Man* (N. Y., 1946) I have examined at length the views of Mr. Hutchins, as well as those of Mortimer Adler, Stringfellow Barr and Scott Buchanan, as expressed in their writings up to that time.

impulse and feeling, the control of action, and the enrichment of the meanings of experience even when we cannot act, Mr. Hutchins derives it from a definition of man's fixed and essential nature.

Man is a rational animal. He is uniquely different from other animals by virtue of his power to think. Therefore, education must be directed exclusively to the cultivation of his intellect.

Now there are several things wrong with the deduction. First, even if we deny that other animals can think—and not all psychologists agree with this—the power to think is not the only differentiating feature of the human animal. There are other differentiating features. Man is the only animal who makes his tools. Man is the only animal with a sense of humor. If we were to derive our educational aims from these differentia, we should have to say that man's education must be primarily vocational or technological, or that it must develop his power to crack jokes.

Second, the nature of a thing is not completely given by what differentiates it. It includes what it has in common with other species in its genus. Man is a creature of emotion, an organism which adapts to and modifies its environment. An education appropriate to the nature of man must be appropriate to the *whole* of man's nature. This would include some things which Mr. Hutchins excludes. The Greeks, whom Mr. Hutchins takes as his model, regarded the end of education, not exclusively intellectual development, but the harmonious development of *all* human faculties. For them a life of reason is no more identical with a reasoning life than the joy of life is identical with a life of joy.

Third, what do we mean by thought? Modern education, to the extent that it is inspired by Dewey, interprets it broadly as creative intelligence in the solution of problems that arise in *all* fields of human experience. But Mr. Hutchins seems to identify thought or reason with academic intellectuality, with verbal skills in the interpretation of texts.

This deductive approach from fallible first principles is carried over into discussion of the curriculum of education. Since by definition all men have a common nature, the education appropriate to this nature must be common, and the means of achieving it—the educational curriculum—must be common, too. Therefore education everywhere, at all times, and for all men (and women) must be the same. Contrast this with modern education which, not by deduction but by inquiry, discovers that men have a great many needs in common and yet vary greatly, that their differences in culture and time reflect themselves in the way their common needs are fulfilled, and that even in the same culture variations among them are appreciable. It therefore stresses the fact that their indisputable common need—the development of intelligence—may be achieved in different ways.

An analogy might make the point clearer. Everyone needs to be healthy. What it means to be healthy, i.e., the *definition* of health, is the same for all men. We might even concede that the *formal* requirement of a well-balanced diet necessary for health is the same for all men. But who will therefore deduce that all men must eat the same things at the same time, or exercise in the same way, in order to be healthy? If there are differences among men, if they live in different climates and must perform different tasks, to prescribe a *common* dietary regimen is to guarantee that not all of them will be healthy. Just as there are different dietary roads to health, so there are different curricular roads to educational maturity. Great segments of these roads, of course, will be common.

I believe it can be established that to be intelligent men must be able to communicate with each other, understand the cultural past relevant to their present experience, and in so doing acquire certain basic skills and familiarity with certain subject matters. But to be intelligent in the *modern* world, their education must prepare them to cope with the *problems* of that world. How best to do this cannot be derived from definitions but must be discovered by inquiry and experiment, which may not give us absolute or certain truth for *all* time but sufficiently reliable knowledge for *our* time. This is a far cry, however, from Mr. Hutchins' all-prescribed curriculum for all men and women whose model, incidentally, is not so much the Chicago plan as the curriculum of St. John's College.

Now Mr. Hutchins is very well aware of the diversity and

variety of human talents. No matter how intelligence is defined or measured there is an enormous variation in human abilities, particularly the ability to understand the great books of the past, a few of which are confessedly beyond the competence of some of the architects of the St. John's plan. He has, therefore, hit upon a novel defense of the kind of education he proposes. According to this argument, since every man in a democracy is a voter, he is a ruler. To be himself a ruler or to elect his rulers, he needs the education which has been universally regarded, except by those who differ with Mr. Hutchins, as the best education. This best education is the education which by prescribed studies in mathematics, languages, philosophy and science develops the intellectual powers of man. It has never been fully tried, but the nearest thing to it is the curriculum of studies as it existed in the aristocratic cultures of the past when few were rulers. Since the best is not too good where all men are rulers, it should be adopted today.

Accused in the past of advocating an education irrelevant, if not hostile, to the needs of men in a democratic society, Mr. Hutchins is now contending that only those who agree with his conception of the best education can be considered consistent democrats. To have "strong faith in the political judgment of the masses with strong doubts of their intellectual capacities," i.e., of their intellectual capacities to acquire the best education, writes Mr. Hutchins, is a paradox. And in criticism of those who penned the report of the President's Commission on Education he says, "They most undemocratically assume that the mass of people are incapable of achieving such an education."

What is paradoxical, to put it mildly, about this argument is that Mr. Hutchins is attempting to settle on political grounds a fact that has nothing to do with politics. Even if the masses were able to profit by the curriculum Mr. Hutchins has deduced for them, that would not be decisive, because they might be able to profit even more from the study of a better one and one more relevant to our times. But the belief that not all students are capable of profiting by the kind of education that Mr. Hutchins regards as best for them is neither democratic nor undemocratic. It is either true or false. Jefferson was no less a democrat because he believed that intellectual capacities are unequal. Democracy in education is the belief that each person is entitled to the educational opportunities necessary to develop his potential capacities to their highest form. It is not the belief that all persons can profitably read Clerk-Maxwell's *Electricity and Magnetism*, Galois' *Mathematical Papers* or Kant's *Critique of Pure Reason*—and this before their twentieth year!

Apparently Mr. Hutchins believes that by flattering the masses with assurances that they can all profit by his prescribed educational curriculum—assurances incompatible with what is known about learning—his proposals will become more acceptable to them. But there is no reason to believe that what was the best education for the undemocratic rulers of the past—if it was the best—is now the best education for the masses. There is nothing inconsistent in believing that the citizens of a democracy are on the whole the best judges of their own true interests, and in believing that the training appropriate for the intellectual or academic elite cannot be made an educational requirement for all.

What Mr. Hutchins is really saying is this: Either accept the rule of an elite or of intellectual experts and give up democracy, or admit that the masses are all potential intellectual experts in a democracy and educate them to be experts. But it is not necessary to be an expert to judge the basic policies proposed by experts. One can choose his doctor wisely without a medical education. It is Mr. Hutchins who is inconsistent here. For, in addressing his appeal for the reform of education to the community, he himself admits that wise educational decisions may be made by those who are not educational experts or who have not been nurtured on the great books. If there are any experts in the wisdom of life, they cannot be mass produced by the same education. It is one thing to say that a healthy democracy rests upon some kind of common education. It is quite another to say that *all* education in a democracy must be common. And it is still something else again to assert that the content of a common education must be unchanging and identical in every respect.

Mr. Hutchins slides much too easily over the fact that the education recommended by him for the preservation of democracy was in the past close to the kind of education found in un-democratic societies. It nurtured an elite which on the whole opposed democracy wherever it appeared. On the other hand, it was the trade unions and the dissenting churches which were the schools of democracy in Europe not the *Gymnasium*, the *lycée*, or the university. Mr. Hutchins is a little embarassed that Aristotle, whose works and ideas are pillars which support the best education, opposed democracy and held that some men by nature are slaves. He explains that Aristotle did not understand his own doctrines. Presumably that is why Plato and Aquinas, as important as Aristotle in his educational scheme, advocated the death sentence for heretics. They, too, presumably did not truly understand the purpose of their own doctrines.

This calls attention to a significant difference in what modern educators call intelligence and what Mr. Hutchins calls intellectual power. If one recommends the study of a subject for the purpose of developing the intellectual powers of students, one cannot believe without deceiving himself that such powers are general and that they can be brought to bear equally well on the problems of all fields. This is the mistake of those who assume that if their employees are slipshod in the use of tools, it is because they did not learn the niceties of Latin or English grammar. The subject matters of different fields are often so far removed from one another that the skills and habits acquired in mastering one field are no index to competence in another. Indeed, do we not often notice today that there is no more agreement about human affairs among those who have developed a common set of intellectual skills in their profession than among those who have not acquired such skills? This would seem to suggest a conspicuous kind of irrelevance between the intellectual skills in language, mathematics, and science, however desirable these skills may be for enlarging our understanding of the world, and the political wisdom and maturity about human affairs which, Mr. Hutchins assures us, is best achieved by what *he* regards as the best education. On occasions one is impressed not only by the absence of political wisdom on the part of those so trained but by their lack of political knowledge.

As modern educators use the term "intelligence" it is broader than the exercise of special intellectual aptitudes. It involves judgment of values, of the relations of persons to persons, and of persons to groups. This is the common subject matter of everybody's experience from childhood to adulthood. The common curriculum of studies that seems most relevant for a democracy would look quite different from that proposed by Mr. Hutchins. Without neglecting the basic skills and subject matter, it would emphasize elements in the student's personal and social experiences which mirror larger relationships, carry this to higher levels of generalization and complexity, and orient liberal education to a consideration of the great social and political problems of *our* time, on which *we* have to make decisions, instead of the social and political problems of past time.[9]

If Mr. Hutchins really desires a curriculum relevant to democratic living and citizenship, he should give greater attention to the development in students of attitudes and emotions necessary to recognize our interdependences, our collective responsibilities and our concrete individual duties. He should encourage the quest for curricular activities and projects which strengthen a behavior free from the twin faults of egomania and servility, which facilitate imaginative identification with others, which teach that an opponent is not necessarily an enemy and that democracy is also a personal way of life. But it is precisely projects and activities of this kind which Mr. Hutchins and other critics of modern education scorn as serious tomfoolery.

I am not suggesting that the formation of attitudes which enter into moral character should be the task only of the school or that it should be the whole task of the school or even the direct task of the school except on the elementary level. Nor do I see why it is necessary to divorce it from the study of organized subject matters and basic skills. If "education *for* democracy" is not to become a mere phrase, we cannot neglect it. Modern education does not neglect it. If it does not educate for democracy well, the only legitimate criticism is that it must do it better and not that it must cease to concern itself with attitudes, emotions, and social relations.

[9]*cf., op. cit.*, Chapter V.

3

In discussing Mr. Bestor's *Educational Wastelands* (Urbana, 1953) we are moving to another plane of criticism—one which is frankly empirical. Although Messrs. Hutchins and Lynd fortify their indictment of modern education by citing some unhappy experiences, they rest their case on other considerations. We have seen that Mr. Hutchins minces no words about it. Since the metaphysics of modern education is bad, its results must be bad.

Mr. Bestor, however, speaks for a large and ever-growing number of individuals who profess to judge modern education by its results. And he is profoundly convinced that the results of our schools, especially of our elementary and secondary schools, are turning out young men and women not only unwilling to think in a disciplined way but unable to do so; not only ignorant about what they should know but, even worse, ignorant of what to do and where to go to repair the deficiencies in their knowledge when they become aware of them. They simply lack the habits of inquiry. "Intellectual training," he says, ". . . has been pushed out to the periphery of the public school program" (p. 44). "Public school educationists have severed all real connection with the great world of science and learning" (p. 47).

The evidence? Some startling quotations from the writings of a school principal or a professor of education, with no confirming evidence that it represents the dominant sentiment among modern teachers or that the results of modern instruction verify it. For example, Mr. Bestor quotes a sentence that, although he characterizes it as extreme, he nonetheless takes as representative of the current mood in American schools. It is a sentence which has been picked up by popular magazines in what seems to be a campaign to scare the parents of the country.

"We shall some day accept the thought that it is just as illogical to assume that every boy must be able to read as it is that each one must be able to perform on a violin, that it is no more reasonable to require that each girl shall spell well than it is that each one shall bake a good cherry pie."

The implication is that this truly horrifying thought is guiding current practices in teaching the fundamental skills in our elementary schools. But what of the studies which show that modern schools do better in this respect than those of the past? All that shows, according to Mr. Bestor, is that, making allowance for improvement in physical conditions and for the increase of the school year, the improvement is not good *enough*. The results of the *Eight-Year Study*? All that shows is that the colleges in which the products of progressive high schools did well were not very good to begin with.

There is some other evidence, but it is difficult to assess. For example, Mr. Bestor quotes some figures from the federal Office of Education which show that smaller percentages of the present student body are enrolled in courses in mathematics and foreign languages than in the past. But today almost everyone is in high school, including groups of children whose intellectual capacities would have been considered in the past as not sufficiently developed for high school and who, had they been enrolled, would have failed their mathematics and language. I am confident that Mr. Bestor would not be willing to degrade the standards of intellectual achievement merely to be able to enroll everybody. What would be more helpful to know is our relative success in teaching mathematics and language today to students of capacities comparable to those who were taught these subjects in the past. Three questions must be kept distinct. Is present-day instruction inferior to that of the past when comparable factors are considered? Can present-day instruction be improved even if it has not deteriorated? Are we failing to give instruction in certain disciplines which would be educationally more profitable to students than the subjects they are now studying?

I do not know the answer to these questions. Mr. Bestor believes emphatically he does. His emphasis, however, seems to me to be disproportionate to the weight of the evidence he submits. I should say in his support that my colleagues in liberal arts colleges are dissatisfied with the quality of the students the high schools send them. I should add, however, that they always have been dissatisfied. I predict they always will be.

Nonetheless, what is apparent from the wide acceptance of Mr. Bestor's charges is that the public does not know what actually is going on in the schools of the country and that they do not understand what modern education is or what it is trying to do. Even allowing for the distortions and caricatures of their detractors, responsibility for the widespread failure to understand the program of modern education rests heavily on modern educators themselves.

Assume for the moment that the true goals of modern education were to become known, independently of whether they were approved or disapproved. Two other things would still have to be known: first, the actual extent to which its goals guide instruction and its methods are consciously used in the school systems of the country; second, the degree of success and failure in the use of its methods as compared with traditional methods. We can answer these questions for a few local communities. I have seen no answers for the country as a whole. A great deal of controversial discussion about current educational matters assumes that these answers are known.

Mr. Bestor believes, however, that there is indirect evidence of the true state of affairs and that it can be found in the curriculums of the teacher-training colleges. He contends that teachers colleges are at best qualified to teach only pedagogical skills—skills that can be taught through relatively few courses. Teaching skills are worthless unless the prospective teacher has mastered the organized subject matter he wishes to teach. This organized subject matter can best be taught by professors of the liberal arts, not by professors of pedagogy in schools of education. These schools, however, not only compel their students to take needless courses in pedagogy for professional advancement, they provide instruction in the subject matter courses given in the liberal arts college. The consequence is that our prospective teachers are ill-equipped to teach the subjects for which they are licensed. To Mr. Bestor the life of the mind is lived only in the liberal arts college: schools of education constitute a kind of intellectual underworld. Since our schools can rise no higher than their teacher source, they cannot educate for intelligence even if they seek to do so. "Across the educational world," he writes, "stretches an iron curtain which the professional educationists are

54

busily fashioning. Behind it, in slave labor camps, are the classroom teachers, whose only hope is rescue from without." He closes with an eloquent plea that his colleagues in the liberal arts colleges concern themselves through their professional associations with "the scientific and scholarly soundness of every major proposal affecting the content and organization of the public secondary-school curriculum." He urges them also to study programs of teacher education and the laws governing certification in order to determine whether proper training in intellectual discipline is given by the first and enforced by the second.

Mr. Bestor's language is provocative and in places needlessly offensive. Whether true or false, his charges are sure to arouse resentment. But whatever their resentments, professional educators should not, I believe, oppose his proposals. On the contrary, they should welcome them as the best way to raise the iron curtain of which Mr. Bestor speaks. They might suggest, however, an addition to the agenda of concern, *viz.*, an inquiry into the effectiveness of teaching in the liberal arts colleges. But even in their original form Mr. Bestor's proposals, if acted upon, are very likely to bear sound fruit. They will at the very least accomplish something that has never been done before, i.e., make the teachers of liberal arts colleges aware of the problems of mass education in a democratic society. Instead of talking about standards in the abstract, they will think about them in the concrete context of wide variations in the natural powers of students, all of whom are capable of some development but not necessarily in the same way. Although he speaks as if teachers colleges usurped their function, he is well aware that it was the refusal of liberal arts colleges to take problems of general public education seriously that was in large measure responsible for the growth of teachers colleges.

It is simply not true that the invidious judgments which, Mr. Bestor reports, are often passed by his colleagues on teachers colleges are the consequence of the *present* character of their goals and curricular content. Unfortunately, these judgments were already reflected in the profound unconcern which liberal arts colleges in the past manifested towards all the great problems of public education. The reason is not far to seek. Until very recently most of the disciplines in the liberal arts college were taught by specialists for future specialists. Chemistry was taught as if all students were preparing themselves for careers either as research chemists or as professors of chemistry. Mathematics and physics were taught as if all students were going to be engineers or college teachers of those subjects. The consequence was that, except for the select few who did become specialists or college professors, there remained no lasting interest in the subject, no sense of its bearing on other disciplines. Even curiosity and the original sense of wonder about the subject were often killed.

The situation has changed somewhat in the liberal arts colleges, partly as a result of the influence of modern conceptions of education. But even to this day I occasionally discover that the cause of concern among some of my colleagues about the education their children are receiving in the public schools is the secret fear that they are not getting an education that will qualify them to be college professors.

Cooperation between faculties of liberal arts colleges and of teachers colleges has been too long delayed. Such cooperation will avoid unnecessary duplication of courses devoted to subject matter. It will make every liberal arts teacher aware that he is an educator, too. It will destroy the idea that there can be a double standard of scholarship, at the same time that it stimulates the scholar to make his knowledge come alive and grow in the students' experience.

4

If one feels a responsibility only to a subject or to a discipline, teaching is the easiest activity in the world, especially if one enjoys monologue. But if one also feels a responsibility to the student, to each student, teaching is difficult. It grows in difficulty with the recognition of the variation in the students' capacities.

As I understand modern education, its aim does not slight intellectual development. It wouldn't be education if it did. But it takes seriously the moral obligation to develop the intellectual capacities of each student by whatever method or route is objectively best. This involves measuring his progress not by some arbitrary norm but in terms of his ability to do better, to widen his cultural horizon, and to improve his intellectual skills. This is not incompatible with recognizing the social necessity of the students' achieving some fixed minimum norms of proficiency before qualifying for advanced work or preparation for careers. If the phrase "responsibility to subject matter" has any meaning, those who use it should acknowledge that not *all* disciplines can be properly taught on certain advanced levels that will make them assimilable to everyone. Within the range of normal variation, however, certain disciplines which all students need in order to live in a modern world and a democratic society may and should be required. Because that variation is still very considerable, curricula and methods cannot be fixed but must be adapted to place, time, and persons. In approaching this task we must bring all the resources of modern psychology and pedagogy into play, not to eliminate difficult things from study, but to make them better understood. This is why, as John Dewey used to emphasize again and again, "the road of the new education is not an easier one to follow than the old road, but a more strenuous and difficult one." He also predicted that if there is a reaction against its aims and methods, it will be because of "the failure of educators, who professedly adopt them, to be faithful to them in practice." Inquiry, of course, must establish whether this is true. *Theoretically*, it is possible that even when progressive educators are faithful to their aims and methods, they may fail to do as well as or better than others. This is still an open question.

One thing seems clear. If modern education is difficult, the preparation of those who engage in it must be at least commensurate with its difficulty. I do not see how teachers can ever know too much or themselves stop learning. I have never been able to understand why a good liberal arts education should not be a *sine qua non* for teaching on any level no matter how elementary. It is not an automatic qualification, of course, because certain qualities of personality are also essential.

No matter how well teachers are prepared, they will still have to confront a great danger intrinsic to the approach of modern education. This danger arises from the fact that in attempting to get the most out of those who are least naturally gifted, the intellectual development of those who are the most gifted is sometimes cramped. Only a tutorial system for each student could avoid this.

But there is another device which modern educators sometimes use, and which is not more widely used because it is feared that it has undemocratic implications. This is the differentiation of students on the basis of their native capacities and achievements in order to prevent the more gifted from being bored by teaching approaches necessary to motivate the less gifted, and in order to prevent the latter from falling behind when the former are given their head. I do not see how this breaches the democratic commitment of modern education in any way. That individuals vary in their musical or athletic prowess is accepted as a matter of course. It is not unfair discrimination to give to those who vary in their learning power different tasks or the same tasks to complete in different times. In many schools this device is widely used. Some high school students cover the course in intermediate algebra in six months; others take a year; a few are encouraged to master the material by self-study. In some English classes four books are intensively studied, in others three. There seems to be no resentment among students who travel at a slower pace, and there is less educational dissatisfaction than there probably would be if they found themselves in the same classes.

This principle can be generalized and applied to colleges too. In each case, the end of education will be the same—the development of habits of intelligent inquiry. But the curriculum and methods by which the end is achieved do not have to be the same even when certain disciplines are required for all. Some critics of modern education do not object to this so long as institutions which depart from standard curricula are not *called* colleges. But it is unimportant what educational institutions are called. What is important is that genuine learning goes on in them, even if they are not degree-granting, and that teachers do not settle for less if better teaching can achieve more.

The best adult education gives us a parallel and many helpful clues. Subjects, methods, and levels of instruction vary. But they all justify themselves to the extent that they contribute to individual growth.

One final word. Modern education will always be on the defensive if it waits for criticisms from those who are hostile to its philosophy before facing its problems and correcting its defects. It is the modern educators themselves who should be the foremost critics of modern education.

5

John Dewey's Philosophy
of Education

On the 100th anniversary of his birth and but seven years after his death, the educational philosophy of John Dewey was condemned by the highest political authority in the United States. In a letter published in *Life* (March 15, 1959), President Eisenhower, who once served briefly as President of Columbia University, where John Dewey taught for more than a quarter-century, wrote: "Educators, parents and students must be continuously stirred up by the defects in our educational system. They must be induced to abandon the educational path that, rather blindly, they have been following as a result of John Dewey's teachings."

This criticism climaxed the offensive from different quarters of the ideological compass against Dewey's educational philosophy. Book upon book, article upon article had developed the same theme. Criticism of the multiple inadequacies of American education was coupled with large, vague but forthright attacks on John Dewey as the prime cause of American failure. Even the Navy and Marines were called in! One of the most strident books in this vein was Vice Admiral Hyman Rickover's *Education and Freedom*, which should properly have been entitled "Education for Victory in the Next War." It is both striking and significant that most of the criticism did not even attempt to come to grips with Dewey's central educational doctrines. Instead, it merely deplored the faults and weaknesses of American education—in the light of the threat to freedom's future implicit in Soviet technological advance.

For all their legitimate, if newly awakened, concern with education, one gets the impression that the most vocal of Dewey's latter-day critics did not themselves exhibit that value of *conscientiousness* in their criticism which they desired our schools to stress in their curriculum. They seemed to be looking for a scapegoat for our predicament rather than for its genuine causes. If they had actually read Dewey instead of denouncing him, they would have observed that he himself had been a lifelong critic of American education, and that on occasion his criticism extended even to that small private sector of American education which was "progressive" in orientation, and took its point of departure from his own principles. More important still, it was John Dewey who long ago foresaw and warned against the very elements that had produced the crisis of our times and set off the current hysteria about the state of American education.

It is generally agreed that the main outlines of our crisis were shaped by the convergence of two great phenomena. The first was the transformative effects of science and technology on society, industry and culture. The second the emergence of Communist totalitarianism as an expanding imperialism which declared the United States to be the chief foe in its crusade for world domination.

During the last 50 years of his life, Dewey defined our age as the age of the scientific revolution. He called upon educators to take note of the vast implications of the scientific revolution, of the changes it produced in our way of life. He urged a searching inquiry into the institutions, principles, and methods necessary to channel and master these changes in the interest of inclusive and humane ends. Calling for improvement of science instruction in elementary schools at the turn of the century, he wrote: "I believe the attitude toward the study of science is, and should be, fixed during the earlier years." He took scientific knowledge as his paradigm of knowledge; and he proposed that its basic *logic* or *pattern* of thinking, as distinct from specific techniques and methods, be adopted as a norm for thinking wisely about political and social affairs. Some of the critics who joined the outcry that Dewey had ill prepared American schools for the challenge of our scientific and technological world were the very ones who not long before charged him with "scientism," with placing undue emphasis upon the scientific mode of experience while slighting other modes. The simple truth is that no one who took Dewey's educational ideas seriously would have been surprised by recent technological advances.

The same is true for the other major explosive element in the situation. During the last 20 years of his life, and most especially during World War II when the Soviet Union was being hailed by professional humanists and scientists, by leading admirals and generals and politicians, as a trusted ally of the democratic powers, Dewey described the nature of the Communist threat to the free world. He did not wait for the Kremlin to put a satellite in the sky to recognize the portents of disaster. He proclaimed them when the Kremlin established its satellites on earth—and even before then. He called for an intelligent foreign policy based on realistic understanding of the nature of Communism, which he had studied intensively from the time of the infamous Moscow Trials in the mid-thirties.

It was the absence of this intelligent foreign policy, for which the politicians, generals and admirals were chiefly responsible, that accounted for the particular crisis that agitated Admiral Rickover and his confreres. During the last war, the American educational system was no better and in some respects it was much worse than it was when the critics attacked Dewey for its failures. But we had enough political gumption to realize what the nature of Hitlerism was—and what its victory would mean to the prospects of freedom. We were able to introduce the emergency research programs which insured our victory.

What happened subsequently? Those responsible for political and defense policy failed to understand the nature of Communism and failed, therefore, to provide the leadership and vision required to contain the newer and more dangerous threat to freedom. They stumbled from error to error, from one improvisation to another, from appeasement to bluster. They were unable to take the initiative with intelligent policies because they lacked a clear grasp of nationalism, of Communism, and of the impact of the new scientific revolution upon the world.

I should not like to be misunderstood as implying that failures and successes in foreign policy flow *directly* from educational philosophy or practice. But precisely such a proposition seemed to be implied by the grand panjandrums of the anti-Dewey parade who were convulsed with fury at what they call progressive education. For what they really were deploring was our truly serious condition *vis-à-vis* the growing power of the totalitarian world—a serious condition that testified to the defect of political intelligence, and sometimes of elementary political knowledge, on the part of those responsible for that policy in the past. If education is relevant to this question, we must look to the education of those in strategic places and command posts. Have those who have neglected the needs of scientific military defense from Pearl Harbor to the present, who have systematically neglected the opportunities for democratic ideological warfare, who have failed to make the United States the leader of the world movement for colonial liberation—have all those politicians, generals and admirals been brought up on progressive education, or in the spirit of Dewey's educational philosophy?

Admiral Rickover and some of Dewey's other critics seemed to be interested in an education that will help us win the next war. If Dewey's educational philosophy had truly guided American education and inspired the architects of American foreign policy, their concern would have been how to avoid a world war and yet preserve and extend the heritage of free society. For this is a corollary of the basic educational aim of Dewey's philosophy—education for creative intelligence in a world of peace and freedom and *danger*.

Despite those who taxed him with lapsing into a cheerful and complacent naturalism because man is "in" and "of" nature, the world as it struck Dewey has at least two outstanding traits. It is a

64

world of danger—which fluctuates in intensity, but is always present—and it is a world of opportunity. The dangers are more obvious than the opportunities because most of the time the opportunities have to be sought for, they have to be made or discovered. In a precarious world, thinking diminishes danger by enlarging opportunity. An education which equips man to live a significant life in a dangerous world cannot be the "soft education" that the Rickovers properly decry. Nor must it necessarily be the "hard education" of technical, mathematical, and scientific courses that, with an eye on Sputnik, they cried up. The world may be dangerous not only because of our ignorance of advanced mathematics and physics, but because of our ignorance of elementary politics, economics and social psychology. Without genuine *political* understanding, the leaders of the Western world could not prevent Communism's postwar expansion, even if they possessed the mathematical and scientific knowledge of an Einstein.

I shall present briefly three leading ideas which seem to me central to Dewey's philosophy of education. They are his theory of experience, his conception of democracy, and his emphasis on scientific method in education.

The term "experience" has many different meanings, but the sense which Dewey gives it makes it relevant to the human learning process. All education is occasioned by experience, but for Dewey not all experiences are genuinely educational. He regards only those experiences to which the individual reacts with an informed awareness of the problems and a challenge of his environment as truly educational. Such a reaction increases our actual or potential power of control in relation to environment or self. For all his naturalism, Dewey is post-Kantian in his theory of experience. Human beings do not merely endure or suffer events or happenings, they actively experience them. To experience them is to take them in a certain way, to react in a manner that expresses the total state of the organism and reflects the cultural and historical situations in which that organism has developed.

To the extent that the organism is passive, it may be trained to react by automatic drill and other forms of conditioning, but no genuine human learning occurs as distinct from animal learning. Some element of activity, of attending and therefore selecting, must be present. Even reading, which seems to take place by passive absorption, cannot give understanding unless the mind reaches out, so to speak, to grasp the sense of the passage. The intercepted light signals and the retinal images are not enough. The meaning and significant content of an experience depend precisely upon this grasp or outreaching of the mind, which responds to, relates, and interrelates the elements of the experience.

Dewey's theory of experience is not derived from arbitrary philosophical premises but from modern psychology. In many ways, experimental findings confirm his view that even what a man observes cannot be adequately accounted for without reference to the active role of the observer, his history and cultural context. As Adelbert Ames and others have shown, perception is not merely a mirroring of what is given but the consequence of some interaction—or, better still, a transaction between organism and environment, self and not-self. It is this theory of experience which underlies Dewey's conception of man as a creature who, although bound by the antecedent conditions of his existence, can within limits redirect and redetermine both the world and himself and become morally responsible for those things which his thought and action can influence.

All this, Dewey would say, is descriptive of what experience is and how we learn by and through experience. But Dewey has a normative approach to what the educational experience should be. He distinguishes between two aspects of an experience, its *impact* and its *effect*. Its impact is the felt immediacy of being exciting or boring, agreeable or disagreeable, pleasurable or painful. The active response in this aspect of experience is of short range. It is atomic or pulse-like and dies with the occasion. The second aspect is its effect upon further experiences. This effect may be measured by the extent to which the learner sees meaning in his present experience, reacts to its possible leads and interpretations, and thus prepares himself to understand better, and to some degree to control, future experience.

This is why, for Dewey, "the central problem of an education based upon experience is to select the kind of present experiences that live fruitfully and creatively in subsequent experiences." To do this a whole series of selections is necessary that results not merely in organized subject matter but in a certain kind of subject matter, not merely in discipline but a certain kind of discipline, not merely in method of instruction but a certain kind of method. But they all have two things in common.

First, they are selected with an eye to the continuity of experience, or, more accurately, to the expected continuities of experience, so that future experiences become more readily accessible to us on the basis of our past experience. This does not mean neglect of subject matter. It points rather to the importance of proper organization of subject matter. And it does not mean that all subject matters are equally important. "The curriculum must be planned with reference to essentials first, and refinements second." What is essential depends on a number of variables. Second, subject matters, methods and disciplines are to be selected so as to maximize the active participation of the learner in the process of learning.

This stress on the element of activity in educational experience is congenial to Dewey's interpretation of "ideas" as implicit plans of action or operations to be carried out in appropriate situations; of "understanding" as congruous and conjoint behavior in partaking in a common enterprise; of "truth" as warranted assertion emerging from the transformative activities of experiment; and of "intelligence" as creative thinking that by sign-using behavior alters situations in such a way as to resolve their problematic character.

Whether these interpretations of "ideas," "truth," "understanding" and "intelligence" are valid I shall not discuss here. Like all other interpretations they have their difficulties. But I stress the character of these interpretations and of Dewey's theory of experience because it enables us to assess some of the criticisms of Dewey's philosophy of education.

I am referring particularly to the view that Dewey emphasizes adjustment to society—if not to present society, then to some future society. Admiral Rickover wrote: "The American people have never authorized the schools to replace education with life-adjustment training and behavioral conditioning. Yet we have permitted the schools to experiment with Dewey's ideas for a long time."

Can misunderstanding be more complete? It would be a more legitimate, even if mistaken, criticism of Dewey to say that the development of intelligence is more likely to lead to estrangement from society or opposition to it or necessarily to a desire to reform and transform it. In order to be intelligent, one must have ideas. To have ideas is to be committed or ready to act on them. To act on them means introducing a directed change either in the environment or in ourselves. According to Dewey, we make our environment in part because our response to it is a selective response depending upon our attention and interest. We make our environment *only in part* because we must accept most of it without thinking—thinking is done only on occasion—and because the results of all same thinking must acknowledge the existence of what exercises compulsion upon what we do. But the world we live in, whether personal or public, private or shared, to the extent that we act intelligently in it, is *partly* of our creation. That is why we are responsible for those features of it that could be different were we to think and act otherwise.

The only person who is adjusted to his environment in the mindless way Admiral Rickover implied is one in a state of torpor, inattention, absence of interest, boredom. To be awake and alive in a world where problems exist means to be alarmed, on guard, ready to do something in relation to what is about to be or about to happen. Ironically, the pejorative educational connotations of "adjustment" may be legitimately applied to the conception held by some of Dewey's critics about the role of students in school and the role of the school in society.

In one of these connotations, adjustment suggests subordination to the *status quo*, not merely learning *about* the conditions of life, but compliance with its norms. The "adjusted" individual assimilates social use and wont, the traditional ways of action, to the compulsions of natural necessity. In the past, education for this type of adjustment was associated with drill, habitual obedience, automatic response, the performance of set tasks under set conditions, the assumption that there is usually only one right way of doing anything and that some person in authority must ultimately define it. This kind of education is more reminiscent of traditional military training than of modern education.

An allied notion of "adjustment" is involved in views which regard the function of education to be the "pouring" or "cramming" of subject matter—honorifically labelled "the great traditions of the past"—into the students' minds, as if they were inert receptacles or containers to be filled rather than powers to be stirred and developed. Such an approach fails to give students a sense of *why* subject matters matter. It also fails to make ideas, people and events come alive in the direct or imaginative experience of those who are learning.

All of these conceptions of adjustment or *self*-adjustment are foreign to Dewey's educational philosophy. For they do not envisage the adjustment of society to the moral imperatives of educational growth. Nor do they adjust the curriculum to the needs and capacities of students in order to achieve maximum educational growth. A curriculum designed and taught in the light of Dewey's philosophy seeks to quicken powers of perception, wherever relevant, into how things have become what they are; into how they may become better or worse; and into what our responsibility, personal or social, is for making them better or worse. It strives to make the student sensitive to the kind of problems he will have to meet in wider contexts when he is through with formal schooling. It is not romantic or utopian. Although it liberates the mind by opening visions of alternatives, it curbs the will and disciplines the imagination by recognizing that not all alternatives are possible or equally probable. Certain objective conditions must be learned and accepted in order to introduce intelligent changes. No one can be wise who is not resigned about something, or who tries to dissolve the stubborn facts in the rose water of myth or hope. But wherever conditions impinge upon men, men can also impinge upon conditions. One can adjust to the weather by letting oneself be rained on or by learning to keep dry in the rain. What is true of weather is true of everything else that is meaningfully perceived in life—even death. So long as one remains conscious, one can determine something important about his own death. We can die like jackals or like men.

Terms like "adjustment" or "non-adjustment," like the terms "conformism" or "non-conformism," are essentially relational. Used without reference to a context, as most critics employ them, they are meaningless. Unless we know *what* is being adjusted to and *how*, what is being conformed to or not, these terms have merely emotive overtones but no cognitive significance. When the context and use are supplied, the only kind of adjustment Dewey would approve of is that which develops independent or creative intelligence.

I do not mean to imply that all criticisms of Dewey's theory of experience are of the same uninformed character as those considered above. His theory of experience is primarily an empirical hypothesis to explain psychological data. Ultimately, its formulations must be tested by observation and clarified by analysis. Its bearing on the philosophy of education is apparent when we consider the ends and methods of education. Certain ends are to be ruled out if, because they run counter to the normal course of experience, they exact too great a price in needless frustration, friction, or pain. But it is possible on the basis of the same theory of experience, Dewey's or any other, to defend different educational ends. At this point we move from the plane of psychology to ethics and social philosophy. An analogy may make this clearer: Certain methods of teaching reading may be ruled out as undesirable because of what we know about the biology and psychology of vision. But even where we agree about the best methods of teaching reading, this by itself will not determine the content of reading or what *should be* read.

Nonetheless, I must confess myself puzzled to understand, in the light of Dewey's own writings, many of the criticisms made by some well-meaning and otherwise well-informed critics of his theory of experience. For example, Professor I. B. Berkson interprets Dewey and the experimentalists generally as meaning by "experience" only biological and social processes of interaction, and excluding ethical and ideal moments. As if the social components of experience are not already drenched with ethical attitudes and values!

This is bound up with the kindred criticism that, because of their attack on fixed assumptions, Dewey and the experimentalists "leave the impression that we can derive conclusions from direct experience without making any assumptions" (Berkson, *The Ideal and the Community*, Harper). This would make Dewey sin against the very first principles of his own theory of inquiry. For Dewey an open mind is not an empty mind. Doubt arises not because we are ignorant but because what we assume to be true doesn't appear to be so. The view that for Dewey thinking starts from scratch and that any subject matter, especially *historical* subject matter, is to be approached with a mind born yesterday is simply quaint. It is a caricature even of eighteenth-century rationalism.

It is a commonplace of the experimental tradition that, as Charles Peirce put it, we cannot doubt all things at once. And it is a simple fact of experience that men and especially children suffer from an excess not of doubt but of credulity and dogmatism. This explains the experimentalists' emphasis not on the absence of presuppositions and assumptions—something must always be taken for granted—but on the importance of developing habits of inquiry as we begin to learn, and the growing importance of these habits of inquiry as the student grows older. As Dewey said in *Experience and Nature*, "What is already known, what is accepted as truth, is of immense importance; inquiry could not proceed a step without it."

The criticism that experimentalism places such emphasis upon primary and immediate experience as to exclude tradition, a sense of history and of the past from learning is a recurrent theme of many different schools of critics. This is evident even when they quote Dewey to the effect that "ours is the responsibility of conserving, transmitting, rectifying, and expanding the heritage of values we have received that those who come after us may receive it more solid and secure, more widely accessible, and more generously shared than we have received it." I am convinced that this kind

71

of criticism is based upon a totally naive view of history and an unjustified fear that when we study the present intelligently we can ever escape reference to history.

Test this criticism by an illustration. Nothing is more topical than the issue of integration in American life or education. No social studies teacher can ignore it as part of relevant subject matter. But who could discuss it intelligently without reference to *historical* factors in politics, law, economics, and ethics? The entire texture of social and cultural subject matter is woven out of historical strands—some short, some long, but all so inextricably and intricately intertwined that we need some principle of relevance to snip their connections to understand what bears on the present. And how can the subject of integration, whether we draw our illustration from what happened at Little Rock or Forest Hills, be evaluated without some defensible commitment to an ideal of democracy, freedom, and fair play; to some conception of federal, states', and individual rights; to rule by majorities, absolute or concurrent, and their relation to minorities? But just as soon as we seek to ground these commitments in history we find that history is not enough. There are many histories, and our selection of guides from among them, Jefferson or Hamilton, Lincoln or Calhoun, Wilson or Debs, expresses in the last analysis a moral judgment that we must show to be viable in the present. We cannot escape the primacy of history when social fact is considered, nor can we escape the primacy of morality where social policy is considered.

What then is the issue? The issue, I make bold to say, is whether we are to accept uncritical history—a traditionalism which under the guise of respect for tradition smuggles in bias and prejudice—or whether we are to accept an approach to history that gives loyalty to truth or the methods of discovering the truth where knowledge of the past is concerned. Dewey would agree with Pascal's statement—although not with his reasons for saying it— that "whatever right antiquity may claim, truth always has a prior claim, no matter how new its discovery."

What, for example, is suggested in the following passage from Berkson's *The Ideal and the Community*: "More is lost than gained when the regime of purposeful activity and critical intelligence is represented as a substitute for, instead of as a supplement to, instilling a devotion to principles and directing toward definite moral ends. The undertone of antagonism to authority, to traditional belief, to doing right for right's sake is likely to lead to loosening of existing standards rather than raising to a higher mode of conduct. In its lack of confidence in the established order, experimentalism unwittingly casts a shadow of distrust on conventional mores and accepted institutional forms *even when these serve valid social purposes."* (Italics mine.)

To me, this suggests the perennial complaint of the traditionalist and fearful conservative against the corrosive effects of intelligence. Experimentalism is decried because it raises doubts about conventional forms *"even when these serve valid social purposes."* But if they do serve valid social purposes, why should critical intelligence sustain doubt? The very language of the passage quoted could just as easily be employed by Prussian schoolteachers or Southern Bourbons convinced that existing institutions serve valid social purposes—and a liberal like Berkson would be among the first to disavow them.

Nonetheless, the assumption of the passage is that children come to school doubting Thomases from homes in which they have been nurtured by a religion of Critical Reason equipped with dialectical weapons. But every teacher knows that they come with the prejudices of their communities prepared to believe whatever they are told, intolerant even of differences in dress, speech, manner and thought. One would think that juvenile delinquency is the consequence of hyper-critical intelligence! The causes of juvenile delinquency are many and what takes place in the schools has precious little to do with them. But to the extent that there is some connection, one can more plausibly argue that the failure of the school to demonstrate the valid social purposes of existing laws and institutions and to bring home a vivid, imaginative and convincing sense of their justifications, makes it easier for students to disregard them.

"Not all who say *Ideals, Ideals,"* Dewey reminds us, "shall enter the kingdom of the ideal, but only those shall enter who know and who respect the roads that conduct to the kingdom." The roads which are to conduct us to the kingdom of the ideal must be built by the best methods of intelligence (or reason or scientific inquiry) available to us. And whether or not we ultimately reach the kingdom is not so important as the direction in which we move and how we move. Agreement on goals and ideals means little in practice unless we can agree on methods and procedures of reaching them. At the risk of being misunderstood, I say that there is greater difference among those who proclaim their agreement about goals and disagree about methods, means and procedures, than there is among those who agree upon the latter and leave open the question of whether they further agree upon "ultimate" ends—if there are such. Every "ultimate end" in a concrete historical context is analyzable into a "penultimate end." For Dewey, just as use of different means results in different ends, so different roads lead to different kingdoms.

What is true of the place of history in education is also true of the place of subject matter and the function of the teacher. There is absolutely nothing in Dewey's theory of experience and education that makes the subject matter and/or the teacher dispensable. The misconceptions about this derive from a misunderstanding of, and sometimes disagreement with, Dewey's conception of democracy in education.

Dewey's philosophy of education, as everyone knows, makes central democracy in education. Although the phrase "democracy in education" has become a shibboleth, so that few will openly declare that they oppose it, it has many different meanings. It is commonly assumed that Dewey's conception of democracy in education encourages, if it does not entail, the cult of mediocrity, and the systematic denigration of intellectual excellence. To assess the validity of this charge, it is necessary to examine with some care what Dewey means both by democracy and by democracy in education.

Democracy in most contexts refers to a form of government or a political process by which those who rule are elected by the freely given consent of a majority of the adults governed. Although Dewey was a democrat in this sense, he did not regard democracy or any other political process or institution as an end in itself. He realized that a democracy could function poorly and that it was capable of acting abominably, *e.g.,* in its treatment of minorities in the South or elsewhere. All his life he criticized the functioning of American democracy in the light of a more basic conception of democracy which he called "moral and ideal."

The essence of Dewey's view was that democracy was committed to an equality of concern for each individual in the community to develop himself as a person. Education was the chief means by which those personal capacities were to be discovered and liberated. Education would enable human beings to achieve their maximum *distinctive* growth in harmony with their fellows. Equality of concern is not the same thing as equal treatment. It is compatible with unequal treatment, provided this treatment is required by the necessities of intellectual and emotional growth in each case. "Moral equality," he says, "means incommensurability, the inapplicability of common and quantitative standards. It means intrinsic qualities which require *unique* opportunities and *differential* manifestation. . . ." The principle of moral equality or ideal democracy is the most revolutionary principle in the world because its scope embraces all social institutions.

Any honest reading of Dewey indicates that individuals come first in the order of concern, and that to be an individual is to be different in some distinctive and important way even though many things are shared in common with others. Conceptually, it is very difficult to express this union of equality of concern and difference of treatment in a formal rule. But we may illustrate it by reference to another institution: In a healthy and happy family where children vary in age, strength and intellectual gifts, it would be absurd for parents to treat them equally—absurd precisely because they are considered equal, valued equally. A family, of course, cannot be taken as a model for a complex society—there are no parents in society—but it illustrates the ethical principle which Dewey believed should be exhibited in the functioning of social institutions in a democracy, or which should be its controlling and guiding spirit. And it is striking to observe how often Dewey uses the family for analogical purposes to make an educational recommendation; for example, his well-known words: "What the

75

best and wisest parent wants for his own child, that must the community want for all its children. Any other ideal for our schools is narrow and unlovely; acted upon, it destroys our democracy."

The significance of this observation is all the more important as an indicator of Dewey's meaning, because the words are such an obvious overstatement. We have never acted on this ideal and have not destroyed our democracy, because democracy so conceived has never really existed. But these words do express in the most emphatic way an entire complex of values, values which must guide our action if we are to approach closer to the democratic ideal. And this ideal rests on the primacy of freedom, on the right to be different, on the right to be an individual—so much so that, although social institutions are recognized as the indispensable means by which personality is aided in coming to development, all social institutions must nevertheless be criticized and reformed in the light of the qualities of human experience to which they give rise. The individual person comes first in the order of significance, not of time.

The educational corollaries which follow from such a democratic philosophy are fantastically different from those drawn by critics who see in it the prolegomenon to an ideological justification for mediocrity. The very contrary is true. Mediocrity is the consequence of imposing one uniform pattern on individual differences, of the attempt to make everyone talk and sing and think alike about the same things at the same time. How can Dewey's philosophy be interpreted as advocating that the gifted child be denied the special attention which would bring his gifts to fruition? Historically, the earliest concern with providing appropriate educational opportunities for gifted children was manifested by educators and psychologists strongly influenced by Dewey. By all means, education must aim at excellence! But is there only one kind of excellence? Must one excellence be sacrificed to another? Must, as Ernest Renan asks, whatever is unfit for the altar of the gods be thrown to the dogs? Or, put more concretely, does it follow that, because we should exert our efforts to provide the educational stimulation that will generate the most fruitful results for students of the highest IQ, we should therefore not exert ourselves to generate the most fruitful results for students of lower IQs? If this is what it means, where is our equality of concern?

We must distinguish between standards of achievement that individuals must measure up to before certain professions are open to them—and from which, both in their own personal interests and those of society, they can be legitimately barred—and the standard of growth and progress that is applicable to each individual. It is the latter which concerns the teacher, insofar as he accepts responsibility for the education of the person. And this means not the elimination or the dilution of subject matter, not the substitution of play for study, not a cafeteria of snap courses—but holding up ever higher goals to be reached by every student until he has attained *his* best. Such an approach is perfectly compatible with some prescribed courses and studies. For if all needs are individual, many of them are at the same time common needs in a common world of common dangers and opportunities. There are some things everyone needs to know; but not everything needs to be known by everybody.

What this democratic conception of education involves is better grasped by contrasting it with the view that would not merely discriminate *between* capacities but *against* them. Such a view advocates a kind of elitist system in which the prizes and the power go to those who by natural endowment or social preferment (the two are often hard to separate) reach the head of their class. It not only differentiates but subtly demeans by suggesting that the hierarchy of intelligence is the key to the hierarchy of human value, which sooner or later determines position in a hierarchy of social standing and political power. Sometimes this view also calls itself democratic, but its spirit as well as its recommendations are altogether opposed to democracy as Dewey understood it.

Let us examine, for example, the view of Professor William Hocking, who has written widely on education. For him genuine democracy consists in *"the democracy of identical standard"* to be applied to all, irrespective of capacities. And he explains his meaning by an analogy: "We do not, in our athletic contests, trim the length of the mile to the convenience of the runners: The

77

democracy of the race does not consist in the assumption that everybody must get a prize; it consists in the identity of the spacing and timing for all entrants. This is what democracy must mean in higher education, and to retain this integrity, there must be losers, and a thinning out of the mass trend to the colleges" (*Experiment in Education*, Regnery, 1954). What this means in practice is indicated by the question: "But where is the college which is willing to flunk 50 per cent of its graduating class?"

Hocking does not explain why democracy means this only in higher education and not in secondary or even primary education. If "every man has a right and duty to be a whole man," as he puts it, why has not every individual a right to that kind of education which will carry him further to that wholeness at any level? And what has all this to do with degrees of certification of professional competence, which are fundamentally socially protective devices? And above all, what has the process of education to do with a race? And even in a race, we do not expect, unless we are Nietzschean, the halt, the blind, the crippled to start from scratch. And if the course of study is to be considered like a race course, who ever heard of 50 per cent of the runners winning the prize? Why not flunk 90 per cent of the graduating class—indeed, why not all except the man who wins by coming in first?

The analogy reveals the unconscious, anti-democratic, almost Prussian, conception underlying this view of education. Education is not a race or combat or a competition, although, properly implemented, these may be pedagogic devices to add zest to learning. If we prefer to use language of this sort, it is better to have the individual run a race against his own potentialities, which, since they grow with achievement, means that the race, like the process of education and self-education, is never finished.

Allied to this conception of education as the process by which prizes and power are won is the view of society as a graded and hierarchically organized society, in which intelligence, not birth, social status or wealth, is the principle of differentiation. No matter what the principle of differentiation is, if it involves hierarchy, official or unofficial, it involves the likelihood of exploitation. It is well to realize that we do not owe the great movements for social

justice and political freedom to the educated classes of hierarchically ordered European societies. On the whole, they sided with
church and king and the social *status quo* during the centuries of
struggle for the extension of human rights. Higher intelligence and
specialized education give both the duty and right to exercise
specific functions in a complex society, but so does not-so-high
intelligence and more general education. Unless there is a
mutuality of esteem and a recognition that there are many kinds of
desirable distinctions, the entire principle of distinction becomes
invidious, a badge of social snobbery and an instrument by which
special interests are furthered. A society in which there are class
struggles between the better educated and the less well educated,
between the more intelligent and the less intelligent, not only
violates the principles of moral equality, but is one in which the
best educated, a small minority, are likely to lose.

There is another aspect of democracy in education which is
intimately connected with modern American education. It has
been travestied and caricatured not only by critics, but by some
unintelligent followers of Dewey. This is the view that at
appropriate levels the student's educational experience—his group
meetings, school projects, class organization—exhibits some of the
values which are central to the ethics of democracy. In a country of
different races and varied ethnic groups in which the family itself
may be the original breeding place of violent prejudice, such
activities are all the more necessary. Whatever "character education" is, it is more likely to take by being lived than by being
preached. Where students are made responsible for some aspects of
their school life, this need not interfere either with the time devoted
to learning or with the seriousness with which it is prosecuted. A
skillful teacher can so organize instruction that often the
educational lesson or project draws all children into it in some par-
ticipating role for which they take responsibility.

The easiest way to make this idea ridiculous is to try to carry it
out with young toughs or hooligans produced by the breakdown of
family and community life in large cities. A pinch of common sense
is sometimes better than a carload of speculative pedagogy.
Although Dewey himself never realized the extent and gravity of

the problem, he did recognize that in the case of disturbed and unruly students who "stand *permanently* in the way of the educational activities of others . . . exclusion is perhaps the *only* available measure at a given juncture, even though it is no solution." (Italics mine.)

Every classroom teacher knows that it requires only one or two such students to make genuine teaching impossible. Nonetheless, the community—or rather, newspapers and educational pressure groups which decry modern education—cites the existence of such elements (which in the past either did not get to school or received short shrift when they did) as evidence of the failure of modern education. Nothing in Dewey's or anybody else's educational philosophy requires the schools to function as psychiatric and/or police institutions. Something should and can be done for such students—a democratic society should be equally concerned about them, too—but they must be firmly excluded, for their sake and the sake of other children, from the normal school environment until they are educationally rehabilitated.

Some of Dewey's distinctive views on education do not follow from his general pragmatic philosophy. On the contrary, he developed the latter, in part, on the basis of his reflection on, and observation of, those processes of education which seemed to succeed best in teaching students to acquire certain desirable skills, habits, values, and knowledge of subject matter. Dewey held the distinctive view that the scientific psychological study of the ways human beings learn, of the effects of individual differences on learning, of the interrelation of interest, insight and effort, gives us more reliable knowledge than the anecdotal methods of uncritical common sense. He held that we should use this knowledge in devising and testing teaching methods. If we wish to teach reading or any other subject worth teaching, there is a bad and a good and a better way of teaching it; there is an appropriate and an inappropriate time for teaching it, in order to get the best results; above all, there is a reliable and an unreliable way of finding out the answers to these questions—and the reliable way is the way of scientific inquiry.

It is beginning to be clear that a good deal of the criticism of Dewey's theories of education is based fundamentally upon a rejection of the view that scientific psychology should be our guide to the problems of effective teaching. For obviously, if the results of modern education (granting that it, too, wants to teach the three Rs) are unsatisfactory as compared with the results of traditional education when dealing with matched children, nothing could be easier than to make the necessary changes in methods and techniques, and no one would be more willing than modern educators.

What is surprising, however, is that the very critics who attack Dewey and modern education for their alleged anti-intellectualism refuse to abide by the consequences of scientific inquiry into matters of disputed fact. They do not even call for such inquiry. A very instructive illustration of this is provided by the Council for Basic Education Inc., an educational pressure group of growing influence. It is the source of many of Admiral Rickover's views on modern education. In one of its official Bulletins (February 1958), it discusses "The Seven Deadly Dogmas of Elementary Education," all of which it derives from what it calls "the official philosophy of education which has prevailed in the past 30 years"—a euphemism for the complex of ideas and theories associated with Dewey.

One of these seven deadly dogmas is listed as the dogma of scientific knowledge. According to this dogma, modern educators believe "that psychological and sociological research has established enough 'truths' about the nature of the child and the learning process to provide infallible guides to methods and even content in the education of the very young." Of course it is only in the minds of these "intellectualists," not in the mind of any sensible educator, that psychological findings provide "infallible" rather than reliable guides to method. The discussion, however, seeks to dispute two pieces of knowledge won by scientific educational psychology as reported in the *The Three R's Plus* (University of Minnesota, 1956). One is that "division by two-place numbers is too difficult for fourth-graders and should be postponed until the sixth"; the other is "that children of average ability do not profit" from the teaching of grammar. (Incidentally, the writer in the Bulletin of the Council for Basic Education does not report the statements accurately. The first asserts that division by two place numbers is too difficult for *average* fourth-graders; the second states that children of average ability do not profit from the teaching of grammar "of the old kind"—that is, formal instruction in parts of speech which have no reference to the expression of ideas. The inaccuracy of the reporting here—and not only here—is seriously misleading.)

The critical response of this exponent of classical and fundamental education to these claims of knowledge is not to challenge their truth on the basis of an examination of how they were reached, or by citation of other data won by controlled inquiry. He begins by denying "this glib faith in the ability of science and the scientific method to discover all truth about Man." But no one asserted that science can discover all the truth about Man. What has been assented is a more modest proposition: Scientific inquiry shows that some methods of teaching some things are more effective than other methods. If this is to be denied, it is not enough to deny what no one asserts—*viz.*, that science can discover all the truth about everything. The more modest claim can be denied only on the basis of specific evidence.

The nearest the critic of modern education comes to providing such evidence is his report: "Fortunately there are still teachers whose own observation and common sense tell them most fourth-graders are not too underdeveloped to conquer the mysteries of division by two-place numbers and that English grammar properly taught is an immense aid to the competent and civilized use of one's own language." The fallacies of this criticism are apparent. No teacher can observe most fourth-graders. He or she can observe only the fourth-graders he or she knows. But this is a very small group; and unless there is reason to believe it is a representative sample—that is, one not specially selected, something which requires scientific inquiry and not merely common sense—it may be an extremely unreliable index of most fourth-graders. Even if some teachers make this report on the basis of a sample about whose representative character we are not in doubt, it would not tell us what most teachers observe. It would, in any event, leave open the question as to whose observations were more reliable. For it is not merely the number of teachers who report observations that counts, but the methods of observation and the controls to which their observations have been subjected.

After all, we are concerned here with matters of fact which are difficult but not impossible to determine with a good degree of probability. Instead of exploring this and similar questions, critics of modern education wish to settle these matters by fiat, impressionism and snap judgment. They do worse. They beg the question because they fail to locate the problem. The question is not whether "English grammar properly taught" is helpful, but how it is "properly" taught—by instruction in formal parts of speech, diagramming, etc., or by instruction through remedial analysis of mistakes in usage and understanding.

What is even still worse than these elementary errors in logic is the attempt to determine what are the facts in the case by resort to political or ethical criteria. "We believe," writes this critic, "that education (which, after all, is supposed to change, remake and refine the human animal) cannot be satisfied with some norm of behavior, but must concern itself with what ought to be." Even if it is true, in other words, that most fourth-graders *cannot* learn some things, they *should* learn them! But is it sensible to urge that one should do what one can't do? Surely we must distinguish between situations where an "ought" implies a "could" and situations where it is inapplicable. A child with normal hearing and vocal cords should learn to sing. But if he develops a bass voice, shall we insist that he "should" continue to sing alto or soprano? If we are dealing with a person who is tone deaf, "should" in this context is pointless.

The trouble with much of our education, John Dewey complained long before his critics, is that most children do not learn as much and as well as they can learn. Modern education, by enlisting scientific psychology, attempts to get them to learn as much and as well as they can. Its *program* is to hold the stick up to the very top level of each individual's capacity, and by engaging his interest, elicit the effort and drive that will take him as close to the top as possible. If it fails in this program, it is not because it is too scientific, but because it is not scientific enough. Of course, there are normative tasks which the school must face, and no one has stressed the importance of the moral aspects of education more than Dewey. But when it is relevant to ask the questions—What ought our behavior be? What is worth pursuing and possessing? What is the best thing to say or do in this situation?—can we improve on Dewey's reply that such questions are to be answered not by habit, not by drift, not by intuition, not by revelation, but by critical intelligence informed by all the relevant facts in the situation? And by intelligence he means the use of the *pattern* of scientific inquiry, as distinct from the specific techniques of specific subject matters. For Dewey, the ultimate authority in liberal civilization is the authority of scientific method, broadly interpreted as the method of intelligence.

This is not the place to analyze all of the alleged seven deadly dogmas of elementary education. They really are not dogmas but leading principles. And their discussion by the representatives of this pressure group betrays the one deadly sin of the life of the mind—the refusal to engage in inquiry in the face of a genuine problem. The real nub of the difference between Dewey and most of his critics of this and allied schools lies in the question of the nature of authority in human judgment. Whereas for Dewey authority is derived from the pattern of the self-corrective procedures of scientific method, for them this authority is subordinate to something else.

Every important thing Dewey said more than a half-century ago about education and society, and education and science (with the exception of some predictions about the future of vocational education), is even more valid today. He began to think about these questions when the social world was rapidly changing. He argued that if education were conceived merely as the transmission of the culture of the past, youth would not really be prepared to meet and master the future. Today our world is changing at an even dizzier pace than he witnessed. The problems of mere survival, not to speak of survival and freedom, are greater than ever before. Nothing but intelligence *can* save us, but the chances that in-

84

telligence *will* are smaller than in the past.

Dewey's concept of intelligence involves the education of emotion, volition and perception, and not merely formal reasoning power or the exercise of what is sometimes called the *mind* or *intellect* considered in isolation from observation, experiment, and practice. "There is no such thing as over-intellectuality," he wrote in *Democracy and Education,* "but there is such a thing as one-sided intellectuality."

If we reject scientific method, the method of free intelligence, as the supreme authority in judgment of both fact and value, what can we substitute in its stead? Every alternative involves at some point an institutional authority which, historical evidence shows, lends itself to abuse, which proclaims itself to be above all interests and becomes the expression of a particular interest invested with the symbols of public authority.

Dewey's educational philosophy must still hurdle some great obstacles before it can be made socially effective. In a sense, this philosophy promises too much. As it conceives education, teaching becomes much more complex, much more of an art than conventional modes. It requires that teachers be much abler than most of them are at present likely to be; and it costs much more than most communities at present are willing to pay. It presupposes the existence of a humanist and scientific society in which all the large problems are being met in the spirit of Dewey's philosophy. The facts are otherwise and are likely to be so for a very long time. Where population is not controlled but grows by leaps and bounds, where practices of segregation and discrimination still exist, where an authoritarian parochial school system parallels the public school, where the presence or imminent threat of war engulfs the community so that the immediate necessities of national security must be given priority—a great deal of Dewey's educational philosophy appears to read like a counsel of perfection. It can do something, but to the literal-minded this will sometimes appear to be not very much.

In a crisis, no one seems to be concerned with the development of individual personalities as the basic categorical imperative of education. The public and even most educators are more concerned with *ad hoc* measures, which although justified are never sufficient. The very reaction against Dewey's philosophy of education is hard to explain in its own terms. If the world were one democratic, freedom-loving, welfare economy, Dewey's educational philosophy could very well become widely accepted as *the* public educational philosophy, although never an official ideology. But that is a large "if," and there are many other "ifs."

This means that unless concerted political and social efforts are made to strengthen the institutional framework of the democratic community, Dewey's educational philosophy may turn out to be inoperative. It is not fortuitous that the Nazis would have none of it, and that the Communists rejected all progressive educational practices as soon as they saw that Dewey's philosophy was more interested in the personalities of children than in their class antecedents. In a racialist community it cannot be properly applied; nor in a slum city which starves its schools, where municipal administration is corrupt, where hoodlums and delinquents terrorize whole neighborhoods. Indeed, to attempt to apply Dewey's educational philosophy under manifestly unripe and hostile conditions may result in consequences worse than those observable in situations where conventional methods of discipline and instruction prevail.

All this represents a two-fold challenge. First, it is not enough to proclaim the virtues of the best system of education for the best of all worlds. We must find ways of making the best of this educational system in a world which is far from the best. We must adapt, modify, improvise in a creative way, using some features in one context and some in another, taking advantage of every opportunity to inch forward, like a New York taxi driver—provided we know the direction we are going. Each educator must work where he is, with what he has, and strive to build up sympathetic public opinion and public support on a local educational level. The intelligent teacher must make the loving parent his staunch auxiliary in this process.

Second, we must remember that we cannot succeed in education without succeeding in fields other than education—in community relations, in industry, in politics. Rates of progress are different in different fields and uncertain in all; but unless we can improve the quality of our local democratic communities, unless we can realize greater democracy in our personal lives and in our face-to-face relations with our neighbors, Dewey's educational philosophy will have only limited effectiveness.

In this sense, the battleground of education is coterminous with the whole of society, for Dewey's educational philosophy entails and is entailed by his philosophy of liberalism. Intelligence in the service of freedom and free man must reconstruct social institutions so that they provide equal opportunity and equal concern for all. Only thus can we provide an educational philosophy not only for present-day America, but also for the future—a future in which, as Dewey envisaged it, "freedom and fullness of human companionship is the aim, and intelligent cooperative experimentation the method."

6

John Dewey
& His Betrayers

During the past few years there has been an open season on the American school system from the most elementary to advanced levels. It has been indicted not only for its failure to teach the rudiments of the traditional disciplines but for its repressive attitudes toward the spontaneous activities and the outreaching natural curiosity of the child and student as learning animals. The schools have been compared to penal institutions not only because of the physical conditions that exist in some ghetto areas but even more so because of the manner, spirit and methods of instruction.

In the past the severest criticisms of the American educational system have come from those who have called themselves or been considered educational "fundamentalists" opposing the alleged inroads of progressive education on the traditional course of study. Today it comes from those who regard themselves as libertarians and humanists and who either profess themselves inspired to some degree by the thought of John Dewey or are commonly regarded by the educational lay public as continuing his influence. I refer to writers like Paul Goodman, Ivan Illich, John Holt, Jonathan Kozol,

George Dennison, Edgar Friedenberg, George Leonard and many others whose views are broadcast and popularized with few dissenting comments in the mass media. These criticisms in various forms are exercising a surprising influence on educators and teachers. Their moods, catchwords, and arguments crop up in the heated discussions about education at school board meetings. They are partly responsible, as I have found in my recent career as a peripatetic philosopher of education, for a phenomenon observable in liberal arts colleges from one end of the country to another, *viz.*, the abandonment of required courses and even area distribution studies as unendurable forms of faculty paternalism, and a violation of "the student's autonomy, his moral freedom and responsibility."[1] The rhetoric is unimportant, but the thought is clear. Since the student is the best judge of his own educational needs, it is a tyrannical imposition from without to require him to take any courses that *he* thinks he does not need.

The extremism of these criticisms is manifested not so much in this move toward a universal elective system in higher education—now called by some merely "longer" education—but in the attack on the lower levels of schooling, in the rejection of any system of compulsory education, and in proposals to weaken and even to abolish the public school, making all elementary and secondary education "incidental"—to use the revealing phrase of Goodman—or purveyed in whatever private schools parents are prepared to establish or support with the vouchers they receive as tax credits for that purpose.

In education as elsewhere extremes often meet. Some of these proposals to abolish the public school and hand over the equivalent tax monies to parents to finance their children's education as *they* deem fit is sure to be enthusiastically applauded by those who are opposed to desegregation as well as by those who wish to perpetuate and extend the parochial school systems. We are reminded that ideas have consequences. Some of these ideas are not only educationally unsound; they are practically dangerous, since they would irremediably polarize the community racially, and

[1]McClintock, *Teachers College Record* (February 1971), p. 409.

separate groups of children from each other at a time when they are
most malleable.

Another point at which extremes meet today is the theme of
my analysis. This is the interpretation of the thought of John
Dewey. It is an open question whether Dewey's educational
philosophy has been more flagrantly distorted in the accounts given
of it by some of his latter-day disciples than by the criticisms of his
vociferous detractors. Both it seems to me have been intellectually
irresponsible in disregarding his plain and easily available texts.
But the moral failings of the professed followers of Dewey are
graver than those of his critics, first, by the very virtue of their
allegiance, which should impose a greater conscientiousness upon
them, and second, because the fundamentalist critics of Dewey
have as a rule seized upon *their* formulations, as professed followers
of Dewey, as evidence of the validity of the fundamentalist reading
of him.

I propose to discuss some central ideas of John Dewey's
educational philosophy that have been radically misconceived in
the current literature of criticism. Before doing so I wish to state as
emphatically as I can that I am no defender of the educational
status quo and that in recognizing the relative improvements that
have resulted from the attempt to educate a *whole* people beyond
the level ever attempted by any culture in the past, I am acutely
aware of the difficulties and problems that have resulted from that
effort, particularly in a society riven by profound social and racial
inequalities. But I am firmly convinced that most of the proposed
cures of latter-day progressive educators are worse than the disease.
They can only end, as is apparent in so many of our liberal arts
colleges, in the debasement of the quality of the educational
experience.

The first misconception of John Dewey's philosophy stems
from the notion that because he stressed the importance of
freedom, he was therefore opposed to authority. Nothing could be
further removed from his real teaching. "The need for authority,"
he wrote, "is a constant need of man" (*Problems of Men,*[2] p. 169).

[2]New York: Philosophical Library.

It is a constant need because conflicts, differences, incompatible desires, perspectives, and possibilities are ever present features of existence and experience. Some authority is therefore necessary. And for Dewey the supreme authority is intelligence. It is "the method of intelligence, exemplified in [but not identical with] science, [that should be] supreme in education" (*Experience and Education*,[3] p. 100). However intelligence be defined, it recognizes that not all forms of conduct are possible or desirable, that restriction and negation are as central to any discipline as affirmation, and that the growth which prepares the way for further desirable growth can be achieved only through a limitation of possibilities. Freedom outside the context of the authority of intelligence is the license of anarchy. The democratic idea of freedom, Dewey tells us again and again, is *not* the right of each individual to do as he pleases but rather "the basic freedom is that of freedom of *mind* and of whatever degree of freedom of action and experience is necessary to produce freedom of intelligence" (*Problems of Men*, p. 61). Far from being an anti-intellectualist, he is more vulnerable, but only to a superficial glance, to the charge of intellectualism.

The second and much more fateful misconception of Dewey's philosophy—because of its educational corollaries— is the equation drawn between education and experience. From this equation it is inferred that experience itself is educative, and that any series of experiences—the more direct and dynamic the better—can be substituted for formal schooling, which is often disparaged as an artificial experience. This equation between experience and education is being translated in some of its crudest forms into recommendations that experiences merely of travel and living away from school be considered as appropriate substitutes for study. In short *having* an experience is identified with knowing it or understanding it.

One hardly knows where to begin in exposing the absurdity of this equation. But one thing should be clear. It should not be fathered on Dewey. For Dewey makes a central distinction

[3]New York: 1938.

between experiences that are "educative" and experiences that are "non-educative" or "mis-educative." The first are those that result in increased power and growth, in informed conviction and sympathetic attitudes of understanding, in learning how to face and meet new experiences with some sense of mastery, without fear or panic, or relying on the treadmill of blind routine. The second may give excitement but not genuine insight, may result in a mechanical training or conditioning that incapacitates individuals when the situations encountered in life change and must be met by intelligent improvisation.

But is it not true, some critics counter, that Dewey believes that we learn by doing? And does not that mean that anything a child or student desires or decides to do inside or out of school is *ipso facto* educational? No, emphatically no! Doing is a part of learning only when it is directed by ideas, which the doing tests. Doing in Dewey's sense is the experimenting that is guided by an hypothesis, not the blind action that never reaches the level of an experiment. In other words, we learn by doing, but it is a simple fallacy of conversion to infer that all doing is a form of learning.

Nothing is so foreign to a philosophy that makes intelligence (an intelligence that does not exclude the arts of controlled observation and disciplined imagination) the supreme authority in experience as the mindless glorification of action for its own sake, not to speak of self-defeating resorts to violence. Nonetheless in a recent address before a University of Chicago club, a Professor Thomas Molnar of Brooklyn College charged that all the "activist excesses" in our colleges can be laid at Dewey's door. Apparently because Dewey believes that ideas are tested in action this has led students to ask, "Why not experiment with society?" and to answer, "And if it does not obey, throw bombs!" To say the least a very peculiar conception of an experiment! Oddly enough this aggressively ignorant interpretation of Dewey's philosophy was sponsored by the Club for Responsible Individualism.

The fallacy that converts Dewey's statement that "all genuine education comes about through experience" into the belief that "all experiences are genuinely educational" is reflected today in two kinds of curricular abuse in our liberal arts colleges. The first is the tendency to assume that for educational purposes any subject matter is as good as any other subject matter and that all intellectual standards or hierarchies or grades of achievement and excellence merely reflect traditional prejudices that must be swept aside from the standpoint of the egalitarian ethic of a democratic education. This is a point of view held unfortunately not only by students eager to reform or reconstitute the curriculum but by some members of the faculty. One recent college reader entitled *Starting Over,* apparently in a fresh start to get away from the prejudices of the past, prepared by two University of California (Berkeley) professors, declares in its preface: "We don't rule out the possibility that Lenny Bruce may have more to teach us that Alfred North Whitehead." They do not indicate *what* we can learn from Lenny Bruce that is of such moment that it dwarfs the many things one can learn from Whitehead. The abstract possibility that one may learn *something* from *anything* or *anyone* cannot serve as an intelligent principle of choice, for it excludes nothing. Since some selection of subject matter and material is inescapable, they have to be chosen on the basis of objective criteria with respect to student needs and desirable objectives.

The key to an intelligent choice is suggested by Dewey in his observation that "the central problem of an education based on experience is to select the kind of present experiences that live fruitfully and creatively in subsequent experiences" (*Experience and Education,* p. 17). If this or any other reasonable criterion is taken as our guide, then not everything goes. There are criteria to determine what is significant subject matter or what subject matters lend themselves more readily than others to significant treatment, and that determine the order and the organization of the materials to be studied. The basic controlling ideas of the new education associated with the philosophy of Dewey flowed from two basic principles which still provide the direction for continued criticism not only of existing practices but of any proposed reforms: first, an equality of concern for *all* children in the community to develop themselves by appropriate schooling to the full reach of their powers and growth as persons; and second, a reliance upon the best available scientific methods in the psychology of learning to discover the means, methods and materials by which each individual child could best achieve this growth.

It should be obvious how absurd it is to attribute to Dewey a belief that *only* the child is important, and not the subject matters that he is taught, and that therefore it is relatively unimportant what he is taught or what his present experiences are so long as they are enjoyed. What Dewey is saying is that without taking into account the "powers and purposes of those taught," their needs, capacities, attention spans, and related phenomena, we cannot rely on the alleged inherent educational value of any subject to become meaningfully acquired in the child's present experience. Enjoyment, of course, is no drawback to learning but it should come from interest, and growing absorption, in the tasks and problems to be mastered. What Dewey says here he believes is scientifically valid; and what he hopes is that the choices of the subject matter presented and the decisions about the way they are presented will have the same *objective* validity that conclusions buttressed by scientific evidence have. Otherwise we tend to fall back on the hunches, intuitions, and impressionistic anecdotal accounts of what has occurred in teaching highly selected children in special circumstances without any objective controls. These accounts constitute the stock in trade of much of the recent writing of our school critics. Such accounts are featured in the press as human interest stories in total disregard of the danger of extrapolating techniques and methods from episodic learning situations to the public school system that must provide structured and sequential courses of study. The assertion that because children learn to speak and walk without formal schooling they can learn almost everything else they need to know in the same way—so popular among the new critics—is evidence of how dogma can put out the eyes of common sense. It is not even true in most cases for learning how to read and write, divide and multiply. There are some skills that if not acquired by formal schooling when young are rarely completely mastered in later years.

The greatest damage of the new dogmas that equate experience and education is apparent not only in what students are offered in the way of courses, and materials within courses, by faculties, but in what they are often permitted to do in fulfillment of their academic responsibilities. Much of this is covered by the euphemisms of "fieldwork" or "independent study." These must be sharply distinguished from the clinical experience that is essential to the acquisition of knowledge and skills in many scholarly and professional areas. Genuine clinical experience differs from the "fieldwork" for which students receive educational credit in that, first, it is related to a definite body of knowledge or set of techniques that the student tests or applies in concrete situations continuous with those they will subsequently face; and second, in that the student's clinical experiences are carefully supervised, his progress checked and evaluated so that he knows in what direction to continue. "Fieldwork" today often means no field except what the student professes an interest in, and work means whatever he chooses to do. The recent revelations of the kind of "fieldwork" done at the New York State University College of Old Westbury under the presidency of Mr. Harris Wofford contributed to the hilarity of the nation (see the *New York Times,* April 26, 1971).

According to this uncontested report, the fieldwork or independent study which students were allowed to pursue embraced

"almost any project that was neither illegal nor hazardous. Among selected topics were 'Migrant Camps and Workers,' 'Liberation of the Ghetto through Economics,' 'Film Study,' 'Guitar-Country Blues,' 'The Craft of Sewing.' . . . One student's project was called 'Creative Candle-Making—learning how to (appreciate) and making candles.' 'The professor's role in this five-credit project was to look at my candles when I made them and receive several as gifts.' . . . The project of one woman student, for five credits, was called 'Poetry of Life.' Her project description read as follows: 'Now I hear beautiful music. Then I paint a mind picture. Later I walk in the wood. Reverently I study my wood, know it. Converse with a poet meaningful to me. Make Love.' "

Not only were all courses regarded as of equal educational significance, a fetishism of equality between teacher and student pervaded all aspects of school life. It sometimes took bizarre forms. "One faculty member met his class under a table so everyone could be on the same level."

These oddities undoubtedly are not representative of all institutions that offer "fieldwork," although the chief architect of this curriculum was rewarded by being offered a post at a more prestigious educational institution. But it marks a tendency that is growing—and that merely substitutes a period of lived experience *for* a period of academic study. Unless undertaken in connection with a *structured* course of study and intelligently supervised by faculty it would be far better to terminate academic study at the point where the student is ready to do his own thing.

The issues I am discussing are raised in a fundamental way when any general requirements are proposed for educational institutions. The new critics of education are against all requirements on the ground that needs are personal and that students are the best judges of their educational needs. I find a threefold confusion in this point of view: the tendencies to assume (a) that desire and impulse are synonymous with need; (b) that when not synonymous, desire is an unfailing index of need; and (c) that because needs are personal, it follows that they are unique and necessarily subjective.

(a) Impulse and desire may sometimes be an expression of need, and desire is often a consequence of frustrated impulse. But our common experience shows that we sometimes desire things we don't need, and that sometimes, especially in an educational context, we discover what we really need only when we have ascertained what our purposes are. One may need to acquire certain skills and knowledge in order to achieve a purpose. But whether or not any particular educational purpose one has is defensible, depends not upon the strength of impulse or desire but upon a rational assessment of the consequences of organizing one's energies in certain determinate ways rather than others. Therefore, as Dewey puts it, "the crucial educational problem is that of procuring the postponement of immediate action upon desire until observation and judgment have intervened" (*Experience and Education*, p. 81). Like Hume, Dewey believes that desires are ultimate moving springs of action but, unlike Hume, he holds that we need not be enslaved by our desires, that they can be governed, modified, sublimated.

(b) If this is true, desire is not always an unfailing index of genuine need. It depends on how and when the desire is expressed, and whether the use of intelligence has disclosed the price to be paid in the present and the future for acting on it.

(c) Finally, even if it is true that the locus of all human needs is personal and individual, it doesn't follow that the student is the best judge of them or is even always aware of the needs required by his purposes. One can draw an analogy here with the medical needs a person has who wishes to live a healthy life. It does not follow that because they are *his* needs, they may not also be common to others. Nor does it follow that he necessarily is the best judge of them. They are objective needs even if they are personal needs, and the physican is usually a better judge of them than the patient.

Apply this to the educational scene, particularly in the light of the encouragement offered by the new progressive critics of education to the present student generation to assert themselves against their "exploiters." Students demand the right to select their own courses on *every* level, and with a kind of democratic belligerence inquire: "Who are you to tell me, a grown person of 16 or 18 years of age, what my educational needs are? How can you prate about democracy in education? After all, I am neither an infant nor an idiot!" To which I believe the reasonable answer is: "We are qualified, professional educators who have been studying the educational needs of our students and our culture for many years. We gladly indicate what we believe your educational needs are and are prepared to set forth the grounds on which we select them, inviting your critical response. For example, we believe that you and your fellow students have a need to communicate clearly and effectively, to acquire a command of your own language, oral and written, no matter what your subsequent educational career will be. You have that need whether you are presently aware of it or not." Another example: "We believe you have a need to understand the essentials concerning the nature of your own bodies and mind, for what you don't know about these matters—as the current drug culture indicates—may hurt you, even kill you. Again, we believe that you have a need to understand something of the history of your own society, the political and economic forces shaping its future—all the more so because you have already indicated that you are aflame with reformist and revolutionary zeal to alter society. Surely you must understand the conditioning social, political, and technological factors of any social change that hopes to improve on the past. Your unwillingness to learn about these crucial matters would cast doubts on the sincerity of your professions. It was Karl Marx who pointed out to William Weitling that ignorance is not a revolutionary virtue. We believe that you have other intellectual needs that are requisite to proper performance of your function as a citizen, especially now that you are or will soon be of voting age. These needs you have in common with all other students and the courses we require are those designed to meet them. We welcome your suggestions. Of course, you have other educational needs that are not common but personal that reflect your own special aptitudes, interests, and aspirations. Here we are prepared to guide you, and help you fashion your own educational purposes and curriculum. Gradually you must take complete responsibility for your education. When you do, your decisions are more likely to be sensible if they are informed."

And so the answer to the students' challenge would go—with whatever modifications or details are required for the gifted or the unusual student who has already met these basic needs.

It should be added here that once the colleges specify the educational needs and requirements of their students, they are under the obligation, in the past more often followed in the breach than observance, of providing the skilled teaching that will make these required subject matters come alive. Not all teaching can be inspired teaching, but good teaching can motivate students sufficiently to evoke an interested response to the structure of what they are studying, and induce them to accept the challenges of continuing study.

So long as colleges are entrusted with the certification and accreditation of students, their faculties have not only a right but the responsibility to set reasonable requirements. At the present time, because of many factors operating on the educational scene, not least the influence of the simple equation between education and experience, the situation is chaotic. It will grow worse. One cannot presuppose any knowledge, skills, or even areas of experience that graduates of our liberal arts colleges have in common. Too many students are in colleges waiting out their time for a degree rather than acquiring an education. It may be necessary to adapt Wendel Barrett's suggestion, at the turn of the century, to award all citizens an A.B. degree at birth so that we can presuppose that those who choose to go on to college have genuine educational interests. More realistically, it may be necessary to set up, as in some foreign countries, national examinations for the degree.

One can recognize a human right to an education, a natural right to learn as distinct from a right to teach, without tying this to a right to the same *kind* of education for everyone at the same time, place or rate of advance. The standards that apply must be applied fairly to all, without any suspicion of double standards in use. But the approaches to the same standards may be varied. Whatever institutional changes are introduced to shorten the curriculum, to permit interrupted study and supervised off-campus study, it is in no way a violation of the democratic principle of equality of educational opportunity to strive to uphold the quality of education.

Most of the criticisms made of the educational establishment by the new progressive critics have been launched from what they declare to be democratic and humanist premises. I want to say a few things about the roles proposed for students and teachers in the democratic reconstitution of institutions of higher learning. We don't hear as much about democracy on the lower levels of instruction as about humanism, which unfortunately gets translated too often into an attitude of extreme permissiveness with the teacher playing a largely passive part. Such a position is more suggestive of the educational philosophy of A. S. Neill, the master of Summerhill, for whom learning, to the extent that it goes on, is viewed primarily as a form of therapy. At any rate, although Dewey loved children, he was neither sentimental nor romantic nor naive about them. He was well aware that because of the crippling experience of their home and street life some children behave in such an unruly way as "to stand permanently in the way of the educative activities of others." He did not hesitate to recommend that in such cases "exclusion perhaps is the only available measure at a given juncture." But he hastened to add immediately "but it is no solution." There is no *one* solution in all these cases. And sometimes there is no solution. Here, as elsewhere, intelligence may be necessary, but it is not always sufficient.

Does commitment to democracy, and to democracy in education, require or justify the recent demands that have been made for codetermination by students, on almost the same footing as faculty, in deciding the curriculum and operating the university? Here, too, we must make some crucial distinctions. In the first instance democracy is a political concept. In a political democracy, however, it does not follow that all the major social institutions can or should be run on politically democratic lines according to which each individual counts for one and no more than one, and where a numerical majority makes a decision that binds the entire community. In a political democracy the army, the church, the museum, the orchestra, the family, and the school cannot be organized in a *politically* democratic manner if these institutions are to perform their proper specific functions. There is, to be sure, a sense in which we can speak of a democratic family, of a democratic army, orchestra, or university. This is the moral sense. This requires in the family, for example, not that children vote by majority rule on all questions affecting them but that they be treated with respect, listened to, given rational answers to their questions, and not humiliated by arbitrary decisions. In a school and university the spirit of democracy can prevail, without students functioning as citizens do in the larger political community, by devising modes of participation that will make more meaningful their educational experience and without establishing a preposterous equation of intellectual authority between the learned and unlearned, the mature and immature. Such an equation is never drawn between masters and apprentices in any field, and in the field of education the overwhelming majority of students, except on advanced graduate levels, cannot be realistically regarded even as apprentices.

The comparison of the academic community with the *political-*

ly democratic community, in an effort to identify common values between them, distorts what is distinctive about the first and misconceives what is distinctive about the second. This is apparent in a recently published study of the role of students in college and university governance by Earl McGrath, formerly U.S. Commissioner of Education, in which he advocates that student membership on all faculty and board committees, including policy making committees, should reach 40% (*Should Students Share the Power?*[4] p. 82). This means that if administrators are represented to any significant degree students would have at least as much authority as the faculty.

In the course of his discussion Dr. McGrath admits that it is "pernicious" to conceive of the academic community, which should be a learning community, as made up of groups with competitive interests (p. 84). But note the thrust and very title of his book, *Should Students Share the Power?* The introduction of the concept of *power* in a situation where it must be shared, and where decisions may affect different interests, is inherently competitive. The more power one group has, the less the other. Extremist student groups are well aware of this when they make "the conquest of academic power" their goal. They wish to do so by depriving faculties of their existing powers.

It is wrong to think of a university primarily in terms of power. Its primary values should be those of learning, truth, and discovery. These are values that when shared are not diminished but enhanced. They transcend the domains of interests and conflict. Questions of power are secondary. In contradistinction to the primary educational values, they cannot be shared without being diminished. They therefore should be conceived and vested in ways that further the primary values. Dr. McGrath himself sees this when he rejects the traditional autocratic control of presidential leaders (p. 47), even when that control is exercised as an enlightened and benevolent despotism, in favor of collegial faculty rule. And the reasons are clear. The faculties, not the administrators, are the

[4]Philadelphia 1970.

purveyors of knowledge, the experts, guides, counselors in helping students to find themselves and to choose their life goals.

At this point, misled by the political democratic conception, McGrath taxes faculties with inconsistency because of their refusal to share the power of educational decision with students. The basic democratic principle, he says, is that "all who are affected by government should have a voice [and vote] in determining its policies and choosing its officers." Applied, as we have seen, to any but political institutions this is nonsense. A democratic family is not one in which the majority of the children determine family policies and elect or reject their parents. And a democratic school system is not one in which the majority of students select or reject what they are to learn or whether they are to learn, who is to teach them and how. McGrath complains that not to share power with students reduces them to mere clients, "to customers who merely buy what is offered" or to "raw material" to be processed. But these degrading commercial and industrial analogies have no justification whatsoever in a properly functioning community of learning. If students were merely clients and customers, before long we would hear the cry of the market: "The customer is always right"—whose upshot is far closer to McGrath's proposal than to any rational scheme of faculty control. Nor is it true that because students are not given power equal to that of the faculty, they are being considered as "raw material" to be pounded, hammered, and whipped into a state of educational grace. Without vesting students with educational power equal to that of the faculty, they are always to be treated as persons, always consulted, always listened to, and given responsibilities commensurate with their growth and maturity in those areas where they have competence, until they reach a point where they can take over their own education.

This brings me finally to the role of the teacher in education. Only those unfamiliar with Dewey's work or who judge him by what embittered critics say about him can believe that he rejects a very active role for the teacher as central to his responsibility or that he excludes him "from a positive and leading share in the direction of the activities of the [classroom] community" (*Experience and Education*, p. 66). Because he eschews the role of a drill master, and refrains from *imposing* adult demands upon the growing child, the teacher's task is more difficult, requiring more intelligence, and consequently more subtle and complex planning than was required in the days where pedagogues ruled with loud voice and big stick.

Some of the recent critics of education give the impression that all that is required for good teaching is a loving heart, that most courses in preparation for teaching are a waste, and that not only in teaching but in all other vocations and professions individuals learn best by the apprentice method or on the job. That anybody can teach something to somebody is probably true, but that anybody can become a *good* teacher merely by teaching on the job is demonstrably false. We may not be preparing teachers properly, but the remedy is not the abandonment of preparation and greater reliance upon volunteers and paraprofessionals but is the improvement of that preparation. Even good teachers can be defeated by social conditions beyond their influence or control, but they can always make *some* difference to some students where "some" may not exclude all.

In assessing and selecting teachers, whatever other qualities and skills are to be sought for, one should look for a sense of concern on the part of teachers, especially on the lower levels of instruction, and a sense of mission on all levels. By a sense of concern I mean something stronger than interest and less than affection. A teacher cannot love all children, and most children, except those that *are* genuinely preferred and loved, can see through the pretense of the profession, for they know that genuine love is discriminatory. Goodman asserts that one must either love students or resent them, but this is typical of his false disjunctions. The good teacher respects all his students and recognizes his equal responsibility for the educational growth of all of them.

It is the teacher's sense of mission that is troublesome because it can easily be transformed into an indoctrinating zeal that uses the classroom for purposes foreign to the process of learning. As committed as he was to democracy in education and education for democracy—where democracy is understood in an ethical not narrowly political sense—Dewey was unalterably opposed to indoctrination. He was explicit about the fact that in the nature of the case every form or system of education had a tendency to develop attitudes and habits of evaluation. He was aware of the great social reforms and reconstructions that were necessary in order for the schools to realize, and with respect to the under-privileged and disadvantaged minorities *to begin* to realize, the moral ideals of the democratic society. And as a *citizen* he was always in the forefront of the battle for reform. But all the schools could legitimately do was "to form attitudes which will express themselves in intelligent social action." This, he says, "is something very different from indoctrination" *(Problems of Men,* p. 56), because intelligence, alone of all virtues, is self-critical. Only those indoctrinate who are unable or unwilling to establish their conclusions by intelligent inquiry. Whatever his own views were, Dewey was confident that if they had merit they would be recognized as valid by those whom the schools in the exercise of their educational function had taught to study and deal with the social world and its problems responsibly, i.e., intelligently, scientifically, conscientiously. He would have regarded any attempt to indoctrinate students with his own social and political doctrines and proposals as an arrant betrayal of his educational philosophy.

Every teacher who takes his vocation seriously must be intellectually concerned about the social conditions that bear upon his activity and that support or frustrate his educational goals. This is what I mean by his sense of mission. If he cares enough about his students, his subject matter, and the effectiveness of his teaching, he must care about *more* than them alone. But in pursuit of that mission, he must not mistake the classroom for the barricades and seek to politicalize the university for a cause that as a citizen in his private capacity he is perfectly free to pursue.

The effort to politicalize schools and universities from within is foolish for many reasons today, the most obvious being its counter-productive character. For nothing is more likely to bring about the politicalization of the university from *without*, and from a perspective extremely uncongenial to that of the new progressive critics of education. In combating this internal politicalization one of the most formidable problems is coping with the teacher, no matter what his discipline, who, encouraged by some of the prophets and seers of the new educational and social order of the future, regards his class as a staging ground for revolutionizing society or for disrupting the local community if its norms of social morality fall short of his own notions of the good society. In pursuit of a political commitment, he is often led to abandon elementary principles of professional ethics, and sometimes to deny, in an apology for his political mission, that any distinction can be drawn between objective teaching and indoctrination.

The following passage is not the most extreme pronouncement of this point of view. It can be matched by others. It acquires a certain piquancy because it appears in a publication of Teachers College (*Perspectives in Education,* Fall 1969) where John Dewey formulated the principles of education for a free society. So far as I know it has not brought any critical response. Says the writer:

> "It is the task of the teacher to educate—to educate for change—to educate through change. To educate for orderly planned revolution. If necessary, to educate through more disruptive revolutionary action."

John Dewey would have been the first to repudiate this travesty of the role of a teacher in a free society. The task of the teacher is to educate students to their maximum growth as perceptive, informed and reflective persons so that they can decide intelligently for themselves *what* is to be changed, *where,* and *how.* It is not the teacher's function to indoctrinate his students in behalf of any cause no matter how holy, to brainwash them into becoming partisans of revolution or counter-revolution or even to prod them to take the stance of radicals or standpatters. To declare as this teacher does—and unfortunately he is not alone—that students are to be educated for and through "disruptive revolutionary action" is to declare oneself morally and pedagogically unfit to inhabit the academy of reasoning and reasonable persons.

It is false to assert, as is commonly done, that the American school system today, especially in our major cities, incorporates the ideals of Dewey's educational philosophy. It is also false to claim that its radical critics today are justified in invoking his ideals for their distinctive proposals.

John Dewey's philosophy has still a great deal to teach us. But it is not the first nor the last word on our problems. To his words of wisdom we must add our own, for we face conditions and challenges that either did not exist or were not so acute in his day.

7

The Ends
& Content of Education

In this chapter I shall restate and defend what I believe the ends of American education should be for our time and our place in history. By our time I do not mean today and tomorrow but the indeterminate historical period before us. When I speak of education for modern man I mean an education for man; but the test of whether it is an education appropriate for man will be found in the experience of *modern* man. I shall present the ends of education from the point of view of (1) a "philosophically neutral" reflective empiricism, (2) a democratic theory of education, (3) an experimental approach, and (4) a secular outlook.

1

How do we go about justifying the ends of education? And what do I mean by saying that I wish to justify them by a "philosophically neutral" reflective empiricism? I mean simply this: that given the kind of world we live in, our society and history, the powers of the human mind and body, certain ends of education are to be justified, not by deduction from metaphysics or theology, but in terms of their fruits in experience. These consequences may be assessed in the light of what we already know or have good reason to believe will be the case in the future, and in the light of common moral values that at the time of inquiry are not in dispute.

For purposes of convenience I divide the ends of education into three overlapping groups: (a) powers and skills, (b) knowledge of subject matter or fields of study, and (c) moral habits, values, and loyalties.

POWERS AND SKILLS

Education should aim to develop students' capacities to write and speak clearly and effectively, to deal competently with number and figure, to think critically and constructively, to judge discriminatingly and observe carefully, to appreciate and respect personal and cultural differences, to enjoy with trained sensibility the worlds of art and music, and to enrich the imagination and deepen insight into the hearts of men by the study of literature, drama, and poetry.

Why? Many reasons may be given, but three generic reasons are sufficient. We must all communicate with each other, no matter what our business and vocation, in a world of increasing specialization. The effective exercise of these powers reduces obstacles to communication where it does not remove them. It enables us to make our experiences more significant and to share them, if we so desire, more readily with others. Man is born to problems and troubles as the sparks fly upward. Whether practical or theoretical, whether it involves a move that may spell life or death or only a move in a chess game, the ability to think increases the power to solve problems. It also increases our satisfaction in doing so. By increasing both power and satisfaction, it multiplies alternatives of choice and makes us freer men. The development of our capacities of aesthetic appreciation and imaginative identification multiplies the occasions for joy and delight in a tragic world. It refreshes the spirit without imposing suffering on other human beings.

110

The values in the light of which these consequences are appraised are not themselves beyond question and dispute. We may believe we can ground them in ultimate intuition, as does G. E. Moore. Or we may agree with Dewey that they can be sustained from case to case, from problem to problem, in an unending continuum of experience. In either case, these values recommend themselves to us more validly than any metaphysical or theological principle that allegedly justifies them.

More controversial is the question whether the powers and skills we seek to develop in education should also include those necessitated by the needs of most men to acquire a vocation and to earn a living. The question here is not whether it is desirable for them to learn what is necessary to follow some calling, but rather whether the schools should help them in their choice of, and preparation for, a calling, or whether industry should do it on the job; if the schools should assume this task, whether they should do it in special vocational institutions or in those of general or liberal studies; and if in the latter, at what point in schooling and with what relationship to non-vocational studies. These questions I forgo for the moment except to point out that the answers depend not so much upon first philosophical principles as upon the character of the society in which our students will live and upon our conception of what constitutes a democratic education—about which more below.

FIELDS OF STUDY

With respect to subject matters and fields of interest, all students should acquire an adequate knowledge (where "adequate" has to be defined in the context of the level of studies) of the physical and biological world—of the forces that play upon and govern man's habitat, limit his place in nature, and determine the structure and behavior of his body and mind.

Why? Again for many reasons. Such knowledge is necessary to make the student's everyday experience intelligible to him. He will not understand much, but he will be more at home in the world. He will better understand scientific method in action—especially if he is properly taught. He will become more acutely aware of the revolutionary impact of science and technology on human culture. If he rises above the level of the earthworm and wonders about human origins and destinies, this knowledge will help him to develop a reflective view of the place of man in the universe, of God's existence, of the meanings and evidences, if any, of immortality and human freedom.

A second field of interest and subject matter is history and the social studies. There is a natural curiosity about one's origins, but it is not universal. In some it must be stimulated. But there is a universal need for all individuals to understand the society in which they live. Every student is a future citizen who cannot make intelligent choices in political affairs, sometimes even in some of his personal affairs, without learning something of the massive economic and social forces—whether it be the presence or absence of oil and rubber, the surge of nationalism, or the pressure of population—that mold contemporary civilization. Whether or not wars begin in the minds of men, ideological differences may well determine whether these differences result in conflict. Educators disagree not about the desirability of instruction in these subject matters but only in the relative emphasis to be placed on the distant past, the recent past, and the contemporary. It seems to me that the key to the wise selection out of the illimitable materials of the past is the notion of *relevance*—relevance to the great issues, problems, and challenges of our age that must be mastered if we are to survive as a free culture. For example, it is far more important to study the nature of communism than the War of the Spanish Succession or even the history of Rome, although in the course of the study of Communism we may find illuminating the study of some aspects of Roman history.

The fact that some selection must be made indicates that here as elsewhere, where choice is necessary, we must be guided by some notion of importance, relevance, or strategic perspective. Not everything is relevant to everything; although all subject matters and all experiences have some worth to someone, they do not all have the same quality or the same worth in the educational enterprise, which seeks to make the individual feel at home in a world of change—mastering events by understanding and action instead of being altogether mastered by events, growing in such a way as not to obstruct further growth in insight and maturity.

What Dewey says of experience seems to me also to be true of the subject matters experienced—push-pin is *not* as good as poetry if we want significant experience; stamp collecting is not as good as geography and history if we want to understand the map of the world today; the study of Greek and Latin words in English use is not equivalent in value or utility to the study of good English usage for purposes of better writing and speaking.

> The belief that all genuine education comes about through experience does not mean that all experiences are genuinely or equally educational. Experience and education cannot be directly equated to each other. For some experiences are mis-educative. Any experience is mis-educative that has the effect of arresting or distorting the growth of further experience. An experience may be such as to engender callousness: it may produce lack of sensitivity and responsiveness. Then the possibilities of having richer experience in the future are restricted.[1]

A third field of study that should be required of all students, particularly in the colleges, is a study of the great maps of life. The value judgments and commitments of the major philosophies and religions that have swayed multitudes, as well as the visions of solitary figures of deeper thought but lesser influence, bear directly upon some of the ideological conflicts of our age. No wise policy can be formulated independently of the facts, but no mere recital of the facts alone determines policy. In the end, a decision with respect to conflicting social philosophies involves a choice among key moral values. Sometimes this is true in what appear to be merely questions of limited means. For example, hard decisions about domestic welfare, foreign aid, national defense in the next decade involve commitment to ideals on which we may literally have to stake our lives. Surely this is justification enough to make a critical and searching study of the grounds, alternatives, and consequences of the great ideals for which men have lived and died.

[1] John Dewey, *Experience and Education* (New York, 1938), p. 13.

VALUES AND LOYALTIES

This last reference is a proper transition point to the aims of education that bear upon moral habits, fundamental loyalties, and what is sometimes called character education. Here, too, the problem is not one of justification but of realization. I do not believe that the intellectual and moral virtues, whether a love of the truth, a sense of chivalry and fair play, a feeling of outrage before cruelty, sympathy for the underdog, or a passion for freedom, can be instilled by didactic instruction. They can be imparted, if at all, only by indirection, by skillful teaching on the part of teachers who care, and by learning well on the part of students the other things encompassed by our ends. How, for example, do we go about developing intellectual and emotional maturity in students? Not by preaching but by setting them tasks of progressive complexity. If, as I have argued elsewhere, the sign of maturity is the possession of habits of reasonable expectation, I do not know how this can be built up except by getting students to learn from lesson to lesson what the world is and what it might be, and relating the possible ideal fulfillments to the limiting conditions that govern men and things. Immaturity may be as much present when we settle for too little, blind to what may be, as when we demand too much, blind to what cannot be.

It is our faith in the educational process as a whole that sustains us in our belief that those who complete their schooling will have acquired loyalties to the enduring values of the human community. Despite those who misunderstand him, John Dewey has placed great emphasis upon this aspect of the continuity between past and present:

> The things in civilization we most prize are not of ourselves. They exist by grace of the doings and sufferings of the continuous human community in which we are a link. Ours is the responsibility of conserving, transmitting, rectifying and expanding the heritage of values we have received that those who come after us may receive it more solid and secure, more widely accessible, and more generously shared than we have received it.[2]

[2]Dewey, *A Common Faith* (New Haven, 1934), p. 87.

The nature of education is such that even when learning is a process of discovery the greatest weight must fall upon the knowledge and wisdom of the past. It could not be otherwise. It takes time for the individual to discover that there are many pasts or many interpretations of the past, and that anything that is genuine knowledge must prove itself in the present, and therefore need not fear challenge. It takes more than time. It takes intellectual courage, the rarest of all intellectual virtues. Those who make a fetish of the past, of historical continuity, of piety before the traditional, live off the intellectual capital of their ancestors' courage. The gabble in the academies about the vice of conformism and the virtue of non-conformism is empty and meaningless. Hitler was the greatest non-conformist of the twentieth century. What we must cherish is not agreement or disagreement but intellectual independence, the courage to hold a position on the strength of evidence no matter what the baying of the crowd.

2

Once we accept these objectives as the ends of education, or any equivalent set, I believe we can easily show that many of the antitheses that plague current discussions of the subject may be resolved. I wish to consider briefly two of them.

THE INTELLECT VERSUS THE WHOLE MAN

The first is the view that the end of education should be the education of the intellect or mind, which brings the retort that it should be the education of the whole person. Both positions seem to·me to be untenable. The intellect or mind is not an abstract, disembodied power. It influences and is influenced by our emotions. It guides perception and is checked by perception. On the other hand, although all aspects of body and mind in a person are somehow related in a pattern of personality behavior, they do not all seem equally important in determining the characteristic

Gestalt. They cannot all be developed and certainly not at the same time. Except when we encounter a Leonardo, we cannot avoid selecting and developing some powers at the cost of inhibiting the development of others. The concert pianist is not likely to be in a position to cultivate his skill as a pugilist for other reasons than his fear about the use of his hands. There simply is not enough time to develop all of our intellectual interests, not to speak of all our practical aptitudes. Development opens up new possibilities, but it is also true that it takes place through successive limitations of possibilities. If the development of the powers of cooking, fishing, and roller-skating get in the way of the development of the powers of reading, writing, and problem-solving, then the first must yield. So much for the development of the whole man.

Let us look at the mind in action. It is never found disembodied, but immersed in concrete problems of discovering and exploring meanings. What does it mean, educationally speaking, to develop the student's powers of thinking in the biological sciences? Anyone who sets out to teach his students to think in these fields is teaching them at the same time how to see, how to observe, how to use instruments, how to discipline his impatience, how to curb his impulse to take short cuts. Is all this part of the mind? Trained observation in every field is an art. It is not merely looking because it is guided by general ideas that structure the field of perception differently from what it appears to the open and innocent mind. Thinking about machines involves knowing how to make things. Thinking is not *merely* reasoning. Otherwise we would have to regard every paranoiac as a thoughtful man. It is not accidental that *thoughtful* and *sensible* are closely related. Chesterton once remarked that pure logic was the only thing an insane man had left.

What does it mean to think about a play, or about a poem, or about people? It means also to feel, to imagine, to conjure up a vision. Not *only* that but *also* that. Why is it that we often say to some thoughtless person, "Put yourself in his place"? To another, "You haven't got the feel or the hang of it"? To a third, "You understand everything about the situation except what really

116

matters"? We do not convey truths by this way of speaking, but we help others to find the truth. If artists and musicians think, as well as music and art critics, their sensory discriminations must be relevant to the thinking they do. After all, we do speak of educated tastes. It is absurd, therefore, to say that the exclusive preoccupation of education should be the development or training of the mind.

Nonetheless, although the antithesis between these two points of view must be rejected, the accent has to fall on one rather than the other. To avoid the implicit faulty psychology associated with the use of the term "mind," I prefer the term "intelligence." Intelligence suggests more than mere ratiocination. It suggests the ability to look for evidence and to discern the likely places where it can be found, and the capacity to weigh it judiciously. The intelligent man knows when it is time to stop reasoning and to act, when it is time to stop experimenting and to declare his results. Of him one never says that he is educated beyond his capacities. He is wise rather than learned because he knows the uses and limits of learning.

CONTENT VERSUS METHOD

The second antithesis I wish to challenge is the one usually drawn between *content* and *method* in education. Shall one cover a great deal of ground or study in depth, stock the mind with useful information or enable it to find the facts quickly on occasion? The danger of emphasizing content rather than method in education is that unless content appears live and meaningful to students, it is transformed into a dull catalogue or inventory of facts. To be live and meaningful content must be related and connected to other content, to problems and issues, and wherever possible to live options. What better way is there of establishing these connections and relations than to show the methods by which conclusions are reached? Where content is stressed at the cost of method, memory rather than understanding becomes the chief aid to educational progress. A good memory is a blessing. But even if it does not become atrophied in the world of automation, it seems as if anything a human being can remember a machine can remember better; but—the power of memory cannot put two memories together to discover something new.

The danger of stressing method *over* content is said to be equally great. It sacrifices content: the student is not required to *know* anything so long as he can talk suggestively about it or around it. This emphasis tends to regard any subject matter as the equal of any other for purposes of developing proper habits of thinking. In some institutions stress on method has often led only to talk about how to talk, to the use of a sophistic dialectic, at which Plato poked fun in the *Cratylus* and *Euthydemus* as the infantile sickness of adolescent philosophers.

I confess that I do not see in these objections much warrant or any danger to learning. By emphasis upon method, I mean upon *critical* method—upon criteria of evidence, norms of validity, rules of consistency, on "how we actually think" and "how we ought to think" in whatever field of study we want students to be informed about. This seems to me more important than stressing what we think, because the how and the what, although distinguishable, are actually inseparable when we think soundly. When facts come into dispute or inferences are questioned, we find ourselves relying on rules or habits that control observation and the movements from statement to statement. In my experience, the most critical thinkers I have known, like my first teacher in philosophy, Morris R. Cohen, have been the best informed. The citing of counterinstances is a phase of critical thinking. Nor does it follow that, because critical thinking should receive the greatest emphasis, any subject is as good educationally as any other for that purpose. To be sure, we can think critically about horse racing and show when it is wise to suspend judgment or hedge a bet or distrust a bookie. But it is possible to learn the same critical lessons by studying subject matter that has a wider range of generality. In some fields—for example, learning languages—I grant that memory is more helpful than critical thought. Finally, those for whom critical method is a kind of verbal sport, a dialectic by which fact is dissolved or the worse made to appear the better cause, have not learned to think critically about language or honestly about purposes. There are stubborn cases in which adolescents are more in need of psychiatry than of philosophy.

The reader will probably disagree with some of the ends of education I have here enumerated or with my relative emphasis. If he does, it will be because of some feature of human experience he believes I have overlooked. He may find some personal or social needs less pressing than I do. He may believe that others are neglected. My contention is that none of his reasonable criticisms will follow uniquely from any theory of ultimate reality. This is what I mean by a philosophically neutral, reflective empiricism in education, and why I propose it as a basis for fruitful cooperation.

3

I now present certain considerations that follow from a democratic standpoint in education. The phrase "democracy in education" has meant all sorts of bizarre things. To some people it apparently means that everything is settled by a majority vote of children in the classroom, not only what to study but what to believe about what is studied. I mean by the phrase simply this: the right of every child to equality of educational opportunity. But this is not so simple. Literally construed, it would mean that we would have to revolutionize our society to establish greater economic equality, for in the homes of the poor and the rich equal educational and cultural opportunities cannot be found. It would mean, as only Plato had the courage to see, the abolition of the family so that all children could be brought up by the best possible educational foster parents. Soberly interpreted, democracy in education is equality of opportunity to achieve through schooling an education commensurate with one's capacities. This is America's contribution to the history of education. It requires that we grant to our neighbor's children, no matter what their social status, the same rights and opportunities to an education that we demand as parents for our own children. Anyone who accepts this principle seriously must acknowledge the great responsibility of the state, as the public agency, to equalize opportunities.

THE MEANING OF EQUALITY IN EDUCATION

To say that all children have the same right to an education that will enable them to achieve their growth as human beings is not to say that all children have the same right to the same education independently of their capacities. It does not mean that they have the same right to attend the same schools. It does mean, assuming they are not subnormal, some education for all. It leaves open how much and how long. It is as absurd to say that some education for all means education for none as to say that nourishment or health for all means nourishment and health for none. It would be absurd even if we confused "some education for all" with "the same education for all."

No matter how generous our hopes for mankind, to be reasonable they must be compatible with the facts of biological variation. Do the facts of biological variation defeat our ideal of democratic education in the sense that it is futile to expect most students to profit by an education defined by the ends we have previously derived? If they do, then, as Jefferson foresaw, the prospects of our survival as a political democracy are extremely dubious. It seems to me, however, that it is quite reasonable to recognize the facts of biological variation in human capacities and still defend democracy in education. It requires that we distinguish between the *function* of schooling and the *content* of schooling, and strive to achieve the same function with different content, where content refers not to ends but to courses and methods and materials of study. These *may* be the same; they do not have to be.

It is not necessary to choose between the view that everyone should be educated in the same way and the view that liberal education is for a small elite while the rest of mankind is to be trained as hewers of wood and drawers of water for their intellectual betters. Those who are tempted by this elite conception always assume that they and their children will be among the elite. When

120

this turns out not to be the case, they usually see things in a different perspective. We can put this to a test by describing a hypothetical situation. Two highly gifted parents, who have achieved academic distinction although they were brought up in underprivileged homes, confirm the Mendelian laws of heredity and rear a family of children whose native intelligence ranges from very dull to very bright. Let us assume that the parents themselves undertake to teach their children, all of whom are equally dear to them. Would they not try to realize the same educational ends for *all* of them? Would they not want all their children to learn to the best of their ability, and therefore in different measure, to speak and write clearly, to read and think effectively, to enjoy music and painting, and the other arts of civilization? Where children's health is concerned, parents naturally provide special medical treatment for the weakest. Where intelligence is concerned, they naturally provide special educational opportunities for the brightest. But they are equally concerned for the health and education of all of them. If they were not, they would be bad parents. A democratic society stands in the same relation to all the children of the community as good parents stand to their own children.

Nonetheless, equality of educational concern on the part of our hypothetical parents would not necessarily lead them to give the same instruction in all subjects to all their children even in varying amounts. What a child cannot grasp about a foreign culture by mastery of its language he may learn by reading books on travel or anthropology. There is nothing undemocratic in diversifying the courses of instruction, the rate of instruction, and the methods of instruction.

4

This brings me to the necessity of an experimental approach. In one sense, an appraisal of any proposed educational end in terms of the consequences of pursuing it is experimental. Such an approach should not be regarded with hostility by those who stress "eternal and perennial values," because if the latter are not grandiose terms, concealing some parochial or partial interest, their validity will be established in the here and now of experience.

Even if an educator claimed that his educational aims were authenticated by an infallible insight, surely he could not reasonably claim to know the methods and means by which they could best be realized. The intellectual scandal of much recent discussion between traditionalists and some progressive educators is the attempt to settle questions in this area not by inquiry or experiment but by dogma.

The phrase "progressive education" is today very much at a discount—and deservedly so—because of the number of educators who thought they could remain progressive while ceasing to be liberal. Originally, however, all it meant was an acceptance of the principle of democratic education, which is an ethical principle, and a reliance upon the findings of scientific psychology about the learning process. These two positions were revolutionary at the time they were formulated, and they still constitute the law and the prophets for modern educators, everything else being commentary. Some progressive educators have deduced what procedure should be followed in educating the young rather than following the lead of experimental evidence. But some of their critics, who have counted only the failures of progressive methods and not their successes, have been even more dogmatic and undiscriminating in their claims, holding the methods responsible for educational phenomena and conditions that must be laid at the door of society. There are critics who tell us that the schools have failed to teach their charges, and failed most miserably with the gifted, and in the same breath concede that their college students as a whole are more serious, abler, more excited by ideas than their precursors in the golden age that existed before the days of progressive education.

There is a great deal of what is called "experimentation" always going on in American education, but most of it is not experimental since it is conducted without proper controls. The result is that we think we know more than we actually do about the best courses to teach and the best ways of teaching them. The fact that something is new does not make it experimental. Nor does the desirability of experimentation mean that we must keep on experimenting about the same things. By this time we already should know what are the best methods of teaching children to read, of teaching chemistry in high schools, of teaching economics in colleges.

Our very metaphors sometimes betray that we are taking for granted what might very well be in dispute. One of our leading traditionalists, Mortimer Adler, writes:

> Human differences in capacity for education can be thought of in terms of containers of different sizes. Obviously a half-pint jar cannot hold as much liquid as a quart or gallon jar. Now the poorly endowed child is like the half-pint jar, and the gifted child like the quart or gallon container.[3]

He concludes not only that each container must be filled up to the brim but that each must be filled with the same rich, thick "cream of liberal education."

The comparing of children to different measures, coupled with the conception of teaching as the *pouring* of the same stuff into passive containers, expresses a point of view that is hard to reconcile with what we know about children as organic creatures and learners whose differential responses determine how much they can assimilate. Even cream cannot be poured into all children with safety, no matter how ingenious our funnels. It would help to change our metaphors. Our experimental task is to find and offer the appropriate curricular nourishment for different types of organisms that will enable them to achieve the full measure of their growth and health. That curricular nourishment may be the same or different. The test is the *function* it performs in the life of the child. The same function will not give us the same result. A dull child will never be able to read as well or as intelligently as a bright child, and an ordinary child will never be able to play as well as a musically gifted child. But both children can be so educated that each enjoys reading and music. Both can acquire something of the grace and taste associated with the liberal arts. They may not both

---

[3]Mortimer Adler, *Liberal Education in an Industrial Democracy* (San Francisco, 1957), pp. 35-36.

be able to do so by studying the same subjects, even though the study of some subjects will be common to them.[4]

"ONE-FOURTH OF A NATION"

How great is the range of student capacities? *The New York Times* (May 4, 1958) summarized a report issued by the United States Army, which recruits from all classes of the population. It stated that 25 per cent of the inductees who have passed their physical tests of fitness lack the *capacities* to be trained for anything except simple manual tasks like cleaning, polishing, digging, and driving. A modern army requires many technical skills. It has a use for individuals with a flair for mathematics, or a knack for building machines, or a feeling for foreign languages. There is no reason to doubt the willingness of the military authorities to recognize the presence of superior and average intelligence and/or aptitudes in the ranks, and the substantial accuracy of the reports of their distribution. It is fairly safe to extrapolate the ratios to the rest of the population

This means that approximately one-quarter of all our students—*One-Fourth of a Nation,* to use the title of Paul Woodring's book—are incapable of completing the requirements of a good academic high school and going on to a liberal arts college. By increasing the number of schools and teachers, decreasing the size of classes, and improving skills of instruction, we can do

---

[4]Before we leave this theme, simple justice requires that I quote a further passage from Dr. Adler. In it he explicates the metaphor of the different containers in a way that departs from the whole emphasis of his previous writings in education. It departs so radically that it may legitimately be interpreted as one of the most dramatic, even if unannounced, conversions to the philosophy of progressive education:

"The main point of my illustration is missed if you make the mistake of identifying the cream of liberal education with the traditional books, subjects, or tasks which once were the substance of liberal schooling when it was given only to the few, and which still constitute, in my judgment, the best materials to use in the case of the more gifted children. The best education for the best becomes the best education for all, not by means of the same materials and methods but rather by achieving the same effect with all children through using whatever materials and methods produce the same results at different levels of capacity." (*Op. cit.,* p. 38.)

How John Dewey would have chuckled! Dr. Adler is still adamant in his opposition to vocational education.

something to bring down this number. Even so, the evidence shows that there will always be a large group unable to profit by the traditional scholarly courses of study. What shall we do with them? Unless they have private tutors it is they who during the period of adolescence obstruct the learning of the more gifted students. Before we answer this question, let us imagine once more, as difficult as it may be, that a child of ours is among them.

It seems only common sense to say that the education of this fourth of the nation should not be so organized as to interfere with or dilute the education of the other three-quarters. Conversely, the education of the latter should not be a ground to deprive the former of *their* educational rights. The problems here are admittedly difficult. They have not been solved. But they are not insuperable. *We should allow these students to remain in school so long as they can profit significantly by instruction.* We should permit universal *access* to secondary and tertiary education without debasing our standards. We should diversify courses of study and individualize as much as possible the curriculum without sacrificing the knowledge and skills that all students should acquire to exercise intelligent citizenship. We should put them in special classes if they can learn better this way. We should instruct them in the skills and subjects that will enable them to begin their vocational experience at an earlier age than their more gifted brothers and sisters—who, sooner or later, must prepare themselves to earn a living too.

SOME PRINCIPLES OF VOCATIONAL EDUCATION

This introduces the complex problem of vocational education, which is often bedeviled by the assumption that where it begins, liberal education must end. Yet we do not make the same assumption about professional education, which is distinguished from vocational education not only because it requires better brains but because it enjoys a higher social status and more money. Until the necessity for earning a living disappears, there can be no reasonable objection to using the schools to prepare oneself for a good living as well as for a good life. The pity of it is that the vocational schools are so bad, worse from the point of view of their own purposes than the academic and general high schools. The reason is partly the confusion between job training and vocational education, and partly the use of vocational schools to provide occupational therapy or temporary shelter to juvenile delinquents. (These delinquents may be victims of society, but what is educationally relevant is that at the moment they are agents of educational chaos. They need special schools to meet their special needs.)

The important points about vocational education seem to me to be these: first, certain fields of study are so general or liberal in character that they must pervade all kinds of education. They bear directly on every student's social and political responsibilities, no matter what his vocation, especially in a community where each man's vote counts for one and no more than one. Instruction in these areas must be given at every level. The student should be made constantly aware that his vocational studies may become a means of dehumanization if no thought is taken of the social contexts and moral implications in which vocational choices are often made. Second, instruction in vocational subjects should cover the basic principles that govern a whole class of practical skills for which the individual displays a bent or interest. Third, we must avoid the invidious social distinctions that accompany educational differentiation; we must recapture the sense, rapidly being lost, of the dignity of useful work. Wherever there is a stigma attached to vocations, it will be attached to education for those vocations. It will be difficult for students themselves to believe that educational segregation for certain vocational purposes, whether in the same or in different schools, is compatible with educational democracy. The doctrine of separate and equal facilities has no justification whatsoever where race is concerned, because of the arbitrary and unjust nature of the criterion. But where we segregate on the basis of intellectual capacity or interest, independently of race, religion, or sex, there is no reason to cry "Havoc!" We must forbear, however, from exacerbating the sting of natural resentment at being intellectually underendowed in a world where survival and power depend more and more upon brains. We can only do this by stressing the truth that everyone counts for something when he is

126

doing honest and useful work, that his dignity as a human being does not depend on his social status, degrees or earning power, and by providing in our affluent society an adequate standard of living beneath which no one should be permitted to sink.

5

What are the ends of education from a secular point of view? The simplest but not the clearest answer is to keep private altars out of public schools. As I understand secularism, its opposite is not religion, because sometimes secularism itself is characterized as a religion. The term "religious" has become so multiply ambiguous that one no longer knows where to look for the irreligious. In addition, there are conventionally religious individuals who are firmly convinced that religion is a private matter and therefore does not belong in the schools. What secularism is really opposed to is clericalism. I shall define clericalism as the belief that the acceptance of certain doctrines about the supernatural is required in order to reach *truths* about man, nature, and society, in order to discover morally valid *ideals*, and in order to acquire certain intellectual *skills*. The ends of education I have previously enumerated roughly fall within this threefold classification of truths, values, and skills.

What have beliefs in the supernatural got to do with the acquisition of skills? No plausible connection has been established between them.

What truths about the world, society, and man depend upon the prior acceptance of religious truth? It may be argued that there is a Christian metaphysics, but who in this age of modern science can show that its acceptance is a necessary condition of belief in a Christian physics or just a physics? Religion has withdrawn from conflict with science by renouncing any pretensions to speak about matters of fact in the dimension of nature. If it resumes the conflict, it must submit its claims to truth to the same arbitrator of method as all other scientific hypotheses. There remains, then, the claim that without some transcendental belief as a supporting or justifying ground, moral values cannot be sustained. Karl Heim, the

Tübingen theologian, goes so far as to assert that the root choice of man is between secularism and theism, and that "secularism, to be consistent, must entirely reject all such words as God, eternity, conscience, ethics, moral rearmament, guilt, responsibility . . . as inadmissible borrowings from a view of the world opposed to its own."[5] However, no proof is given that moral judgment rests upon any theological belief. On the contrary, it is demonstrable that if any moral attributes are predicated of supernatural powers or entities, they are derived from the autonomous judgments of men. Men always have built and always will build gods in their own moral image.

This fact is no way precludes the intensive examination of religion in the course of study. On the contrary, neither past history nor present society can be understood without an intensive analysis of the role of religious movements, traditions, doctrines, wars, and conflicts. To the extent that religion in Santayana's phrase "is an imaginative echo of things natural and moral in human experience," we can appreciate it as poetry. To the extent that religion makes claim to a distinctive knowledge, we can consider it in our study of philosophy. For educational purposes, is it not sufficient to approach religion as a creation of the human spirit without assuming that it is a revelation of the Divine Spirit? What more can reasonably be required without introducing into the schools of the nation the strife of private faiths? And this at a time when our more intimate contact with other cultures reinforces the wisdom of a more catholic approach to the religions of the world.

Those who believe that religion can serve as a unifying principle around which to synthesize the subject matter of education seem to me to ignore both the nature of religion and the pluralistic commitments of the American tradition. I have more sympathy with those who see in religion an avenue to an experience that sustains human allegiance to ideal ends, especially when these are threatened with defeat. Religious experience may offer support to human ideals, but it is not the sole source of such ideals nor can it

[5]Karl Heim, *Christian Faith and Natural Science*, translated by Neville Horton Smith (New York, 1953), p. 231.

ever be the guarantee of their validity. The educational experience itself, when teachers have both skill and vision, may become both source and support of the love of truth, the love of justice, the love of beauty, and the love of human freedom. This is all the public religion we need, in both peace and war. For it enables us to hope without illusion, to fight without despair, and to stake our life in defense of the things that make life worth living.

8

Reason & Violence–
Some Truths & Myths
about John Dewey

1

In writing about John Dewey, I am aware that I am offering an interpretation of his thought, and that like all great works of the mind—in art, literature, philosophy—there are a variety of interpretations possible, not *all* of which can be true, but all of which may be *false*. In extenuation of my own interpretation, allowing that there may be others, I can reinforce my reading of John Dewey's texts by memories of discussions about many of them while they were being born. In the face of conflicting interpretations of Dewey's philosophy, I feel, somewhat oddly for a secularist, like the clergyman behind the lines in the last war who, to his surprise, found other brother clergymen active in his own sector. One of them, in a friendly overture to forestall the suspicion that he was poaching on the first clergyman's spiritual preserve, observed: "How wonderful to find ourselves here—all of us doing the Lord's work." "Yes," the first clergyman drily observed, "Yes, we are all serving the Lord by our presence—you in your way, and I in His."

131

Nonetheless, I make no claims to esoteric knowledge of Dewey's philosophy comparable to the first clergyman's claim of esoteric knowledge of God. Almost everything I say should be granted by any careful interpreter of Dewey, or even critic of Dewey, who reads him in order to understand him. But alas! Not all critics read Dewey with the aim of understanding him, and, judging by the volume, quality, and substance of most popular criticisms of Dewey, much of it seems written by people who have never read him.

It is sometimes said that the culture of a country can be judged by the men it honors. This is an uncertain and somewhat ambiguous proposition because it depends on *how* a man is honored. To have one's visage stuck upon a postage stamp is no longer the prerogative solely of kings and presidents, but a mark of recognition for achievement. But to recognize and honor an achievement does not mean that the culture in which that achievement has come to fruition necessarily has been profoundly influenced by it. Philatelic recognition these days is bestowed for many different reasons. The honor accorded to heroes of action, and especially to heroes of thought and vision, may express the *hopes* of a culture rather than its actualities.

The fact that a commemorative stamp has been issued for John Dewey is evidence that he is on his way to becoming a legendary figure, that he is honored in official quarters. It would hardly justify the inference that John Dewey has become an Establishment figure, or that our culture markedly reflects the impact of his revolutionary thought. Indeed, the most vehement of those who assert that American culture today does reflect the impact of his thought deplore it in the extreme. They would probably contend that a stamp of 30 cents in Dewey's name represents too high a valuation on his philosophy. They would probably object to any stamp honoring him, even one for 2 cents. For they believe, as one academic critic has put it, that John Dewey "applied his talents and his longevity to wrecking the educational philosophy which had been built up through 25 centuries of classical and Christian experience."

This is almost a tribute! Think of it! What a mighty force, even if only of destruction, John Dewey must have been to destroy 2,500 years of classical and Christian experience. What giants he has overcome in destroying the legacy of Plato, Aristotle, Augustine, and Aquinas! And when we ask how this was done, in what this destructive force consisted, we are told that it flowed from the alleged Dewey doctrine that "all forms and rules are evil."

Now the supreme irony with this, as with so many other criticisms, is that any familiarity with Dewey's work would have shown that he was the last man to hold that "all forms and rules are evil." The nearest thing that he ever said that could possibly be misinterpreted—but not by a literate mind—as implying the view that "all forms and rules are evil," which would simply be a glorification of chaos, is that "not all forms and rules are good." But who in his senses can deny that "not all forms and rules are good?" Certainly not any exponent of the classical or Christian tradition!

The truth is that John Dewey was a firm believer in authority and of forms and rules, and a strong critic of the revolt against authority that made a fetish of freedom conceived as lack or absence of form, rule, and control. To him, the central question was what *kind* of authority, what *sort* of form, what *type* of rule shall we acknowledge—the authority of force, the authority of revelation, the authority of social tradition, the authority of the market, the authority of war, or the authority of *organized intelligence* responsive to human needs, to new social forces, and their hopes and aspirations? No social life, no cooperative human effort, no institutional practice is possible without "forms or rules." That goes without saying! And it is far from crying up freedom as an end in itself, which could just as well become the free-for-all of the Hobbesian war of all against all. John Dewey stressed, in ways from which we can still learn, that until, in his own words: "there is an intimate and organic union between authority and freedom," human life undergoes violent pendulum swings from one form of oppression to another, with the spokesmen of the old forms crying for "law and order" and the spokesmen of the new forms crying for "freedom and justice," which may turn out to be masks for the law and order of revolutionary terror.

John Dewey's academic critics never understood that for Dewey "authority stands for the stability of social organization by means of which direction and support are given to individuals, while individual freedom stands for the forces by which change is intentionally brought about." Change we shall have in any event, whether we seek it or not, whether we fear it or not. The question is: Shall we change blindly, haphazardly, or purposively? When change is uncontrolled, authority naturally takes the form of traditional institutions and the old rules and forms. The result is repression of "variable and fresh qualities, of the qualities of initiative, invention, and enterprise." As these expand and burst their social and cultural fetters, and as these fetters are experienced as fetters, authority becomes the enemy, especially in the form of the State. The end result is not the triumph of individuals but of individualism in which the strongest, the wiliest, the most forceful individuals find fulfillment in complete independence from, or indifference to, other individuals, sometimes even at the price of their sacrifice. This was especially true in the economic sphere of society in Dewey's day. As a democrat, Dewey wanted for all human beings not the freedom to strike out blindly, the freedom and power to control other human beings by the control of the things they depended upon, but the freedom of all to grow to the full reach of their compatible, nonexploitative powers.

That is why Dewey would have looked with a troubled eye on those contemporary apostles of freedom in all their discordant and colorful motley for whom any kind of authority or control is anathema. "We need," he says, "a kind of individual freedom that is general and shared and that has the backing and guidance of soundly organized authoritative control"—one informed by intelligence and inspired by the shared values of communication—a communication that can generate the sympathy without which intelligence, if it is too cold, detached, and abstract, is not intelligent enough.

This particular myth about John Dewey, that he had no place for authority or form, was originally circulated in the academy, and is one of a large number of misconceptions, some of them mutually incompatible, that still thrive there. For example, there are some critics of Dewey who still insist that he wishes to teach students to adjust themselves to the life and society around them, and there are others who charge him with anti-intellectualism because he allegedly wishes to adjust society to the needs of its children.

If these are the myths that circulate in ivied halls and university towers, can we be very much surprised about the character of the myths that are prevalent in the marketplace? For a large part of his life, Dewey deplored the use of the term "pragmatism" as ruinously misleading. The sad fact has been that Dewey's thought has more often been assessed in the light of popular misconceptions of pragmatism than the meaning of pragmatism assessed in the light of a sober reading of his thought. One cannot tell anything about what a person *believes* if he is called a pragmatist by others. Actually, the term has acquired such a variety of uses that it is today employed to describe a person of whom we cannot even tell what he is likely to do. Walter Lippmann, who once knew better, in explaining his only hesitation about endorsing Nixon, writes that the trouble is that "Nixon is, as they say, a 'pragmatist'—which means that he might do anything."

If Walter Lippmann is guilty of such sleaziness of thought, can we be surprised at General Eisenhower, who had never heard of John Dewey before he came to Columbia but nonetheless blamed him for the fact that the Soviets put a space satellite in the sky before we did? Dewey's philosophy was made a scapegoat by Admiral Rickover, and shortly after by a brass hat among the Marines. Today this military crusade has been continued by Dr. Max Rafferty who, although a civilian, is a warrior in spirit. For ten years or so, he ran against John Dewey in every election, using him as a King Charles's head, scaring the voters into electing him each time except, fortunately, in November 1968. Among other things, he charges John Dewey with the death of that revered institution of our ancestors, "the little red schoolhouse."

Critics of this caliber knew no more about the real nature of the little red schoolhouse than of developments in the psychological study of learning, and of industrial society that made "the little red schoolhouse" an anachronism. Dewey knew "the little red schoolhouse" first hand. He once wryly observed that "far from being a center of educational enlightenment, 'the little red schoolhouse' of our ancestors was a struggle of wits and often of main strength between pupils and teachers."

It was not only with respect to Communism, the study of science and technology, the revolution in schools and schooling that Dewey saw earlier and more deeply than his fellow citizens. It was he who warned of the coming crisis of our cities, and urged already in the twenties a planned ecological development that would provide a humane environment for human beings. Indeed, his whole emphasis on democracy in education, and his analysis of what it means, presupposed that democratic changes in the social and economic order, if they did not accompany progressive changes in education, would not lag far behind.

2

Even when it is understood, John Dewey's philosophy has manifold technical difficulties, not all of which have been satisfactorily resolved. I wish first to speak of the chief respects in which he has been radically misunderstood both by those who invoke his name and those who scorn it.

The first large misunderstanding might be regarded as the literary man's fallacy, were it not shared by so many who are not literary. This is the view that Dewey's philosophy expresses and suffers from the cult of the practical. Dewey is regarded, in a minor critical tradition that runs from Lewis Mumford to Joseph Wood Krutch, as a man of liberal faith who cannot reach the home of the human spirit because his models for mind and thought are derived from engineering. Engineering is a discipline whose actions are completely subordinated to antecedently set ends—usually set by others. The test of success in engineering is practice, getting the job done, the achievement of useful goals. Since Dewey, too, speaks of thought as "practical," what is easier than to suggest that both ends and means should be tied down to the practical and useful?

What is overlooked is that for Dewey being practical, where good thinking is concerned, is not a goal but a career of action. It is not defined merely in terms of success, or of getting results, or even of usefulness. The presence and practice of thought is the ordered activity that spells out the difference between having an idea and not having an idea with respect to the problem in hand. Responsible thinking commits us to a way of conduct or behavior. Ideas are plans of action, and true ideas are those whose consequences are in accord with the logical consequences predicted. The idea is to practice what a hypothesis is to the experiment that tests it. When we speak of ends or goals being "practical," this introduces an entirely different sense of practical. Dewey is a critical behaviorist. He anticipated what is sound in both the behaviorism of J. B. Watson and Gilbert Ryle, refusing to reduce thought merely to muscle movements in one case, and merely to proper linguistic locutions in the second place. For Dewey, thought, one cannot repeat too often, is not for the sake of practice. Practice stands for symbol-using behavior, action, experiment in the process of thinking. This is a far cry from the Philistinism of holding that thinking to be true must be useful. Truths may kill us and lies may be consoling, but they are truths and lies nonetheless; but whether truth or lie, the evidence that warrants the judgment of what they are is found in the consequences of what we do in the course of *finding out*.

The second current major misconception involves an issue around which controversy and violence have erupted. It will not be long before some hostile critic, wishing to cite some dramatic event to symbolize the eclipse of John Dewey's philosophy, points to recent incidents at Columbia University, where Dewey taught for a quarter of a century. In the name of "participatory democracy"—a concept that Dewey fashioned—some students have attempted to transform the university into an instrument of their revolutionary purpose or to destroy it in the attempt. Although their actions, which encompass words and deeds hitherto associated with the language and behavior of the gutter, are clearly dictatorial, they have "rationalized"—in the bad sense of the term—their assault as inspired by a desire to enstate the process of "participatory democracy."

Anyone familiar with Dewey's philosophy would repudiate this appropriation of the phrase in the context of activist student behavior as a grotesque caricature. It is true that John Dewey, continuing a vein of thought already found in Jefferson and Mill, stressed the desirability of the widest participation in the political life of democratic society. But he never conceived of all the institutions of a democratic society as functioning by the *rules* of political democracy. For Dewey, democracy was a way of life—one whose spirit could be and should be realized in all human institutions. But he was a canny Vermonter, and when he spoke of democratic family life or democracy in education and education for democracy or democracy in culture or economics, he did not mean the principle of one man-one vote, mechanical equality in power of decision for everyone, the young and old, the inexperienced and experienced, the qualified and unqualified alike.

This raises the difficult question of leadership in a democracy. Some apostles of direct democracy deny need for leadership or assert that all persons should be leaders. But where all lead no one leads. Where there is no intelligent leadership democracies may perish. One may well be suspicious of all leaders. One may even grant the great *dangers* of abuse of power involved in delegation of authority so skillfully but speciously developed by Parete, Mosca, and Michels to prove democracy impossible. The dangers only reinforce the necessity of finding mechanisms to limit the excesses of leadership. This means that where political leaders are responsible to those who lead, the source of their moral, as distinct from legal authority must be some superiority of insight or function freely acknowledged by their fellows.

The situation, of course, cannot be the same in a non-political context. Leadership in any institution to which we can legitimately extend the term "democratic" must be grounded only in the authority of function, of superior knowledge or skill. In the classroom, the role of the teacher and students cannot be equated if they are to learn properly. In the family the guiding role of parents, cannot be shared with immature children. In laboratory and university the judgment of senior professors of intellectual distinction cannot be equated with that of assistants.

John Dewey was for many years the Honorary President of the League for Industrial Democracy, whose youth group, before it parted company with the mother organization, was the S.D.S. He would have found it utterly incomprehensible that a group that was prepared to use any means, fair or foul, peaceful or violent, to achieve its ends, even to ally itself openly with totalitarian groups, should speak in the name of participatory democracy. For Dewey's conception of democracy was essentially committed to the continuity of means and ends. Some of his most valuable analysis consists in his annihilatory critique of the totalitarian doctrine, found among many who do not recognize themselves as totalitarian, that the proclamation of a noble-sounding democratic ideal or goal justifies the use of any means, no matter how undemocratic or violent, to achieve it.

This brings me to the crucial question of the use of intelligence in social action. There are some who believe that Dewey believed that intelligence should always be a *substitute* for force in human affairs, and that intelligence is sure to prevail when so used. Such individuals write with a mixture of irony and glee when they are unfriendly critics, with sadness and a touch of despair when they are sympathetic, that Dewey's philosophy has been invalidated by the growing resort to force and violence in American life. They often say: "Events have bankrupted Dewey's view that intelligence is the central value in human experience. If you want to get things done in this world, *in the end,* it can only be by force or violence or the threat of force and violence. See how quickly reforms come, not when the appeal is to good will or intelligence or compassion or love but to fear of riot and burning cities." Or, as I have heard some students say, to go from the larger to the smaller context, "administrations and even faculties never listen to reason unless they fear something. And it is not the fear of the Lord that makes them yield to student demands, but the fear of Berkeley and Columbia."

139

Let us face this challenge, because it is honestly made and has a ring of plausibility about it. But once more, let us judge Dewey's thought here by what *he* says, not by what others imagine he has said. And the first thing we discover is that Dewey has *never* counterposed the use of force as such in human life to the use of intelligence. In one form or another, force is necessary to give effect to our reflective ideals, and to repulse the use of force by those who would prevent us from giving effect to them. Dewey was never a pacifist. He supported the First World War against imperial Germany and the Second World War against Hitler, and yet his ideals included a warless world. "Squeamishness about force," he said, "is the mark not of idealistic but of moonstruck morals." But what he urged upon his fellow citizens was the realization that there is force and force, that one can use not only military or physical force but the force of industry, commerce, money, self-interest, scientific inquiry as well as the force that lies "in the actualities of human companionship." Physical force or violence recommends itself to us only because of a failure to use other forces sufficiently or in time, because, in other words, of a failure of intelligence to know what and how to use other forces available. More important, even when physical force or violence recommends itself to us, Dewey asks merely that we be intelligent about its use, which means aware of the consequences and costs of its use in comparison with other alternatives. But here is the rub! How many make the comparison? How many ask themselves what consequences the legacy of fear and hate, which is the result of the use of violence, will have on the ends or goals in behalf of which the violence is used? Is it not interesting that the injunction "think about violence" sounds almost like a contradiction in terms? Why? Because most social violence, the kind to which we are accustomed, as well as the new expressions of it, is blind. It rarely survives reflection—and that is why those in a violent mood shrink from reflection. You *may* get your way by violence, but *may* means *may not;* and even if you get your way, the cost or price may turn out greater than any of your gains. Is it true that reforms come quickly by violence, or are they delayed or canceled by the backlash of counterviolence? If you fire the slums because you cannot abide the slow rebuilding of them, are you sure you will get better housing, and if better, is it worth the cost in death and suffering? Is it true that administrations and faculties never listen to reason? Is it true, the reflective student must ask, that I will get a better education if I act as the students at Columbia did? John Dewey was not a moonstruck idealist. But for him, the intelligent idealist was not a fanatic who says: "My goal justifies the use of *any* means," but one who recognizes that in human experience men have many goals, and that the consequence of using any means to further *one* of them may destroy the possibility of achieving most of the others. In many situations in which violence is used, this is precisely what happens.

There is one theme related to violence that Dewey never wrote about at length, so far as I know, but that nonetheless lay close to his heart; for in conversations with me over a quarter of a century he would raise it and return to it whenever some event and movement gave it relevance. This was the American Civil War, in whose shadow or aftermath he came to critical self-consciousness. He once told me that next to the religious crisis he went through in relation to his mother, the most lacerating emotional crisis was a political one with his father—a veteran of the army of the Potomac—when he and his brother announced they were voting for Grover Cleveland, a Democrat, the first Democrat to be elected to the Presidency after the Civil War. To John Dewey's father, this was tantamount to betrayal of the great cause for which he had fought. Dewey believed there was no historic necessity for the Civil War, although he recognized that after John Brown's raid at Harper's Ferry, it was too late for Lincoln's solution, which was to liberate the slaves by purchase. Dewey was no admirer of John Brown, and he felt that Emerson, whom he greatly admired as a moralist, was acting out of character in his extravagant defense of Brown. Dewey felt that Lincoln's solution would have cost less even in money than the actual cost of the Civil War, the most terrible of human conflicts in human history up to that time, not to speak of the hundreds of thousands of lives lost and the immeasurable human suffering, the bitter legacy of Reconstruction, and of the exacerbated situation since. For it would have enabled

141

the community to offer an *economic solution* to Negroes after liberation, which the impoverishment resulting from the Civil War made impossible.

I am not qualified to speak with confidence about the historic possibilities of the Civil War, but I am confident that Dewey's approach to the question of violence in human affairs was affected by his assessment of the Civil War and by his early emotional reactions to it. Between the two world wars, John Dewey spent many years in the movement that sought to outlaw war as an instrument of social policy. The considerations that moved him with respect to war were all the more weighty in his judgment on civil war—which is the fiercest and most inhuman of all wars—as an instrument of social change in a *democracy* where other modes of affecting change, albeit more slowly, are available.

For Dewey, the use of intelligence in the modern world will not necessarily result in a series of tepid tea parties. In un-democratic countries, we can expect Boston tea parties. But when democratic processes are in existence, there is no room for them. Boston tea parties take place or should take place in order to *establish* such processes. But even in the best of democracies, intelligence may have to use a varied number of legitimate forces to curb outbreaks of violence. The anarchist ideal of a world without a state, and therefore without any body of force, when all men will accept the rules of reason and love and all conflicts will disappear except those that can be resolved by such rules, is a mischievous myth. For it has no basis in the nature of man and society as presently constituted, and in any plausible conception of them for the future. What we can reasonably expect from the use of intelligence is the progressive diminution of coercion or violation in human affairs. Marx, Lenin, and Trotsky assumed that man's increasing power over things will necessarily diminish man's power over man. But events have showed that man's power over things may lead to power over man so pervasive that his very mind and spirit become progressively enslaved. For Dewey, we can take nothing for granted. Our task, step by step, even when we take very large steps, is the piecemeal reduction of violence in human affairs as too costly, psychologically and materially, and therefore unintelligent. Here as everywhere else in human experience we must pursue not the best or absolutely perfect—for it cannot serve as a guide to practice—but the "better." The only caution to bear in mind is that "the better" is not only the enemy of the "good," but that it can become the enemy of the "still better." For Dewey, to speak paradoxically, it was not the quest for the good that was the starting point of action but the quest for "the better."

9

Conflict & Change
in the Academic Community

Among the current myths that circulate about the American
college and university is the view that they have been very
conservative institutions, hostile to educational change and
cloistered off from the tumults and troubles of the marketplace.
On the basis of my own experience as student, teacher, and
administrator, covering a time-span of more than a half-century, I
can testify to the injustice and inaccuracy of such a characteriza
tion. Much of that period has been spent, together with colleagues,
in prolonged and agonizing reappraisals of the objectives of higher
education, particularly liberal arts education, and the refashioning
of the curriculum of studies to achieve these objectives. The very
diversity of our institutions with respect to methods, content,
requirements, and standards of instruction is weighty evidence of
the experimental nature of American education, and its sen-
sitiveness to a wide variety of educational needs. From the multi-
versity to the denominational college all are in need of educational
improvement. The present ferment within them may provide the
occasion for accelerated change and continued improvement but
only if we do not assume that every change is *ipso facto* an

improvement. Institutions like human beings change for better or worse.

At the same time during the last half-century the governance of universities and colleges has on the whole been transformed from administrative absolutisms with respect to educational issues to academic communities in which faculties possess preponderant powers if and when they choose to exercise them. Although the structure, legal and otherwise, of our colleges and universities is today in debate and in transition, the proper resolutions of this and allied problems seems to me to be clearly dependent upon the prior determination of what the educational function or goal of the institution should be.

The history of American higher education, then, shows no hostility to change. The all-important question today is how changes are to be effected—by coercion or the threat of coercion or by reflective discussion and debate. Unfortunately, there is a wide-spread tendency to introduce reforms not in the light of a considered analysis of basic issues but in terms of what will restore order and prevent further physical disruption of the campus—as if this were the primary criterion of what the best higher education for modern man should be, as if the absence of physical tur-bulence—the freedom from arson, bombings, violent confron-tation—could be anything more than a necessary condition for the *locus* of a liberal educational experience.

I have been a lifelong critic of American higher education mainly on the ground of its deficiencies as an instrument of liberal education whose ideals I regard as perennially valid. (The "perennial" must not be confused with the "eternal."[1])

Before addressing myself to current challenges to the ideals of a liberal education, I wish to take sharp issue with those who confidently assert that today's graduates are better educated than their predecessors. If the perduring quality of the liberally educated mind is the pursuit of freedom through the arts of

---

[1]In my *Education for Modern Man* I have offered a program of positive reconstruction of the college curriculum along the lines of John Dewey's educational philosophy whose validity seems to me more apparent today than when it was originally published.

intelligence, then by and large we must frankly recognize that liberal arts education has failed dismally. When arson, obscenity, violence, confrontations, classroom disruptions and hooliganism, and cognate activities are present, the legacy of liberal education is absent. Nonetheless, I find it significant that some apologists for radical student activism should contend that despite the means that it employs, this movement is designed to reinstate the traditional values of liberal arts education betrayed by its faithless faculty servitors. This reminds me of nothing so much as the contention of advocates of almost all totalitarian philosophies that despite their dictatorial means they are "really" committed to democracy in a "higher" or "truer" sense.

By a liberal arts education I mean an education whose curriculum has been designed to help students develop those powers and resources—intellectual, emotional, cultural—that will enable them to acquire in a greater or lesser measure:

(1) a perspective on the events of their time with which to meet the challenges of present and future experience

(2) a constellation of values or a set of meanings or a calling or a developing center around which to organize their lives

(3) the knowledge, ideals, and techniques necessary for them adequately to perform their duties as free citizens of a free society

(4) a cultivated sensibility and inner landscape so that they can live a rich and significant personal life in a continuous process of self-education.

These are generic ideals whose connotations embrace an indeterminate number of special and temporal goals. It should be quite clear that the commitment to a liberal arts education does not entail a single and fixed curriculum for everyone. On the contrary: just as the ideal or pursuit of health is comparable to quite different regimens of hygiene and diet for different individuals, so a liberal arts education will have not only an historically varied content as society becomes more and more complex but will be reached by varied paths reflecting the experience, capacity, needs and interests of the student.

Today this conception of a liberal arts education, which I regard as a basis and sometimes an accompaniment of all higher professional education, is under attack from many different quarters. I wish to consider some of them.

The first of the many threats to liberal education is the popular view that the curriculum of our colleges should be oriented to meeting the *crises* that periodically arise in society, that threaten to set the world aflame or to imperil our national survival or health of the economy. This crisis-oriented approach to education assumes that the course of liberal study can and should be so organized that we can win a war or end it, prevent recessions or inflations, extend civil rights, rebuild our ghettos, stop the population explosion, prevent pollution—whatever may be the "good cause" that we as citizens rightfully deem to have overwhelming priority at the moment.

In view of the extent to which the colleges and universities of the country have responded to appeals to gear their curricular offerings to special situations and emergencies, the complaint that institutions of higher education have been academic cloisters and ivory towers, uninvolved and unconcerned with the troubled fate of man and society, borders on the grotesque. It is typical of the looseness and irresponsibility of much of the writing about the state of American higher education today. If anything there is a greater need of ivory towers for competent persons who wish to live in them, especially when we recall the great benefits to mankind from those who have inhabited them in the past. Even practical effects are best achieved by indirection. On any but the most philistine conception of human culture, the larger community has an ever present need for its seers, prophets, and lonely men of vision who sometimes seem maddeningly irrelevant to the intellectual and social fashions of the moment. We cannot breed such men but we should not prevent them from functioning by denigrating them or depriving them of a hospitable environment. They are all too rare under the best conditions.

It is one thing to aim to develop through curricular means the attitudes and capacities necessary to think and act intelligently in periods of crisis. It is quite another thing to believe that the special knowledge and skills required for the mastery of specific crises can be acquired in advance of their appearance. It is one thing to plan a curriculum of studies with an awareness of the social trends and problems that are shaping the future and that are certain to affect the lives of generations to come. It is simply utopian in the bad sense of the term, i.e., unrealistic and self-defeating, to imagine that a curriculum must necessarily keep up with all the specific trends and changes that are cried up as important in the great news media, which often emerge into and fade out of public consciousness with bewildering suddenness. It is one thing to develop a *readiness of response,* an ability to move promptly and intelligently in grappling with successive problems. It is quite something else to become petrified in a specific posture, however excellent it may have been with respect to some previous complex of problems.

This particular myth that colleges and universities can anticipate through curricular panaceas, the specific *crises* of the future and help master them, not to mention crises of the present, overlooks the most patent truths about the history of past crises and of the kind of social action necessary to resolve them. It is a myth that has been attributed with some justification to modernists who have invoked Dewey's name but have either not read or not properly understood him.

The opposite of a myth, however, can be just as mythical. Some traditionalists argue, in contradistinction to the above, that the best preparation for social change is the immersion in a fixed curriculum or program of studies. For example, Robert Hutchins writes: "If one neglects history in favor of current affairs, first he will never know history, and second he will not understand current affairs." (Oscar Wilde put this more felicitously a long time ago when he wrote: "He to whom the present is the only thing that is present, knows nothing of the age in which he lives.") We should applaud this recognition of the value of knowledge of history and the plea for its intelligent study. But then Hutchins goes on to add: "The part of the schools is not to expedite current affairs but to initiate students into timeless affairs." One cannot help asking: How can the study of timeless affairs help us to understand historical affairs that by definition are not timeless? Surely there is a distinction between the enduring, which is part of historical existence, and the timeless!

An intelligent modernity does not require that we redraw the maps of learning each year or decade or even generation at *every* level. The past, even interpretations of the past, do not change that much. Intelligent revisions and adaptations of the curriculum are always in order, and if better methods and techniques of learning and teaching are available, let us employ them as soon as possible. But not all knowledge becomes obsolescent at once!

There are more serious threats to the future of liberal arts education, as I have described it, allied to this ill-conceived notion that the university be crisis-oriented. They are more serious in that they challenge the supremacy of the authority of reason, or better, the authority of intelligence, which gradually has emerged as the *ideal* of the secular university. Quite often it has been breached by different pressure groups which in behalf of some private faiths or vested interests have struggled against its recognition. This ideal is intimately related to the conception of the university in the words of Karl Jaspers, "as the place where truth is sought unconditionally in all its forms." It is an ideal that, like the value of intelligence in reflective moral experience, is the only valid absolute because it is self-critical, aware of its own limitations. The view that American institutions of higher learning stress intelligence and the rational process too much is another bizarre notion of the educational underworld for which no rational evidence is advanced. A much more formidable case can be made for the opposite view.

Today the challenge to intelligence takes the form of the renewed cult of raw experience, of glorification of action, passion and sensual absorption as if they were immediate avenues not only to excitement but to truth and wisdom. Hoary errors in the history of thought have been revived to buttress this view when those immersed in its cult deign to defend it. "We learn by experience," it is said. "We learn by doing. We learn by going into the fields, streets, and factories—by marching, demonstrating, fighting, etc." One might just as well say we learn by living, and that the longer we live the more educated we are.

This is absurd on its face. But even if it were not, it is apparent that one does not need a university to acquire this kind of education—if one calls it an education. Life is not a school except as a dubious metaphor. There are many ways by which reality may be experienced or encountered, all legitimate in their context, but the knowing that gives us understanding and truth is a distinctive mode of experience. It is not true that we learn *by* experience. We learn *through* experience, and only when we have the capacity to learn. And what we learn through experience is more likely to be valid when we confront experience with a prepared mind. It is the cultivation and development of the prepared mind and its attendant functions of trained observation and disciplined imagination which is or should be the objective of all schooling, and especially schooling on the college and university level.

It is true that ultimately we learn by doing. But we must add, at the risk of wearying the reader, only when the role of ideas or hypotheses is central. Their presence is what distinguishes the intelligently learned man from the learned ass, from the dogmatic autodidact, and from those long on experience but short on wisdom.

Effective schooling of the prepared mind requires clinical experience that may take the student out of the classroom to amplify the meaning and test the validity of what he has learned within it. But it must be intelligently planned, supervised, and carefully assessed. Emphasis on clinical experience, where appropriate, cannot be overstressed. It is analogous to the experimental approach. It is a far cry, however, from current demands that uncontrolled, diverse, helter-skelter forays into "life" and "experience" be recognized as integral and valid elements of university education. The demand that "action Ph.D.'s" be awarded, that graduate students receive credit for leading rent strikes, organizing the unemployed, fighting pollution, and that undergraduates be granted academic recognition *merely* for the experience of traveling or living abroad is a *reductio ad absurdum* of this view. One may as well give them academic awards for sex and marriage.

Another challenge to liberal arts education is implicit in the demand that the research, teaching, scholarship—in short its total curricular activity in whole and part, be "relevant." What nonsense is covered by that term! The cry for relevance extends from the simple demand that the teacher talk sense to the demand that what he teaches, regardless of his subject matter, help achieve the classless society. Strictly speaking, the term "relevant" is relational. We must always ask: "Relevant to what?" Normally in the life of mind what is taught, if the teaching is good, is relevant to a *problem*. Problems themselves are relevant to domains of experience. The problem of *who* first propounded the theory of organic evolution or the labor theory of value is irrelevant to the problem of its validity. One man's problem may be irrelevant to another man's purpose or interests without affecting its significance in its own field. In a well-ordered university, where the scholarly faculty makes the educational decisions, after consultation with students and community leaders concerned with curricular content, the existence of certain fields of study in a university is *prima facie* evidence that the field is deemed to have educational significance in the light of the objectives of liberal arts study. Any attempt to control the relevance of studies except on educational grounds is an intolerable interference with academic freedom.

Most demands that higher education be "relevant" are either politically motivated or inspired by narrow utilitarian considerations. I shall discuss the political motivations below. The others are open to the easy retort that narrow utilitarian considerations are irrelevant not only to the ideals and delights of liberal arts education but to the multiple, indirect, and enlarged social usefulness of what is not immediately useful. Einstein's special theory of relativity had no earthly use when it was first propounded. But it was highly relevant to a genuine problem—the negative findings of the Michaelson-Morley experiment. The current demands for relevance would have driven Einstein and many others out of the university. Whitehead used to celebrate the perpetual uselessness of the theory of numbers and symbolic logic. Although they have now found a use, they have always had a sufficient justification to those who enjoy the games and beauty of abstraction.

Related to these challenges is the critical challenge to liberal arts education that stresses the importance of immediacy—the demands that the curriculum offer solutions to complex problems that can lead to early if not overnight transformations of our

society, economy, law, and culture. Radical activist students are
properly aware of the distance between the goals of the American
dream and our current achievement—something that they have
learned in large part through the despised curricular offerings of
the present. They are not properly aware—indeed, they aggressively ignore—the fact that American society has again and again raised its sights and periodically redefined the goals of the American
dream. They have, therefore, systematically ignored the distance
covered in removing the obstacles to political and social equality,
and despite the great problems and injustices still remaining, the
magnitude of the social gains. Disregarding the fact that American
colleges and universities have been the great centers of outspoken
criticism and dissent in American life, they have pictured them as
an exploitive institution of the Establishment, caricaturing the
whole notion of the Establishment—a vulgarized Marxist view of
"the ruling class"—with their charge that the organized working
class is part of it. In consequence, they have demanded not only
that their instruction be relevant in relation to their purpose but
that it be oriented to reformist even revolutionary objectives vague-
ly defined but completely and explicitly critical of every aspect of
American history and culture.

The truth tends to be the first casualty of every war and
crusade. One-sided criticism can distort the truth every whit as
much as apologetic accolades. On several campuses the classes of
professors who have not taken a sufficiently critical stance to one or
another aspect of American culture—in the eyes of *enragé*
students—have been disrupted. There is no record of student interference (which would be deplorable) with the instruction of
teachers openly sympathetic to the Viet Cong or to the totalitarian
despotisms of Castro, Mao Tse-tung, or the Kremlin with their
holocaust of victims. It is not surprising, therefore, that these
radical activists and their faculty allies have denounced the ideal of
"objectivity" as a bourgeois myth. To challenge the ideal of
objectivity, difficult as it may be to reach, as a chimera is to
renounce the ideal of the truth which is the *raison d'etre* of the
liberal university. To deny that the concept of objectivity is
intelligible is incoherent and self-contradictory, for it would

prevent us from distinguishing between historical fiction and historical fact, and make groundless and arbitrary even the radical activist's litany of alleged American crimes.

An unexpectedly formidable challenge to liberal arts education has been nurtured by some liberals so acutely aware of the failures of the liberal tradition to achieve its promise, that they have betrayed its perennially valid ideals—sometimes out of simple confusion and sometimes out of cowardice—moral and physical. I refer to the failure to recognize *the human experience* or the human condition as the basic source and orientation of the curriculum, and the resulting and growing fragmentation of the curriculum into isolated blocks of study, into "Black Studies," "Afro-American Studies," "Chicano Studies" "Third World Studies." The black experience, the African experience, the Third World experience, the Jewish experience, the Irish experience, etc., are all part of the *human* experience and as such worthy of inclusion in those areas and subject matter whose understanding is required to achieve a proper liberal education. The revision of the traditional liberal arts courses in history, literature, art, and the social sciences to do justice to the various ethnic expressions of human experience has long been overdue and is currently being undertaken. That is one thing. The organization of special blocks of study often open in effect only to members of minority groups, controlled and organized by these students and their representatives breaches important assumptions of liberal education as well as the principles of academic freedom. Here I stress only the educational aspect of the question. The Black experience is neither necessary nor sufficient to understand the truth about slavery any more than the experience of white Southerners is necessary or sufficient to understand the truth about the Reconstruction Period, or experience in Fascist or Communist countries is necessary or sufficient to learn or teach the truths about their terrorist regimes. I find it highly significant that the powerful criticisms of the proposals for *separate* courses of study for black students, made by distinguished Negro educators like Kenneth Clark, Sir Arthur Lewis, Bayard Rustin and others, have provoked no considered replies but only derisive epithets. Many administrators who have supported the demand for autonomous Black

Studies programs have done so not on supportable educational grounds but out of fear that their campuses would be torn apart. Professor Henry Rosovsky who did pioneering work as Chairman of the Harvard Committee on African and Afro-American studies in devising an undergraduate major in Afro-American studies with the *same standards of academic excellence* that obtained for other majors flatly charges that the action of the Harvard faculty reversing the report of his committee and in effect giving black undergraduate students "powers hitherto held only by Harvard *senior faculty* and denied to junior faculty, graduate students, and non-black undergraduates" was adopted in the face of threats and violence.

To make exceptions to principles of equity as well as valid educational policy in order to compensate for historical injustices is an inverse form of racism just as objectionable to sensitive and intelligent members of minority groups as traditional forms of racism. To lower standards of judgment and excellence, to dilute content and subject matter as a form of intellectual reparations is to restore and compound the infamies of the double standard. The student is just as much a second-class academic citizen if an institution discriminates in his favor on the basis of his skin color as he is when it discriminates against him on the same basis.

There are dangerous tendencies in the admission policies of some institutions which mistakenly believe that democracy in education requires that all groups in the population be represented proportionally among the student body and faculty. A case may be made for the view that in American democratic society everyone has a human right to the kind and degree of schooling from which he can profit and which will facilitate the growth of his intellectual and cultural powers to their fullest. But a right to an education no more carries with it the right to a specific kind of education or to the same degree of education for everyone than the right to medical treatment entails the right to the same kind of medical treatment no matter what one is ailing from. Here as elsewhere individual need, interest, capacity should be the determining considerations. Democracy, we cannot repeat too often, is not a belief in the moral equality of those who are the *same* or *alike* but in the moral equality

155

of difference—whether they are physically different, racially different, or intellectually different.

The liberal arts conception of high education is based upon a belief in the community of educational interest among teacher-scholars and learners and administrators. This conception is being threatened by something analogous to a "class struggle" view according to which the university is a factory in which students are processed and exploited by their teachers and administrators. But knowledge is not a commodity of which one can say that the more one has of it the less remains for others. It belongs to the family of values of which it is true to say that they are not diminished but enhanced by being shared. Education is not in the first instance a quest for power, whether student power or faculty power, but a quest for truth, a means for growth, spiritual enlargement, and maturation. Where a community of educational interest prevails in the university this does not preclude difference, sometimes sharp differences about a multitude of things. But so long as the class struggle conception of education does not enter to disrupt rational exchange of views, all of these differences are negotiable in the same way by which we seek to resolve scientific differences. This is why the university can be both a conservator of values and attitudes as well as an innovator. It cannot legislate for the community, certainly not for the democratic community. It serves that community without being either a servant or master of it.

All the challenges to liberal education I have considered come to a head in frank espousals for the politicalization of the university. By the politicalization of the university is meant the direct involvement of the university as a *corporate* institution in the controversial political and social problems of the day. The radical activists of our time speak out of both sides of their mouths on this question, sometimes condemning the university for allegedly already being politically involved, and as guilty of betraying the ideal of non-involvement, and sometimes—the real burden of their song—condemning the university for being involved on the wrong political side. Not content with having won the right for individual faculty members to espouse any political cause they wish without prejudicing their position in the university community, they seek to

156

draw the university *as such* officially into the endorsement, teaching, and organization of programs for social reform and/or revolution of the society on whose largesse and support the university ultimately depends. Since these activists assert that no program of social reform or commitment can dispense with an ideology, they are proposing that universities cease making a fetish of objectivity and neutrality and become ideological institutions.

This is a recommendation which if acted upon can result only in educational disaster. If the universities attempt to politicalize themselves, and instead of studying, proposing, and critically analyzing programs of social action seek to implement these programs as part of an agenda of social action, the unconverted larger community will not only withdraw its support but purge or suppress them. The universities will lose their hard won relative autonomy and be politicalized with a vengeance but from an ideological quarter hardly congenial to the radical activists who will be swept away together with their liberal allies. Although I am convinced that the consequences of politicalizing the university will be suicidal, I do not wish to base my criticisms of the proposal on these grounds but in terms of the values of the liberal arts traditions.

The attempt to line up the university *as such* behind some particular program of reform or revolution testifies to a failure to establish a consensus or win agreement to positions on the basis of argument and evidence. There is very little that a university can do as such that a faculty of persuaded individuals acting as an independent group in their own name cannot do as well. Where a university takes a stand on capitalism or socialism, or war and peace, or methods of urban reconstruction, in the nature of the case the position of the minorities that cannot accept that stand becomes precarious. They appear as malcontents and troublemakers sabotaging the larger commitments of the university.

Once the university becomes politicalized, the students, too, become politically polarized if they have not already reached that state. Students and faculty then join forces in ways already familiar to us not only in the universities of some foreign countries but on some of our own campuses. Factionalization among extremists leads to a kind of competition among them to implement the

157

corporate policies more vigorously and to push the university into the forefront of the struggle to radicalize society. The effect of ideological commitment on departments—on the appointment and promotion of faculty personnel is to produce one-sided and unbalanced presentations and criticisms. The normal frictions and conflicts that operate even when the university is uncommitted and permits all the winds of doctrine to blow freely on the campus become exacerbated to a point where professional competence, which should be the first and main criterion in matters of this kind, is subordinated, under all sorts of pretexts and rationalizations, to ideological considerations. The canons of professional ethics and integrity are celebrated in the holiday rhetoric of convocations and commencements but are abandoned in practice.

That politicalization of the university constitutes an obvious threat to academic freedom is acknowledged. Sometimes in an effort to minimize the danger, advocates of politicalization narrow the scope of the "political" to grave issues or to periods of crisis. But the definition of grave issues depends on how intensely human beings feel about them, and the world is always in crisis. More often, and especially among students and junior faculty, academic freedom is regarded as a kind of class privilege of professors that can readily be sacrificed or compromised to further larger ideological goals or purposes.

It may sound harsh but there is convincing evidence that it is true: Academic freedom in the United States today is threatened not so much by fundamentalist churchmen, reactionary businessmen, and political demagogues, as much as it is by ideological fanatics among students and faculty. It is ironical that they owe their presence in the university and the fact that they are given an opportunity to proclaim their ideological wares to the very principles of academic freedom which they violate and undermine by their disruptive activities. They ignore the truth that genuine tolerance does not entail tolerance of the actively intolerant.

No one can reasonably defend the *status quo* in American higher education. For one thing there is no such thing as the *status quo*. For another, the growth of American universities in the past has not always been guided by a critical and self-conscious philosophy of education. Many activities and enterprises could more appropriately be housed elsewhere. The university cannot be all things to all men, an instrument of every purpose, without losing its intellectual dignity and authority and ultimately its honesty. Everything depends upon the methods of change and the direction of change. I take it for granted for the moment that the methods will be through the rational and autonomous decisions of its faculties uncoerced by political groups from within or without. If I am mistaken about this and the fate of the university is a function of which political groups triumph in American life, academic freedom both of *Lehrfreiheit and Lernfreiheit* will be eclipsed.

The direction of change that holds the greatest promise for deepening, enriching, and developing the great humanistic and scientific legacies of university education lies in liberalizing the curriculum and processes of teaching and learning in the light of the ideals of the liberal arts tradition. These legacies may stem from the contributions of socially privileged and elite groups of the past. Today our technology makes it possible for *all* men and women who are willing and able, to partake of them, to contribute to them, and to find some meaning and enjoyment in them. The liberal arts tradition is strengthened by the principles of academic freedom and in turn draws support from them. For both keep open the pathways to new truths and new visions of excellence in man's unending quest better to understand himself, society and the environing world.

10

The De-schooled Utopia

We are beginning to understand that the rhetoric of revolutionary extremism is not simply a put-on or a form of exhibitionism or an outburst of politicalized aesthetic fury that titillates the penthouse *rentiers* of the New Left. Not only have ideas consequences, words have consequences too, even if the ideas they express are vague and somewhat incoherent. The inflammatory language of the Black Panthers and the blood-chilling manifestos of the Weathermen may be empty of serious content. There can be little doubt, however, that they have had a profound effect on the behavior of some of their initiates. The terrorism of the word—even revolutionary bull—prepares the way for the terrorism of the deed.

Something analogous is observable in the field of education. Paralleling the extremist position and inflated rhetoric of the revolutionist decrying the possibility of democratic social reform is the development of extremist positions in education decrying the possibility of intelligent school reform. Here, too, what was listened to with indulgence as an exaggerated expression of a universally shared dissatisfaction with the present state of schooling is beginning to have practical consequences. The existence of the school itself and the system of compulsory public education has come under fire in the United States. The professional teachers and their organizations are becoming the scapegoats of our discontent. Permanent tenure is under fierce attack in many quarters as primarily a shelter for incompetence at public expense. At the same time we are told that everyone has a natural birthright not only to learn but to teach. Every citizen is not only equally concerned with education, he is equally an authority about what should be learned and how. Those educational authorities, especially the professional teachers and administrators, who are dubious about this are really authoritarians masking themselves as adepts in the pseudo-science of pedagogy. In the interest of freedom we must abolish schools whose inhibiting and demoralizing effects on the personalities of their charges are worse than those of our military and penal systems.

The most recent expression of this view is found in a slight volume, *De-schooling Society* by Ivan Illich.[1] It is a book whose absurd extremism warrants little attention from anyone endowed with a normal portion of common sense. The only reason for taking it seriously is that some of its positions are influencing the new radical critics of American education who, without subscribing to Illich's panacea, are accepting some of his assumptions about schools and schooling to fortify their attacks on current educational theory and practice and on professional teachers as "buttresses of the Establishment." Also disquieting is the fact that Illich's views seem to have won the endorsement of some officials of educational institutes who purvey advice for liberal fees to the school systems of the nation.

Illich's thesis is a simple one—so simple that the reader hesitates for a moment in concluding that he really means what he writes. But he does. Our schools are unmitigatedly bad. All of them? Well, almost all. Then why not try to improve schooling by taking as a model the best schools? This is hopeless, a trap, says

[1]*De-schooling Society* (New York, 1971).

162

Illich. The "hidden curriculum" of schooling, of any formal schooling, inspires the "myth" that certified teachers—bureaucrats all—can use scientific knowledge to impart "humane and efficient" education. The only remedy is to abolish all formal schools and with it all compulsory education.

What do we put in its stead? Reliance upon "self-motivated" learning, upon the processes of self-education in freedom through natural association with those who already possess skills and knowledge or who are willing to cooperate in a quest for them. This will be facilitated by four interrelated networks or "learning webs." The first will make accessible to children and students the necessary things and processes (in libraries, museums, theatres, factories and farms); the second will facilitate the exchange of skills among learners; the third is called "peer-matching": persons will advertise their educational needs or interests "in the hope of finding a partner" for mutual advantage; and, finally, diligent use will be made of a Yellow Pages of self-selected and self-advertised Educators-at-Large who will list their skills and addresses and the price of their services.

The only thing clear about the operation of these networks is that the government will pay the costs. Left completely vague is the answer to the question: Who will supervise and direct this educational experience and provide for the sequential organization of subject matters and acquisition of skills without which no discipline can be mastered? Something like the invisible hand that guarantees the harmonious adjustment of the needs of buyers and sellers in the free market is presupposed. But even less than the free market in commodities, the free market in education may not meet genuine and desirable needs while gratifying some that are not so desirable. Some of the proposals for peer-matching are suggestive of the techniques used by genteel and literate prostitutes in arranging assignations through the columns of literary periodicals. Although Illich admits that his networks of learning may be abused, he is convinced that the perils of schooling are far worse because of their restrictions on the freedom of natural self-motivated learners. How the child who is not self-motivated is to learn is left unexplained.

It is not only the school which in Illich's view prevents "personal, creative and autonomous interaction" among learners and teachers but all the major institutions of society: the state, the church, the army, the medical services, the political party, the media, the family as we know it. "Not only education but society as a whole needs 'de-schooling.'"

One would imagine therefore that before any significant change in education can be effected we would need a total social and cultural revolution. Nonetheless Illich holds that the de-schooling of education can succeed in relative independence of the other equally necessary "de-schoolings."

Despite the extremism of his position Illich writes with an astonishing confidence and dogmatism, piling one questionable statement upon another in reckless disregard of evidence, logic, and common sense. "Middle-class parents commit their children to a teacher's care to keep them from learning what the poor learn on the streets." But parents—poor ones no less than those of the middle class—usually commit their children to schools and teachers in the hope that they will learn what they can't learn at home or in the street. (Illich seems unaware that a child who is well taught at home is not compelled to attend school.) "Teachers more often than not obstruct such learning of subject matters as goes on in a school." In order to know this Illich would have to know how much reading, writing, arithmetic, geography, history, etc. most children learn *without* benefit of any schooling. Since he does not and cannot know this today, his remark simply slanders school teachers whose dedication to their students is no less than his own. Teachers are painted as monsters sadistically exploiting and oppressing children whose "chronological age disqualifies [them] from safeguards which are routine for adults in a modern asylum—madhouse, monastery, or jail." They need the constitutional protection of the First and Fifth Amendments!

Why should all schools, not merely authoritarian ones but those that are avowedly liberal and progressive, be charged with totalitarian oppressiveness? Because they all operate with the idea that "one person's judgment should determine what and when another person must learn." Yet, surely, when the other person is a growing child and not an adult an informed and sympathetic determination of what and when he should learn is no more improper than determining what and when he should eat. What is wrong is the imposition of the same learning (or feeding) schedules on children independently of their special needs and interests. But there is a world of difference between individualizing the curriculum and, as Illich proposes, abolishing it.

Actually it is both foolish and cruel to rely for education on the casual, chance encounters of the young. Illich's assurance that the young always learn something from their experiences or become aware of their needs through raw, unstructured experience is not less absurd than his implied view that with respect to health they should be liberated from the ministrations of compulsory medical care. The young are no more always aware of what they need to know in order to grow to their full powers than they are always aware of what to do and what to avoid to achieve health. In either case what they don't know may sometimes cripple them for life. If they waited until they experienced an acute need before learning certain things, they would discover what so many foolish adults have discovered who waited to see a doctor until they had an acute need for one, *viz.*, that it was too late or costly to remedy what ailed them.

The basic question in education, explicitly denied by Illich and other New Left critics, is: "What should individuals learn" in modern society in order more readily to achieve their maximum growth as persons? The basic problem in teaching on every level (except the graduate school) is how to motivate the individual to learn joyfully yet thoroughly what he should learn—as well as what he wants to learn—until he is mature enough to take over the direction of his own education. This, of course, is a gradual process that recognizes that each learner has individual needs as well as common needs.

For Illich and those he has influenced, on the other hand, the planning of new educational institutions must start with the question: "What kind of things and people might learners want to be in contact with in order to learn?" A parent who actually lived up to Illich's dictum might well find himself in difficulties with the

165

Society for the Prevention of Cruelty to Children (if that worthy group hasn't also been abolished). Children might want to be in contact with anything from live wires and drugs to the glazed ridges of tenement roofs; they may never recover from the effects of learning about them and kindred things. Conversely, they might *not* want to be in contact with children of different races, religions, or nationalities. And yet such experiences of mixing and contact might be necessary to cure them of their prejudices and helpful in avoiding the stereotyped judgments of their elders. On Illich's view, whether anyone learns anything worthwhile is purely a matter of chance. On a more sensible view, our world is too dangerous to take such chances.

The flaws in this smart, silly book can be traced to a number of assumptions explicitly made by Illich but also widely held by other romantic critics of the school system who draw back from his extremist remedies. He assumes that because children learn to speak their own language casually without going to school and without explicit instruction, they learn most other things in the same way. To be sure, children have learned to speak and walk without schooling or explicit instruction since the emergence of man from more primitive species, but all human history testifies that they do not learn to read and write as effortlessly. Before compulsory schooling was introduced the vast majority of mankind remained illiterate. Illich holds no brief for illiteracy but he assumes that literacy can be more readily acquired by abolishing schools and relying upon the casual operation of his networks to effect mastery of elementary skill. To claim that we will all learn from and teach one another as need and interest manifest themselves is to invoke pious hope that flies in the face of overwhelming evidence. Not everyone who knows something, even when he knows it well, can teach it, not to mention teach it effectively. Not everyone who is able to teach is willing or in a position to do so. Even speech depends upon the models imitated and can be immensely improved by proper schooling.

Further, some skills are best learned in youth, like writing and arithmetical computation, as well as certain habits of work, and of thoughtfulness for others. Anyone who has seen a grown man, who has been raised in some foreign culture where no ball games were played, writhe as he vainly tries to throw a ball, understands the point. Accidents have been known to happen to persons who never having learned, when children, to differentiate automatically between left and right paused too long at the shouted advice to turn out of the path of an oncoming car.

Illich "hopes" that education will improve after society is de-schooled. But his conception of "hope" indicates that he has not liberated himself from metaphysical superstition. He sharply contrasts "expectation" with "hope," and downgrades the former because it means "reliance upon results which are planned and controlled by man." Schooling is a form of expectation, since it uses plans and controls, and is therefore bad. Hope "means trusting faith in the goodness of nature." It is interference with nature and human nature that produces evil. Disease presumably is the product of medicine, not the consequence of natural causes. If Illich had the courage of his hope, he would opt for the free market as well as for education free of schools in order to avoid any kind of planning and controlling of the economy.

Illich has a flair for drawing absurd conclusions from truisms. "We have all learned most of what we know outside the school." From which he infers that schools are therefore unnecessary. But unless the kind of learning is specified, it is just as true to say that most of what we learn outside of school we learn *because* of the skills, knowledge, and training we learned in school. Obviously, since formal schooling is comparatively recent, human beings have learned most things, for better or worse, in the course of living. In a sense they always will. But this by no means invalidates the benefits of schools. Schooling can make a difference to what we bring to an experience to make it educationally significant. Illich pretends that "schools are designed on the assumption that there is a secret to everything in life" and that only teachers hold the key to it. The truth is that the assumptions of modern schooling are much more modest. They are: that much knowledge and many skills are interesting and useful in helping people cope with their experience and in enhancing the quality of their lives; that they can be learned by systematic schooling more easily than by casual encounters with things and persons or by reliance on "the goodness of nature"; that the acquisition of knowledge and mastery of skills requires a grasp of sequential order in subject matter; that teachers can be helpful in the process of learning until students are in a position intelligently to choose their own patterns of growth.

Illich disputes all this. He claims that schools and teachers prevent children from learning by chaining them to alternating routines of trivial play and drill. According to him we tend to romanticize what we have learned in schools. No one, he claims, really learned how to read in school. We learned outside of school from parents or older siblings or from the boy across the way. He leaves unexplained how, in the U.S.A., entire generations of children of immigrant parents, who could neither speak, read nor write English, learned English more or less adequately. He has read about all the weaknesses of the American public school; but he is ignorant of its achievements.

The animus against school teachers extends to a point where he resents and deplores reliance upon official certification by the state of the capacity to teach or to practice any profession. For all his talk about autonomy and independence and creative rediscovery in education he bemoans the passing of "personal discipleship." The Yellow Pages of Educators-at-Large will probably have a special supplement on gurus. Not unaware of the dangers, he nonetheless would abandon all official restraints or controls on those who hold themselves out to be healers of the sick in mind and body. Their expertise would be determined by popularity polls of students, patients, and clients. "The right to teach any skill"—including surgery and engineering?—"should come under the protection of free speech." For him academic freedom is not the right of *qualified* teachers to be free of ecclesiastical, political, and administrative interference. Academic freedom is a human right; it does not have to be earned. His open society therefore would be an open society for medical and educational quacks without any safeguards for their victims that intellectual scepticism, the by-product of effective teaching, can produce. Never mind the casualties! Of course, schools of medicine, engineering and education today have their casualties, too. But the remedy for poor schools is better schools, not their abolition.

What makes Illich's proposal to abolish schools gratuitously foolish is that some of his suggested webs of learning, with appropriate revisions and safeguards, are in use today as supplementary aids to basic schooling. Compulsory education is an institution, not a process of learning. Students can no more be compelled to learn than to love. Compulsory education expresses the responsibility of society to all its children, especially where parental responsibility is absent. It does not go on forever. By the time students have reached the school-leaving age, they should be in a position to choose freely and intelligently the kind of continuing education, in school or out, they wish to pursue.

The meeting of extremes in politics is an old story. The voice of Bernardine Dohrn and the Weathermen is hardly distinguishable from that of Charles Manson and his Family. In education the mindless Right that opposes public education sounds very much like some factions among the mindless Left. For both the state is always the enemy whose interference with the natural order must be resisted even if it is the order of anarchy. The case in general for compulsory education, not necessarily through one kind of school or any formal school, is even better than the case for compulsory vaccination which in Illich's eyes must also appear as an abridgement of human freedom and a betrayal of hope "in the goodness of nature." In a democratic community the right to learn is a human right. The community owes a responsibility to all children to provide them with the opportunities to develop their powers to make informed and reflective choices not only for the sake of their survival but its own. Under certain circumstances this responsibility may override the rights of parents who are either indifferent or hostile to their children's development.

It is significant that in democratic societies the centers of dissent have usually been the schools and the schooled. Nor is it fortuitous that sophisticated apologists of oppressive regimes in the past have been hostile to universal compulsory education out of fear that "the lower classes," having caught glimpses of the great legacies of human culture, would seek to enlarge their share of it. Nothing would please those who are opposed to desegregation in American education today more than the abolition of compulsory schooling. Like so many other contemporary reactionaries on the New Left, Illich talks a great deal about freedom but neglects the principles of intellectual authority and organization necessary to negotiate the conflicts of freedoms. The result is that his free society is one in which everyone is free "to do one's thing" no matter if the consequences result, as in all anarchist utopias that rely on the goodness of nature, in the universal loss of hard-won freedoms.

11

Some Educational Attitudes & Poses

The attitude of American intellectuals toward education is a subject of considerable complexity. I cannot begin to do justice to the theme in these largely autobiographical remarks. There are different kinds of intellectuals, and there have been changes over the years both in their degree of concern and in the causes of their lack of concern with American education. The term "education" in its comprehensive sense embraces much more than formal schooling or pedagogical activity on all levels, but I shall use it in this latter, restricted sense. I am confident that some day a scholarly work will appear which will explore with the latest tools of research and, I hope with good judgment, the chief facets of this vast question. My reflection on the subject will be casual and impressionistic, part of the materials to be evaluated.

By and large in the half-century during which I have observed the intellectual scene, I have found American intellectuals profoundly uninterested in the nature of American education, its problems, controversial issues, and conflicting philosophies. I use the paradoxical expression "profoundly uninterested" to suggest an awareness of their lack of interest, a willingness to remain unconcerned despite efforts to arouse their interest. During the twenties, American education in all its aspects was damned and dismissed by many American intellectuals, especially the literary intellectuals, as part of the culture of the "booboisie," as the appropriate institutional breeding grounds for the generation of George Babbitt. American democracy itself, which had put Coolidge, Harding, and Hoover at the helm, was contemptuously characterized as "the dictatorship of the booboisie," a phrase coined, I believe, by Mencken, who was to end as an even more bitter critic of the Roosevelt era than of the decade of normalcy.

The hostility to the externalism, commercialism, nationalism, and isolationism of American life was automatically extended to American education, conceived as an integral part of popular culture. It wasn't necessary to be familiar with what American educators wrote and with the actual practices of the school—the impact of scientific psychology was increasing—to dismiss American education with some off-hand denigrating remarks. It was the culture and education of Europe which were exalted, again without much understanding of the actual character of European schooling and its institutional structure. Very few American admirers of European culture knew or cared that above the elementary levels, European education was an education of and for an elite, and that if a similar system had prevailed here many of the American intellectuals who admired it from afar would not have been eligible for a higher education. They were content to believe that the culture of Paris, centered in the Academy and the Left-Bank, was the culture of France, and the culture of France, the culture of Europe.

This invidious and absurd contrasting of American and European education was until recently a constant feature in the attitude of American intellectuals, the writers and critics, whose concern with large and general ideas was not analytical but predominantly personal, social, and political. These were intellectuals who did not take ideas apart. They considered them primarily as "expressions" of social forces, sometimes of personality, and later as weapons in political struggles. *The Partisan Review* was the most influential of the periodicals that served, so to speak, as house organs of the intellectuals. But I do not recall its publishing any article *strictly* on American education except one by the German emigré writer, Hannah Arendt. This was a lecture she delivered at the University of Bremen which began, "I do not know anything about American education." What she said proved it. My point is not that her article should not have been published but that a contribution by an American educator on this theme would have been scorned. Haughty ignorance of American conditions need not deter European intellectuals from talking about America. They can always find an eager and respectful audience among American intellectuals. (At the time of the Little Rock riots, Hannah Arendt defended the rights of parents to send their children to segregated schools, white or black, and asserted that the basic deprivation of Negro freedom in the U.S. was laws forbidding intermarriage—a subject that was and still is of the lowest order of concern to Negroes in their struggle for civil rights. I mention this only as evidence of unfamiliarity with the American scene.)

Nor was the situation very different during the thirties when many American intellectuals were caught up in the movement of social protest. This was the decade in which a considerable group repudiated social reform as too superficial a remedy for the crisis of American society. They regarded the legislative reforms of the New Deal as utterly inadequate, as comparable to slapping a fresh coat of paint on a house about to collapse from dry rot. Yet for all their espousal of the cause of social revolution, they were singularly indifferent to the character of education in the revolutionary society about to burst on the world. They ignored—most of them were not even aware of —the interesting controversies beginning to rage in the philosophy of education, and the problems of theory and practice engaging professional educators. The latter were regarded with unconcealed disdain as pedagogical bores and hacks, and, with the rare exception of a few who had made contributions to other fields, no more qualified to be considered intellectuals than the neighborhood physicians.

The intellectuals talked, wrote, and cheered revolution, and encouraged those who could to dramatize, paint, and sing it. But except for a handful whose critical attitude soon isolated them, they

173

thought very little about revolution. They left their "thinking" to the leaders of the Communist Party and their spokesmen in intellectual circles, mediocre minds incapable of fresh and original thought and fearful of it in others, intent primarily on keeping the confidence of those appointed by the Comintern to safeguard their orthodoxy. They sought to do this by parroting the latest directives received from authoritative sources. Most of the thousands of writers and artists and progressive-minded professionals organized in the various Leagues and Congresses were perfectly content to retire from thinking even in their own fields, and merely to devise projects and slogans for the line handed them by their political mentors. They shrank from taking issue with the nonsense about class literature, class art, class science, class this, and class that in the subjects of their competence. How much more unready and unwilling were they to challenge the current party line in politics and economics! How often would one be told after criticizing the theory and practice of dual trade-unionism, or the theory of Social Fascism, or the simplistic pieties, contradictions, and irrelevancies of historical and dialectical materialism: "Who are you to set yourself up against Browder (or Foster)? And perhaps you consider yourself a better student of Marx than Stalin or Lenin?" There was little attempt made to meet any arguments except by denigrating references to the critics as "Talmudists" or "Trotskyists," or, as one literary editor of an important periodical put it, "disgruntled New York Jews who want to be generals." Even those who were impressed by the criticism, silenced if not convinced, would say: "You may be right. If you are, you ought to join the Communist Party and change it from within. If you don't you are insincere." Their idea of sincerity was to dissemble what one believed until one could safely criticize, precisely what the continuous Communist purge of deviationists and semi-deviationists made impossible.

In an atmosphere of this kind it is not surprising that my suggestion that Dewey's educational philosophy provided a basis for a continuing revolution of the whole of American society was greeted with incredulity. And when I argued that its political and psychological possibilities carried greater promise for the development of an American socialist movement than domestic or imported varieties of vulgar Marxism, this was regarded as the worst kind of revisionism. According to my reading of Dewey's conception of democracy in education, it entailed the responsibility of the community for the growth of all its children to their full reach and power as persons. This could serve as both normative premise and as goal for a continuous and permanent social revolution, for the continuous reconstruction of all our major social institutions, especially the economic system.

Dewey himself had come to realize this—not without prodding from me, I can say not too immodestly. I had contended and still do, that only in a democratic socialist economy in which housing, schooling, and vocational opportunities are planned in relation to the needs of individuals, and not made dependent upon the vagaries of the market, could the educational ideals of *Democracy and Education* be realized. By the time he published his *Liberalism and Social Action* Dewey had come around to accepting this, and, with an eye on the hate-mongering, violence-inciting, neo-Nazi groups then cluttering up the political landscape, to emphasizing that the method of intelligence was not milk-and-water reasonableness but toughness with those who resorted to force to negate the popular will. But after his study of the Moscow Trials and his bitter experiences with the hostility and indifference of large numbers of ritualistic American liberals to criticisms of Stalin's regime of terror, Dewey drew back from further exploration of the social corollaries of his underlying philosophy of education. He was committed to piecemeal solutions that did not exclude large-scale social changes and, under some circumstances, even revolutionary changes. But he became increasingly suspicious and critical of revolutionary changes conceived as "total solutions," and of the disregard of the means and instrumentalities by which they were achieved. There were some who dismissed his own educational ideals as utopian in that they could no more be implemented than the ideals of Robert Owen before some revolutionary changes had transformed the existing order in its entirety. Dewey regarded as much worse than utopian, conceptions of an ideal society that were not continuous with programs

175

and methods of action in the present, that failed to give some purchase in the struggles to solve present problems. Such ideals he regarded as purely verbal allegiances, and very dangerous to boot, because unrelated as they were to any specific practice, they could be invoked to sanctify any practice. Dewey distrusted those who regarded democracy merely as a means of realizing socialism, instead of testing proposed socialist measures as a means of extending and deepening democracy.

What was required, among other things, were detailed studies in depth of the educational system on all its levels. This meant more than fresh analyses of the curriculum to purge it of racial and ethnic prejudice. Inquiries should have been undertaken into the effects of existing social and economic institutions on the functioning of schools—the effects of the technological revolution, the population explosion, and the migration and displacement of families, for instance, upon the distribution of educational opportunities. Such inquiries should have culminated in imaginative proposals for practical changes for which wide political support could have been organized. The labor movement could have been mobilized not only for support of programs of social security but for broad educational reforms.

But this research was precisely what most radical intellectuals were unwilling or unprepared to do. It was much too prosaic; it smacked of busy work, of Fabianism, of the unexciting publications of the unexciting League for Industrial Democracy. It has been characteristic of American intellectual radicalism from the early thirties down to the present that it has been primarily an expression of a mood of protest, opposition, and aspiration. Its greatest intellectual effects and triumphs have been rhetorical. And although there have been heroic individual episodes and actions, there has been a singular lack of enthusiasm for developing specific programs for legislative action around which, with the help of the organized labor movement, educational and political campaigns could have been waged. Even fundamental analyses of developments in the American economy—a critique of welfare economics from the point of view of public welfare, for instance, or studies of the promise and inadequacies of economic aid to

176

underdeveloped countries, of the impact of automation on employment, or of the growing power and changing nature of the corporation (subjects one would have thought crucial to the understanding of our present capitalist society)—were either not undertaken or left in the main to professional economists and semi-public agencies. This was true, not only of the American intellectuals whose political syndrome in the thirties and forties was a positive tropism toward the Soviet Union, but also of a much more gifted group of radical intellectuals, largely literary, who were so intent upon preserving their revolutionary purity, despite the absence of any revolutionary program, that they would denounce with equal ferocity—when they did not draw an equation between them—the cultures of totalitarian Communism and the imperfectly democratic West, a West in which they enjoyed a greater freedom and opportunity than ever before to influence their fellow citizens by presenting better programs for living and learning. They, too, were indifferent to basic educational issues and problems.

Nor was there less indifference to the philosophy of education, until quite recently, among professional American philosophers despite the early example of James and Dewey. Here and there during the thirties a philosopher would criticize the overweening arrogance of Hutchins, Adler, and their neo-Thomist allies in their attempt to derive educational corollaries from metaphysical premises. But on the whole the philosophy of education was regarded as a "soft subject," like the philosophy of art, to be left to the cultivation of those who found the severe discipline of logic and epistemology too taxing. When in the forties I published my *Education for Modern Man*, some of my colleagues saw in it merely a foray into an unrelated discipline despite the obvious truth that any discussion of the ends of education that goes beyond sociological description inescapably involves a normative approach to human values, a central and continuing concern of philosophy from Plato to the present.

The contributions of professional American educators did little to interest the bulk of American intellectuals. Dewey was known to them as a public figure who had been part of the cultural landscape when most of them appeared on the scene. His writings on war and peace had put him in the thick of public events. His philosophical contributions which ranged over many of the disciplines in the social sciences and humanities commanded respect even when they elicited little understanding. Lewis Mumford, for example, interpreted Dewey's stress on the reconstruction of experience, personal and social, in order to liberate, enlarge, and enrich human energies, as a rationalization of the *status quo*, an acquiescence to dominant American values, and as a plan for personal adjustment to contemporary institutions. The "proof" of all this was that Dewey had critically supported the First World War. But at least American intellectuals were aware of his existence as an educator. His professional colleagues in education were either unknown to most intellectuals or ignored by them. The reasons for this were many and obvious. The interests of the professional educators were for the most part narrow and highly specialized. They were unaware of the moods and enthusiasms and currents of thought among intellectuals. Even when professional educators had strong social interests, they showed no sensitivity to the multiple ways in which these interests could be expressed in literature, drama, and art. They concerned themselves little with the problems of the creative medium and with the clash of traditions in criticism. To the intellectuals American professional educators appeared insular and parochial, if not Philistine—too much absorbed in the latest fiddle-faddle about reading, child psychology, and curricular innovation to warrant receiving serious attention.

My own relations with professional educators, except for George Counts and John Childs, were always ambiguous. They welcomed me enthusiastically because of my critical rejoinders to unfair and uninformed attacks on modern education by Neo-Thomists, classicists, and purveyors of salvation in this world and/or the next. But they were puzzled by my interpretation of Dewey's educational philosophy and by Dewey's endorsement of it. I recall two incidents sympotomatic of these ambiguous relationships. On the occasion of one of Kilpatrick's birthdays, I was invited to participate in a discussion of the significance of his contributions to education, which was to be put on records that could be replayed in schools of education throughout the country. I was reluctant to accept but finally yielded because although I had never read much of Kilpatrick, I assumed that our views about modern education, drawn from the same source, were the same. Besides, it seemed a good idea to do something for the morale of progressive educators, who were under fire on various grounds from fundamentalists, patrioteers, and real estate boards. The theme was "The Resources of Education." The other four participants had spoken and mentioned many interesting ways in which students' experiences and environments could be used as aids in learning and in furthering significant educational growth. The devices and procedures suggested were not radically different from those I had used when I taught in elementary school or high school while doing graduate work.

But to my surprise no one mentioned what I regarded as one of the most important resources in education, and I began by saying, "Another powerful and widely useful resource in education for the cultivation of the imagination and the enlargement of intellectual horizons is the reading of books," or words to that effect. I got no further. Excited interruptions from all sides demanded to know what I meant. I was asked what relevance books had to the project method, and was lectured about the dangers of using books as a substitute for experience. All this to the apparent embarrassment of Kilpatrick himself who was present but said nothing, and to my own amazement that my innocent and commonplace remark should have provoked such dismay and commotion. The recording was broken off. When it was resumed I rephrased my remarks carefully to indicate that the reading of books was, of course, supplementary to the other resources of education, that there was reading and reading, and that a good teacher knew how to stimulate the student's interest in sustained and critical reading by giving him various projects related to it. But even my amended contributions had spoiled the recording. The next day the woman in charge of the arrangements telephoned and requested rather peremptorily that I appear for a rerun. She made no bones about the fact that she thought I was in the wrong educational pew and would just as soon leave me out but that Professor Kilpatrick had specifically asked that I be invited. It had been his idea in the first place.   I begged off and, when I had a chance, dipped into Kilpatrick's books.   I got the bizarre impression that in *Education and Experience*, Dewey had been aiming his shafts at those apparently under the influence of Kilpatrick.

The second incident occurred when Harold Taylor was appointed President of Sarah Lawrence College and I was invited to address the faculty and students on the philosophy of education. My critique of the conception of an ideal curriculum of required courses for everyone everywhere as comparable to the prescription of a required diet for everyone everywhere was warmly received. But when I went on to defend *some* curricular prescriptions for all students on the ground that although all student needs were individual some needs were common—like the effective use of English, understanding of logical relationships, knowledge of historical traditions, intelligent awareness of the social forces shaping the present and future—a pained hush fell on the audience.   Taylor stiffened and reddened.   He later said something about Dewey's "left-hook" becoming a "right-hook," and the only question I recall was whether I considered myself a progressive educator.   Sarah Lawrence obviously did not.   Since that time I have never been invited to Sarah Lawrence to talk about anything again except half-heartedly by some student organizations in search of "a conservative speaker" who will take "the negative side" in a forum on peace or academic freedom or civil rights.   However, I was once told by a member of the faculty that it was not so much my educational views which gave offense as the fact that my critical attitude towards the Soviet Union and its foreign policy was deemed too inflexible.   I am confident, or rather, hopeful that the climate of opinion has changed, and that today an analysis of educational issues would meet with a more discriminating response and not with blind and emotional labeling.

American intellectuals will probably come to take a greater interest in the nature of American education for at least two reasons.   The issue of desegregation in education has become central and has raised difficult problems of establishing equality in education while preserving or improving its quality. The interest of liberal intellectuals in these questions is reinforced by the necessity of thinking about the education of their own children, very few of whom, incidentally, attend public schools. More important, the Berkeley revolution has inspired the mistaken notion that it developed primarily because of the dissatisfaction of most students with their educational experience. Although this belief is untrue, the Berkeley revolution, among other things, has led intellectuals to think about at least some problems of higher education. The so-called "free universities" will die aborning except as adjuncts to sectarian political movements. But the ferment produced among administrations and faculties, who are running scared before any manifestation of student unrest, may develop some sound and fruitful educational proposals.

The professional educator should welcome the belated discovery of his colleagues from other disciplines that they, too, are educators. He should rise to the challenge of new interest, and a new intellectual audience, to reaffirm what is valid in his past views and to project bold and imaginative ideas for improving the character of education on every level. The current emphasis on linguistic analysis can be helpful in clearing away some confusions in the formulation of problems, the statement of plans, and the articulation of insights. But the point of departure should always be some problem, plan, or insight. New vision will not arise merely from linguistic refinements. These must be inspired and controlled by genuine problematic situations. To sow in education linguistic distinctions developed in other fields and for other purposes will result in little but a harvest of dry thistles.

12

The Humanities
& the Taming of Power

Some years ago, the academic dovecotes and the literary marketplace were stirred by the appearance of Sir Charles Snow's book on *The Two Cultures*. In it he argues that the failure of the predominantly humanistic education in the past to provide a thorough, even if elementary, knowledge of the sciences, has produced a cleft in our culture that, if not soon bridged, might result in disaster for the Western world. Although it was the state of education in England which chiefly exercised him, his criticism of the trend of humanistic education was widely interpreted as a valid impeachment of the dominant tradition and practices of the higher learning in Western Europe and the United States as well. In this country, coming as it did in the wake of the shock of, and frenzied reaction to, the Soviet triumphs in space, ushered in by the launching of Sputnik, Sir Charles' pronouncement affected the public mind with an added impact. This explains in part something much more surprising than the contents of the book itself, *viz.*, the uncritical nature of the reception originally accorded it.

One of the most baneful consequences of its influence was the widespread acceptance of its implicit assumption that the division between the scientific and humanistic disciplines is both exclusive and exhaustive. It seems to me to be neither. The sciences themselves were born of philosophy, when philosophy was unabashedly a quest for wisdom, and therefore have traditionally been considered an integral part of the liberal or humane arts. This is conspicuously illustrated by the role that Plato gives them in the curriculum of studies prescribed in the *Republic* for the education of those entrusted with the virtue and happiness of the state. It is also exemplified in the content of the medieval quadrivium and trivium. The affinity between the sciences and the liberal arts may be rediscovered anew by anyone who, even at second hand, familiarizes himself with the dramatic advances of modern science, and experiences the liberating—and sobering—effects of the new vistas of the cosmic deep opened up as manned satellites explore space, to mention only one pending breakthrough. Very few of the substantiated claims made for the study of the humanistic disciplines, cannot be equally well sustained in behalf of effectively taught non-specialized study of the sciences. Viewed in this way, that is, from the standpoint of the adventure of ideas, of important ideas, and of their bearing upon man's conception of himself and of his place in a universe, the division between the sciences and humanities is not exclusive.

We can, however, take a narrower view. Instead of regarding as essential the function and effects of studies in the economy of mind, we can focus on their specific content or subject matter. When we do this, it becomes clear that Snow's division between the sciences and the humanities is not exhaustive. For from the point of view of human life in a civilized society, the social studies comprehensively defined, are at least as important today, possibly more important than the study of nature or of the great classical works of the past. The revolutionary impact of science on society is not a normal concern of the professional scientists whose excursions into affairs of state have revealed no consensus of social judgments. On the other hand, the study of new doctrines of social and political salvation, which have so largely inspired the wars and revolutions of the twentieth century, and their corollary strategies of the conquest of power, are incomprehensible to those who approach them with

184

no other preparation than knowledge of the traditional humanities. It would not be difficult to show that Sir Charles' naive and callow attitude toward the cost of industrialization in the Soviet Union and elsewhere reflects an unfamiliarity with a whole spectrum of historical and social problems outside the ken of the natural scientist and the traditional humanist. The division, therefore, between the two cultures, the scientific and literary-humanistic, is not exhaustive. There is at least a third culture in addition, *viz.*, the complex of studies that bear on the contemporary conditions of the good life in the good society today.

The recognition of this is of the first importance. Despite its remarkable technical triumphs, science has in recent years been subjected to a fierce attack, and the scientist often denounced as an enemy of mankind because of the past uses and possible future uses of atomic power. But, I submit, the scientists have been unjustly criticized on this score. To the extent that Hiroshima, Nagasaki, and their consequences are to be deplored, to the extent that the war was won and yet the peace lost, responsibility lies at the door not of the scientists but of those who made the fateful political and social decisions that spawned the series of mounting crises from 1945, when the United States was at its peak as a world power, to the present. In perspective these decisions seem to be even more gratuitously ill-informed than their few critics at the time, as caustic as they were, declared. Not the bankruptcy of science is established by the increasing threats to the peace and freedom of the world but the bankruptcy of the political and social policies of the statesmen of the world who thought that Mussolini was at worst a harmless buffoon, who despite his theatricality had brought order to chaotic Italy, that Hitler could be appeased, that his *Mein Kampf* was merely ranting nonsense, that he would be sobered by the responsibilities of power, that Stalin could be handled like Jim Farley, that at the time of the Potsdam Conference not Communism but British Imperialism was the chief enemy of democracy—this on the eve of the liberation of India—and that we could withdraw our forces from Korea with the assurance that the Communists would abide by their covenants, that Stalin who had acted as if treaties were like pie crusts—made to be broken when convenient—was a man of his word. It was the "third culture" which was the one most neglected, and we are paying for the consequences of that neglect.

All sorts of comparisons and contrasts may be drawn between cultures—a term whose range of reference is too large to be explored here. We speek of high culture and low, the culture of cities and of rural areas. But with respect to the sense of culture with which Snow is concerned, I believe far more illuminating contrasts can be drawn than the one he draws between the sciences and the humanities. These are the differences between the pure and applied or technical disciplines, between the theoretical and the professional, between the professional and the commercial—distinctions which are hard indeed to draw since they are of degree, but which exist whether we approve of them or not. They run through all the sciences and humanities alike.

For purposes of my discussion, I shall understand by the humanities those subjects, or those aspects of any subject, that are concerned with a normative consideration of human values. The humanistic disciplines in this specific context are those that primarily direct themselves to the nature, origin, career, and conflict of values in human experiences, that reflectively consider ideas and ideals of what is of most worth in life, and that give course and direction to experience. Particular sciences take note of or assume commitment to certain values—e.g., physics assumes the value of truth, medicine the value of health—but the humanistic studies, literature, philosophy, and history, are focally concerned with the understanding and evaluation of these values in the constellation of ends.

This concern is expressed in two generic ways—in a creative and appreciative dimension. The humanities in their creative dimension propose goals and project ends for man. They suggest new possibilities, new visions of excellence. In their appreciative dimension, which is most important because most human beings are consumers rather than creators of value, the humanistic studies work on us through our imagination. Their appeal is to the whole man. Their message burrows under the closed doors of sensibility and feeling. By dramatizing the situations in which we feel akin to all human creatures in their need, agony, or hope, they surmount ideological or doctrinal walls by which fanatics fence themselves in. They sometimes reach the heart and, in ways we still do not understand, open the shutters of the mind against which arrows of argument have failed. To be sure, any subject, whether it be astronomy, zoology, or the theory of numbers, properly taught can enlarge the imagination, but the humanities enlarge the imagination in a unique way by making us aware of ourselves in our fellow men and of our fellow men in ourselves. "If we were all seated at the same table," a great English story teller once wrote, "no one would go hungry." This is one of the profoundest observations ever made, despite its apparent obviousness. No one could eat his fill with good conscience in the presence of others whose aching need for food is reflected in their hungry eyes. In a very real sense, we are all seated at the same table but the table is so long, running to the ever-receding horizon, that we cannot see the faces of our fellows and sometimes are unaware of their presence. The task of the humanities, among other things, is through the cultivation of the imagination to help us see the faces of our fellow human beings who are beyond the range of ordinary physical vision. They evoke within us a power, call it inner vision, call it sympathy, to see the face of a fellow human being in the stranger. No particular policy flows from this, but it is an invaluable, if not indispensable, aid in the *quest* for intelligent policies. The task of the humanities is not merely to teach us to see and appreciate what is common or similar in ourselves and others, but also to appreciate and to tolerate where we cannot appreciate, *compatible* differences. It is for this reason that the words "humanities," "humanism," and "human-itarianism" constitute a family of terms.

The second main task of the humanities is to criticize and evaluate human ends, to bring to bear all of our humanistic knowledge and insight on the values we profess or to which we are already committed by our institutional arrangements and allegiances. The critical examination of ends, the survey of existence from the standpoint of reflective value, has defined the mission of philosophy from Socrates to John Dewey. It is at this point that we encounter a methodological roadblock thrown up by some philosophers who deny that we can be rational about our ends, and who, when pressed by the evidence that we can support ends by good reasons, fall back step by step to the view that we cannot be intelligent about our *ultimate* values or ends. This is the view of Bertrand Russell. Together with other philosophers he defines rational behavior merely as the employment of appropriate means to achieve certain given ends. Therefore, by definition, ends are beyond rational assessment, and we can at most be rational about means, never about ends. "There is no such thing as an irrational end," writes Bertrand Russell, "except in the sense of one that is impossible of achievement." Russell might agree with Socrates that an unexamined life is unworthy of man but he would insist that it is not unreasonable to refuse to examine one's life, and that what is worthy or unworthy of man has nothing to do with reason.

Russell's position seems to me to be unacceptable on many grounds. To begin with, there are many ends impossible of achievement that are not irrational—e.g., omniscience, universal love, and complete impartiality in establishing justice in the affairs of men. They are not irrational because of the desirable character of the consequences of trying to achieve them. Secondly, leaving this point aside, if the *fact* that an end is unachieved or un-achievable is a valid ground for rejecting it, why cannot the *fact* that the realization of an end hurts too much or costs too much also constitute a valid ground for rejecting it? Thirdly, as the foregoing already presupposes, human beings are committed to *plural* ends. Any one of these ends may be intelligently criticized in virtue of the consequences of the means used to achieve that end on the cluster of *other* ends to which we subscribe.

Fourth, no one in fact puts all ends on the same nonrational basis, and if he did he would not survive for long. As an abstract possibility, if we discount history, and the needs of men for health, knowledge, and security, and start from scratch without memory, like the Platonic shades that have drunk of the waters of Lethe, the ends of a Gandhi and Hitler may be regarded as inarbitrarily ultimate. But men cannot escape from history and from their biological and social heritage. Historically, there is an enormous presumption in favor of the validity of some ends, say kindness, over others, say cruelty, because of their different effects on the clusters of other values to which at any given time men find themselves committed.

Finally, it is possible to challenge the view that taken in specific contexts there are such things as ultimate values. It may be the case that every allegedly ultimate value, when considered in the concrete situation in which we choose, turns out actually to be penultimate. Russell himself has always stood ready to defend his choice of allegedly ultimate values when problems of basic policy in personal, social, and international affairs arise. A person who offers good reasons for his position, thereby indicates, if he is not merely rationalizing, that he has grounds for choice that, if successfully challenged, place his ultimates in jeopardy. The moral life of man is an ongoing affair in which means determine his ends as much as ends determine his means, a process in which reason operates as much in the choice of ends as in the choice of means. The phenomenology of moral predicament has its locus in the conflict of ends when we seek a reasoned answer to the question: "What should we do?"

2

Let us now bring to bear some of our considerations on the problems of war and peace and the alternatives open to us as we mobilize power for one or the other. The first point I want to make is that the moral quality of power rests on the values in behalf of which it is used. Power can never be an end in itself in any rational life. It has the neutrality of an instrument or tool which becomes good or bad as we use it in relation to things or persons. Although in general it is legitimate to say that increased power over things is good but increased power over human beings is bad, there are times when it is unwise to have too much power over some things and unwise to have too little power with respect to some men. Power in relation to other human beings is not necessarily the same thing as coercion. Nor is coercion necessarily the same thing as cruelty for there are just and unjust uses of power. Those who decry the use of power in human affairs, who proudly say "No" to

189

power as such, will be compelled to forswear all realistic possibilities of realizing desirable goals against resistance or preventing the realization of undesirable goals. That is why power itself can not rightly be declared an evil. For when power becomes an evil, there are times when it can be limited only by other power. And that is why whoever fears power cannot tame power, and why whoever fears power fears life, and tends to withdraw from it, leaving the world to those who love power, even when they are the morally worse.

It is these considerations which make one of the noblest attitudes that human beings can take toward other human beings defective when it is absolutized, when, independently of causes, consequences, and contexts, it refuses to use power to limit or stop power. I refer to the attitude of pacifism which when absolutized takes the form of nonresistance to evil power, or more accurately, passive resistance to evil power, either on the ground that the exercise of all power is intrinsically evil or on the ground that no human being who is short of perfection has the right to pass moral judgment on any other imperfect human being, no less violently restrain him.

In face to face relations, there is a great deal to be said for such a position on common-sense grounds. Sometimes one can overcome an enemy by loving him. False pride stands in the way of seeing this; but, if one reflects, he will agree that psychologically it is impossible to hate someone who gives every sincere evidence of affection or genuine friendship. However, even in face to face relations there are obvious limits to the extent to which this attitude may be carried. There may not be time to return good for evil; the evil-doer may not be convinced of his wrongdoing, and the evil action which impends may not be forestalled by the contagion of sympathetic understanding. Even in such extreme situations, however, there are some great souls who love man so much that they prefer to suffer violence rather than to inflict it, even in defensive action, against another human being. Sometimes they let themselves be martyred rather than take the life of another human being, regardless of the other's guilt or evil character.

Such a fetishism of nonresistance runs the risk of a still greater evil if it is not practiced with intelligence, if it is hypostatized into an absolute. Where only the individual's own life is concerned, we may still honor and admire the man who chooses his own death rather than the death of someone unworthier than he is who has threatened it, because he has set a standard of selflessness and integrity and veneration for life that may help all men to become worthier, and in the future to find substitutes for violence, and to strive to diminish if they cannot altogether eschew violence. But suppose the situation is one in which some power-obsessed creature, or some desperate character who believes he has nothing to lose, or someone full of hatred for a family, a group, a town, a whole people, one can find many illustrations in these tortured times, threatens to destroy other innocent human beings. Suppose the absolute pacifist can stop him only by destroying him. The situation is no longer one in which he faces the grim alternative: kill or be killed. For in that case he lets himself be killed rather than take the life of another. The situation is one in which either he must destroy a man about to commit a horrible and wicked action or let other innocent creatures be killed. The absolutist at this point who refuses to kill out of love of his fellow man makes himself co-responsible for evil, for the murder of the victims—and not all his radiant consciousness of righteousness at not sullying his hand with the blood of the would-be murderer—prevents the blood of the murderer's victim from being on his head. Any individual who could stand by out of fanatical devotion to an ideal of nonresistance or peace and permit those who are near and dear to him to be tortured and killed by someone whom he could stop by destroying is either more than man or less. In either case, however he appears in God's eyes, in human eyes his guilt is heavy. He is truly a fanatic in the sense in which Santayana once defined a fanatic as a man who having forgotten his goal redoubles his effort. For the goal here—love of man, humanity, kindness—is mocked by the corpses which result from his redoubled resolution not to act.

Here we have an illustration of how a value is tested by the consequences of achieving it. In social affairs, however, the situation is enormously complicated. The problems that arise, especially of peace and war, do not depend upon face to face relationships. The force of personal example is less. When we make decisions in social and political affairs, it is the pre-eminently humanistic discipline of history that must become, not our guide, our values are our guides, but our aid in determining how and when to act on them.

The study of history is important in curbing and taming power because life is not a laboratory in which we can perform and repeat experiments. Yet we can and must learn from the past if we wish to choose wisely. Even our very memory takes the form of an historical judgment. And although the occasions and situations in which power is potentially oppressive change, the human beings who exploit them do not change as rapidly. It is very instructive to observe how central the study of history has been in the curriculum of studies drawn up by the great humanists of the past. Thomas Jefferson in his *Notes on Virginia* was the first to outline a scheme of free public education. Chief of the required courses in this scheme of public education is the study of history. History for Jefferson was an education in human liberty. He held the sanguine view that those who studied history would be forever on guard against the corruption of power:

> But of the views of this law none is more important, none more legitimate, than that of rendering the people the safe, as they are the ultimate, guardians of their own liberty. For this purpose the reading in the first stage, when *they* will receive their whole educations, is proposed, as has been said, to be chiefly historical: History, by apprising them of the past, will enable them to judge of the future; it will avail them of the experience of other times and other nations; it will qualify them as judges of the actions and designs of men; it will enable them to know ambition under every disguise it may assume; and knowing it, to defeat its views. In every government on earth is some trace of human weakness, some germ of corruption and degeneracy, which cunning will discover, and wickedness insensibly open, cultivate, and improve. Every government degenerates when trusted to the rulers of the people alone. The people themselves therefore are its only safe depositories. And to render even them safe, their minds must be improved to a certain degree.

This is rather a naive view of history. It overlooks the fact that like Scripture, history can be quoted in behalf of all causes.

Nonetheless, historical knowledge although hard to come by is attainable. We neglect it at our peril. We may be skeptical about the sweeping character of any particular conclusion. But properly qualified by the recognition that history is not geometry, that we are dealing with probabilities, that history never repeats itself in all its details, we may reach conclusions that are true beyond reasonable doubt—conclusions which the logic of law and common sense tell us may be strong enough sometimes to support a capital verdict. And Jefferson was not wrong in believing that the study of history could help safeguard our freedoms. It will not give those who have no desire for freedom a passion for it; but it can give those who treasure it, insight into more effective measures of defending it. History alone is never sufficient: it is always necessary.

It is to history that we must go in order to determine the conditions under which the ideals of passive resistance are likely to be effective in social relations. "Appeasement" was once an honorable word like the term "collaboration." It is only when "appeasement" has failed or when it has been practiced in such a way as to aggravate the evil it would forestall that it takes on opprobrious connotations. Appeasement sometimes has been successful in preserving peace without loss of dignity and self-respect and freedom. The most conspicuous illustration of successful appeasement was the campaign of passive resistance against England led by Gandhi and his followers. But what were the conditions of its success? First, the opponent was dedicated not to the destruction of the Indian people but to the preservation of the *status quo*. Therefore he was committed to improving the conditions that made for a stable society. In consequence, there were many advantages to British control more widely acknowledged today than in the past. But these advantages were not enough. An Indian judge who owed a great deal to British rule once said to his English colleagues, "You gave us justice, roads, hospitals, the British peace: but you took away what we now value more: our self-respect." Secondly, the opponent in this case himself cherished the values—self-respect, freedom, dignity—which inspired the Indians to resist. In his heart he knew he had no case. For his own moral ideals were being invoked against him. Thirdly, it followed, therefore, that there were some things that he would not do, there were some means which he would never employ in order to achieve victory. When the Indians lay down on the railroad tracks to prevent the movement of British troops, the trains did not move. That is why passive resistance cost less in human life and suffering than active resistance would have done. It was more humane and more intelligent.

But suppose the enemy had not been the British with their humanist traditions but the Japanese or German Fascists, or the Chinese or Soviet Communists? What would the outcome have been? We know the answer in the light of what actually happened. With the exception of the desperate rising in the Warsaw ghetto, six million Jews practiced nonresistance toward Hitler. Many of them went to their end—when they knew it was their end—singing psalms to their God. Did this soften the hearts of their tormentors? When the Russian kulaks—farmers who had more than one cow—protested passively the policy of collectivization, those who were not left to starve were herded into concentration camps where they were worked to death. When the prisoners in the concentration and work camp Kolyma lay down on the railroad spur of the N.K.V.D. those trains moved.

Appeasement is not only inappropriate in situations where common values are lacking. It may actually be an invitation to aggression. There is hardly any question but that strong tendencies of pacifism in England in the thirties fed the policy of appeasement toward Hitler, and that the latter was emboldened to go further and further after Munich. Indeed, he ended up by believing he had been tricked into the war since he had never anticipated that England that would not fight for Czechoslovakia would fight for Poland that geographically was even farther removed. Today there are still many well-meaning persons who believe that a policy of appeasement toward Communism will be more successful than the policy of appeasement was toward Fascism first in Spain and then the rest of Europe. Some are even prepared to urge unilateral disarmament on the West instead of insisting on multilateral disarmament or reductions in armament. They seem unaware that despite many historical changes the two major Communist movements reveal a persistent combination of absolution and a degenerate form of pragmatism, i.e., an inflexible dedication to political ends with a maximum flexibility in the use of means and tactics. The kidnapping of the vocabulary of democracy is only one strategem in such tactics. Another is the organization and exploitation of peace movements despite the contemptuous pronouncement by Communist theorists that pacifism is an expression of capitalist decadence.

3

History and literature are sources of perennial and fascinating interest because, among other things, they give us insight into the nature and condition of men as we experience them in their customary political and social habitat. At their best the historian and novelist enable us to see into the hearts of men, make us aware of the ambiguities of their motives, of the deceptive depths of their speech, of the latent corruption of the best of men and the possibility of grace and regeneration in the worst. It is in this sense that they give us not a truer psychology of the human animal but a completer one than the textbooks of academic psychology no matter what the standpoint from which the latter are written. The world as seen by the seasoned historian and literary critic is not one in which credulous myths flourish about the natural goodness of man. And although he does not subscribe when he is intellectually sophisticated to any metaphysical or theological view of natural evil, he does know that whatever its causes, evil exists.

What we expect from historically trained intelligence is a certain sophistication and skepticism that unfortunately is rarely found among pure scientists who, shocked into a laudable interest in political and social affairs, sometimes conclude that all that is necessary to understand these complex affairs is simple good will and the same straightforward methods of thinking with which they are acquainted in the scientific laboratory, seminar room, and study. But the problems of men are different from the problems of atoms and galaxies, genus and species, not merely because they are at once both more complex and individualized, not merely because they have an historical dimension, not merely because the subject matter is more intimately affected by the way it is handled, but because the rules of interpreting *human* behavior, the criteria of valid evidence of *human* designs, the presumptions of integrity of *human* witnesses are different. Although the formal pattern of logical and scientific inquiry is the same in both fields, the differences in subject matter are reflected in different methods, approaches, and degrees of probability.

The scientist who turns without historical preparation to inquiry into human affairs is apt to bring his code of inquiry with him. In the ethics of the laboratory, the unspeakable sin is to misstate a fact. The normal presumption is that all inquirers are seeking to establish a truth rather than to further a cause or gain an advantage. Outside of laboratory situations, men are not so simply motivated, and it is distressing naiveté to postulate that the good faith which is presumptively present in the scientific community also obtains in the community of those who hold and wield power, especially political power.

It is notorious that eminent scientific men have been hoodwinked by fake mediums and other charlatans whose impostures have been most effectively exposed by the Houdinis and other professional magicians whose art is deception. Consider the number of eminent scientists throughout the world who have been taken into camp by Communist causes and fronts, who have put their names to extraordinary documents like the ones which gave circulation to the infamous falsehood that the United States had waged germ warfare in Korea and similar canards. To a scientist, the arena of historical-political-diplomatic affairs is a bewildering world because it is one in which even the telling of the truth may sometimes be the most effective way of deceiving or misleading one's opponent, if it is a partial or selected truth.

The incursions into political affairs on the part of representative figures and periodicals of the American scientific community, with some outstanding exceptions, make very depressing reading, whenever they concern themselves with problems regarding the *possibility* of Communist evasion of disarmament conventions and test-ban agreements. They regard it as unsporting, ungenerous, and sometimes even dishonorable to be suspicious of Communist professions unaware that according to canonic Leninist doctrine the good in any specific situation is that which contributes to the strength or victory of the Communist movement, the bad is that which results in weakening or defeating it. Just as there are some invulnerably innocent minds who argue that since the Communist Party *calls* itself a political party, then in all relevant respects it really is a political party like the Republican, Democratic, and Socialist Parties, and must be treated as such, so there are some who read their own professional high-mindedness into the behavior of their opposite numbers in the hierarchy of rank of the Soviet Empire. They even assume that their own independence in selecting or rejecting fields of inquiry and in expressing views on national policy, exercised without fear of any government sanctions in an open society, is just as possible in a totalitarian society.

Here is not the place to document the political innocence of some scientific minds but I cannot resist quoting from an article by an eminent scientist in which he presented "The Case for Ending Nuclear Tests" and which he published in August 1960 in *The Atlantic Monthly*. He admitted that another American scientist, apparently one of the exceptions, had been fearful that the Communists would adopt evasion schemes to nullify a test ban. He confessed that as a leading negotiator he felt embarrassed about presenting to the Russians this conjectural possibility of evasion on their part, because, he said, it "implied that we considered the Russians capable of cheating on a massive scale. I think they would have been quite justified if they considered this as an insult" (Vol. 206, p. 46). This was in August 1960. In early fall, 1961, the Communists violated their solemnly proclaimed nuclear test-ban on such a vast scale that it was technically demonstrable that they had been cheating for many months prior to the event. They probably had been doing so at the very time when this article—which dubbed the imputation of such an action by Communists as a gratuitous insult to them—was published.

The unprepared and unhistorical scientific mind when it turns to social affairs is almost always attracted by blueprints in which

197

efficient use is made on paper of resources among which men are one, and so long as the scientific enterprise itself is not threatened, costs in human freedom, dignity, and ordinary human suffering are unwittingly ignored because they are not easily quantifiable. The result is a tendency to social utopianism, for which a critical study of history is usually the best corrective.

What makes so many proposals to preserve the peace of the world utopian and abstract is the failure not only to think historically but to apply some psychological truths which we have won by reflecting on our experience, to complex political issues. The psychological approach by itself, of course, is far from adequate as a sole guide in understanding what happens in history and in making history. But so long as history is made by men a grasp of psychological facts is a necessary condition of wise policy. Disregard these facts and very often the precise opposite of what one intends is likely to be the consequence of what appears on paper to be a generous and enlightened program of action. For example, properly troubled by the danger inherent in an unchecked nuclear arms race, Bertrand Russell declared a few years ago, that the West should renounce nuclear armament *unilaterally*, even if this means the world triumph of Communism and all its evils.

Although Russell subsequently sought to modify this position, in effect he reaffirmed it.

Now what can the reasonable reaction of the shrewd leaders of the Communist movement be to a pronouncement of this sort? After all, in the ordinary situations in life, if a dispute arises and someone says to us: "If you persist in refusing to compromise, I shall have to yield, reluctantly yield, but yield nevertheless," would this not tempt us, if important issues are at stake, to remain firm? After all, we have been promised capitulation if we simply stand on our position and wait. Assume we sincerely believe we are right. How much more likely is it, when the question at issue may be the life and death struggle for the extension of the Communist system, that the men of the Kremlin steeled by their dogmatic doctrines will dig their heels, in, once they hear of the likelihood of *unilateral* disarmament, refuse reasonable compromise, and raise the ante as the West makes one concession after another? A position like that of

Russell's would almost certainly have reinforced the intransigence of the Kremlin in negotiating questions of disarmament because it promised them realization of their political goals without the necessity of their taking risks for it. Fortunately the West ignored Russell's advice as it did his counsel a few years earlier to drop atomic bombs on the Soviet Union if it did not accept American proposals to internationalize atomic power.

It is the humanistic discipline of history which reinforces the lesson won by a humanistic psychology by providing the counter-evidence that the great Communist powers will take no serious risks, if they can avoid it, of war. They retreated in the past whenever they have met firm resistance at Berlin, at Quemoy and Matsu, at Cuba. They are proud that they cannot be provoked. They have a complex mythology which makes it easier for them to play a waiting game if necessary. They need but look at the map to find reassurance that they are no longer being encircled but are doing the encircling. They worship at the altar of History, which is something different from learning from history. Strategic retreat for them is always easy not only because they have no free public opinion to placate but because they believe History is on their side. This explains why "the balance of terror" has kept the peace. War is not likely to be avoided by appeasement or unilateral disarmament. For it is when preponderant power tempts aggressors to move quickly and suddenly for victory that the danger of war is greatest. Once this is understood we can move toward multilateral disarmament under proper controls.

Common sense and logic reinforce history and psychology in teaching us that we cannot substitute slogans for policies, and if we do, we deceive ourselves and others. A few years ago, Mr. Eisenhower, or one of his speech writers, got off a famous phrase: "There are no alternatives to peace." And time after time we hear the same slogan repeated among groups whose dedication to peace cannot be called into question. But what can such a slogan mean? If there are no alternatives to peace, what would our policy be if the Cubans under Castro were to launch an attack against other American countries? Would we permit Israel to be destroyed by an aggressor nation? Would we suffer this for the sake of peace? If there is no alternative to peace, the Federal Government would have to climb down before the law-violating mobs in the South. The truth is that there are always alternatives and that we must choose among them. The choice is hard because every basic choice we make sins against some value. But choose we must. For the refusal to choose in such situations is itself a choice. In this lies the tragic sense of life.

As I understand the philosophical bequest of the humanities to the modern world, it reinforces our awareness of the indispensability of human choice in every moral situation, and the dignity of human choice as constituting the glory and tragedy of man. Indeed, the operating effectiveness of human choice is what we mean by *freedom*.

The issue of freedom so conceived is *not* free enterprise—but the freedom to choose the economic system under which one wants to work and live.

The issue of freedom so conceived is *not* grounded in religious faith or faith in the Judeo-Christian tradition. The issue is not one of religion *versus* atheism, religious belief as opposed to disbelief, or the religious values of the West as opposed to the great non-Christian religions of the East. It is simply the freedom to choose one's faith according to one's conscience.

Nor is the issue one of productivity which was central in the kitchen debate between Nixon and Khrushchev over what system could outproduce the other. Regimented peoples, even slaves, may sometimes in some respects outproduce free men precisely because they live in the condition of regimentation in a command economy which can mobilize all its resources at any point. What of it? It has no bearing on the freedom to choose one's life.

The history of the defense of human freedom makes plain that ultimately the refusal to risk one's life for it spells its death in struggles against enemies who are prepared to die for their cause. It is, or should be, by now a familiar story. Those who make survival the be-all and end-all of existence in politics, in order to safeguard their property, their position, or their life, will lose their treasures, their status, and often their life as well. For in this precarious world there can be no absolute safeguards or guarantees except at the cost of what makes life itself worth living. The humanist tradition goes back to Aristotle who taught that it was not life itself which is worth living but the good life; it goes back to the Stoics who taught that the essence of liberal civilization is the refusal to accept a life which makes human dignity impossible. "Whoever says that life is worth living under *any* circumstance has already written for himself an epitaph of infamy." In the end power can be tamed, if at all, by the human spirit which alone is the carrier of cosmic value, and by the use of intelligence in the service of human freedom.

It was all summed up in Thucydides' simple but eloquent account of life in Athens as a school of civilization to all of Hellas, and valid today for all of mankind. "Think what she has the power to be," he says, "and become her lovers. And remember that the secret of happiness is freedom, and the secret of freedom is courage."

201

Part II:
Problems in
Professional Education

13

Ideals & Realities
of Academic Tenure

General acceptance of the principle of academic tenure came as a result of many hard fought battles in the market place of public opinion, and sometimes in legislative chambers. Until quite recently, however, whatever gains were made with respect to academic tenure seemed immune to the periodic changes in policy that result from economic recession or from financial stringency in particular institutions. Even during the depths of the great depression in the thirties, although in some institutions salaries were frozen or reduced, where academic tenure was recognized no proposals were made to abandon or weaken it.

In the past few years the situation has markedly altered. Academic tenure, both its theory and practice, has come increasingly into question and in some regions of the country under open attack. A conjunction of factors accounts for the change: economic recession, public and legislative reaction against student violence and other excesses on college campuses, the view that this behavior has been tolerated, if not condoned, by faculty bodies and in a few cases actively encouraged by some of their members, and, finally, a growing belief that the quality of teaching was in the long run being debased by the practice of academic tenure rather than strengthened. It is not necessary to sort out the relative weight of these factors, or to determine to what degree the plea of economic hardship masks other considerations, to recognize the existence and broad scope of the challenge.

Once the challenge to the principle and practice of academic tenure is raised, the grounds for supporting or opposing them should be rationally considered regardless of what the causes of the challenge are. Failure to distinguish between the causes and grounds of opposition to (or support of) academic tenure results in the emergence of stereotyped attitudes among some highly vocal participants in the debate and a disregard of genuine problems that exist for both sides. In some quarters it is enough that a conservative group or individual has raised questions about academic tenure to make it a sacred part of the Bill of Rights. This is the typical stance of many members of the American Civil Liberties Union as distinct from the days when Roger Baldwin and Norman Thomas guided its destinies. Some of those who react this way seem to be unaware that the most outspoken criticisms of the tenure system in higher education have come from the leadership of the same extremist student groups who have frankly declared the politicalization of the university to be their goal. Realizing that for all educational purposes, the faculty *is* the university and that the vast majority of the faculty is not at present politically radicalized, they have demanded (a) that students have equal representation and power on all departmental committees, including curriculum, appointment and tenure committees; (b) that teachers be appointed for limited periods, three or five or seven years, at the termination of which their contracts and tenure would be renegotiated; and (c) that in determining the pedagogic worth and effectiveness of the faculty, student evaluations be given decisive weight. Since according to the educational philosophy of this group, the most important component in evaluating the "relevance" of a teacher's knowledge or pedagogical craft is the presence or absence of a "progressive" political orientation, it is clear that attacks on academic tenure from this quarter are implausible rationalization for a political purge.

On the other hand, there are some conservative groups and individuals who downgrade or reject principles of academic tenure because they regard it primarily as a shield for radical teachers to politicalize the university and subvert society. It is important that the more influential they are, the more they realize that academic tenure is not only a shield for dissenters against the *status quo* but a shield for its defenders or for those who are neither one nor the other but who pursue their professional inquiries regardless of where the chips fall or what fancied social and political implications are read into their conclusions. One can mention certain departments today in some well-known universities in which the principle of tenure is the chief obstacle preventing a complete take-over by radical doctrinaires. Academic tenure and freedom are always in danger in times of social stress, tension, and fear, and not only from one source. To be sure, history shows that universities have played important roles as loci and agents of revolutionary change. It also shows that they are among the first victims of revolutionary repression, and when an historical backlash develops, of counterrevolutionary repression.

It is not altogether unlikely that in the future strong threats to academic tenure and freedom may come in some local communities from elements in the population that regard universities with their liberal traditions that stress continuity and orderly change, as obstacles to "progressive" and "enlightened" social change, as they interpret these terms. Even on the tertiary level of public and private education, "tribunes of the people" inside and outside the academy have been heard to refer to academic freedom and tenure as a vested right of a privileged class with a low order of priority when it conflicts with "the rights of the people."

These considerations reinforce the basic argument in behalf of the practice of academic tenure and override the weighty objections against it. This basic argument which has been called by one leading scholar "the only justification for the system of academic tenure" is that "the social products of academic freedom . . . can be guaranteed only by the instrument of tenure."[1] The word

[1] Fritz Machlup, *Academic Freedom and Tenure*, edited by L. Joughin (Madison, 1967), p. 326.

"guaranteed" is perhaps too strong. That academic tenure is a "safeguard," that its presence strengthens the defense of academic freedom against its detractors, outright opponents, and innocent, albeit well-intentioned misinterpreters of its meaning, is hardly questionable. But it weakens the case for academic tenure as well as for academic freedom to make exaggerated claims for it. If it were true that the growth of new knowledge and fresh imaginative perspectives depended mainly upon the presence of academic freedom, it would be hard to explain the great scientific and artistic achievements in all the centuries preceding our own. For the principles of academic freedom in the time span of human history were formulated only yesterday. Further if academic tenure is a *sine qua non* of intellectual independence and nonconformity, how to explain the fact that the extremist elements among faculties today are drawn for the most part from the ranks of untenured junior teachers, some of whom have endorsed and not seldom encouraged student disruption? In some institutions in recent years, there have been marginal cases in which tenure has been won not despite, but because of, the instructor's revolutionary stance in consequence of the administration's fear of a violent confrontation with militant students who have rallied to the cause of the instructor.

For educational purposes it is sufficient to claim that academic tenure is *historically* justifiable because it strengthens the defenses of academic freedom against elements outside and inside the academy that would impose some doctrinal orthodoxy upon those pledged to the quest for truth.

Why, then, the growing dissatisfaction—if "opposition" is too strong a word—with the system of academic tenure in recent years, and the invidious distinctions often drawn between the vocational security of members of the academy and the relative insecurities of other untenured professional livelihoods? Why is it that although in the past, there were sharp conflicts on whether particular individuals were *worthy* of tenure or whether they were being denied tenure on grounds irrelevant to their professional fitness, *today*, over and above such conflicts, the very concept of permanent tenure is under sharp scrutiny, and in a few places under open attack?

206

So far as I can see the reasons are twofold. The first is the obvious fact—obvious to anyone familiar with the academic scene—that permanent tenure, once acquired is rarely, if ever, lost regardless of scholastic or pedagogic performance. One does not have to agree, as I do not, with the recommendations of Utah's Governor Rampton to modify conditions of tenure, to acknowledge that he is right in his contention that permanent tenure has often become a shield and shelter for the incompetent, for those who have failed to develop, or even to remain on the same level of performance that originally was the basis of the judgment in their favor. In the half-century I have spent in the academy, I have never heard of a tenured professor dismissed on the ground of professional incompetence. If not on the basis of the laws of chance, then on the basis of extrapolations from other fields of achievement, one would naturally expect that a certain small percentage of those awarded tenure would fail to live up to the anticipations that entered into the decision to award permanent tenure. This is particularly true for the last decade and a half when the tremendous expansion of the facilities of higher education resulted in the hasty recruitment of teaching personnel. Nonetheless my own testimony on this score can be matched by colleagues in every region of the country. What is more significant and disquieting, there is no evidence of even an organized *effort* on the part of the overwhelming number of institutions of higher education to check up on the teaching and research capacities and achievements of the tenured staff. Strictly speaking, "permanent" tenure is never granted but tenure up to the age of retirement subject to dismissal only for sufficient or adequate cause. Professional incompetence, properly established, would constitute such cause. The great scandal has been the failure of institutions of higher education to check on the level of professional competence after tenure has been granted.

This failure inescapably leads to breaches in the responsibilities that tenured professors owe their students, their discipline, their colleagues—responsibilities that are correlative with the rights bestowed by academic freedom. There is no need to catalogue these breaches of responsibility. I mention only for illustrative

207

purposes the teacher who persistently fails to teach his subject. There have been notorious cases in which tenured professors have time and again devoted very substantial portions of the class hour to fervent denunciations of causes or persons (or to paeans of praise of them) that have little or absolutely nothing to do with the subject matter of their disciplines. And although some clever administrators have been able to get some of these errant professors to retire on grounds of health or to bow out with some other polite fiction, once they prove obdurate there is nothing that can be done, short of embarking upon the full scale hearings spelled out by the provisions of due process in establishing adequate cause for dismissal which, when the cause is alleged professional incompetence, administrations have been notoriously loath to do.

There are some good reasons why administrations and faculties do not enforce existing provisions against tenured professors who have failed to make good as scholars and teachers. The first is that in contradistinction to the situation in most other vocational fields dropping a tenured teacher on grounds of incompetence is a sentence of vocational death. Most colleges will take a man from Harvard who at the end of his probationary period goes out rather than up but not even a junior college will hire a former tenured Harvard professor, if there were any such, who has been dropped for incompetence. There is all the difference in the world between the failure *to win* tenure and the failure *to keep* tenure. Failure *to win* tenure may often be interpreted as the fault of the institution to recognize special talent or as a consequence of a change of educational policy. It is far from fatal. But failure *to keep* tenure bears only one construction except where the principles of academic freedom have been clearly violated. That is why everyone who envisages the possibility of losing tenure would infinitely prefer to be dismissed as a heretic or a victim of political prejudice than as an incompetent. For in our vast, uncoordinated complex of institutions of higher education, there is sure to be room for heretics and victims but not for publicly stamped incompetents.

The second reason why administrators and faculties are loath to drop tenured colleagues on grounds of professional incompetence is that after tenure has been won the criteria of competence and/or incompetence seem less firm and objective than the criteria used to determine eligibility for tenure. This seems a paradox to academic outsiders but only because they regard teaching and research as the only valid criteria for preferment. Perhaps they should be. But in sober fact, once a man has won tenure, after five or seven or nine years have elapsed, it is not only his publications and teaching that are weighed in the scales of the judgment of his peers but his collegiality, his willingness and ability to do committee work, to relieve more productive scholars of chores, and his contributions to building up the public image of the college in the community.

Furthermore, the scholarly life is no more necessarily cumulative in its achievements than the creative life. The critical as well as the constructive spirit sometimes manifests itself in fits and starts. There are slumps in performance terminated by leaps of achievement. The normal tendency of the humane person toward a colleague in danger or distress is: "There but for the grace of God go I." It is compounded by the realization that few people are so good that one cannot easily find someone better. Without permanent tenure no man's job is safe if the university or department decides to follow the policy of some museums—to replace the good things they have by something better and sometimes by something just as good but different. And once social ties have been established, as almost invariably they are, between a person, however incompetent, and his colleagues, dropping him for incompetence is tantamount to a kind of genocidal attack on his family. No wonder we hear so rarely of actions against tenured faculty members!

These considerations do not justify the tolerance of incompetence among tenured faculty. I submit, however, that they help explain it.

There is another relatively novel cause for the growing disquietude about tenure. After all, it is an old story that a man who gets a reputation as an early riser can sleep late the rest of his life. This is the price of all permanent tenure systems in any area. But what has become more noticeable in recent years is the emergence within the academy of ideological commitments, a hardening

209

among some faculty members of attitudes and points of view independently of evidence and argument, an open avowal of partisanship in behalf of "noble causes" sometimes expressed in crusading zeal for change, other times in intransigent resistance to change. More ominous for the future is evidence in some academic quarters of a contemptuous repudiation not only of the political neutrality of scholarship, but a criticism of the very concept of "objectivity" as either hypocritical or unattainable. There is a growing belief that, whatever may have been true in the past, the predominant intellectual orientation of the American academy today is one of doctrinaire, ritualistic not realistic, liberalism. It has been charged that this ideological predisposition not only profoundly influences the basic values of student bodies in one direction, but that in hiring and promoting staff to permanent tenure, undue weight is assigned to factors unrelated to strictly scientific or objective norms of teaching, research, and publication.

It is hard to assess the validity of such beliefs and I, for one, am unconvinced that, aside from some departments of some universities, this situation obtains generally. It is incontestable, however, that such beliefs are becoming prevalent. It probably accounts for an item in *The Chronicle of Higher Education*[2] which reported that one professor of philosophy had requested the Board of Trustees of his institution to rescind his tenure appointment and grant him a two-year renewable contract instead.

> "The original purpose of tenure," he wrote, "to protect faculty from arbitrary and improper pressures applied by trustees, has little relevance at New College. The problem is that the institution needs to be protected from doctrinaire, rigid attitudes *within* the faculty, and not the other way around" [my italics].

In all likelihood the new radical doctrinaires are more visible than the old conservative doctrinaires but from the standpoint of a university dedicated primarily to the objective quest for truth and to the principles of academic freedom and responsibility, both are equally objectionable. Whatever remedies are adopted must come from within the academy and respect the right of its tenured faculty

[2] June 16, 1969.

to be wrong and wrong headed, heretical and crotchety, provided only that there is no violation of professional ethics.

The basic question is whether and how we can eliminate or substantially reduce the admitted hazards of permanent academic tenure. The statement of the Utah Conference on Higher Education makes several commendable suggestions to encourage the continued growth and professional development of members of the faculty. Nonetheless I do not believe that these will result in the elimination of the unfit even if it leads to their identification. For unless I have mistaken the temper of my academic brethren, I doubt whether they possess the psychological ruthlessness publicly to stamp unfit their erstwhile colleagues and friends. And unless I have failed to assess the intestinal fortitude of most administrators, I doubt that they have the gumption to press publicly, and in a sustained way, charges of unfitness against tenured faculty members for whose original acquisition of tenure they may have been co-responsible. Whenever a tenured faculty member is threatened with dismissal on grounds of incompetence, as distinct from a charge of moral turpitude, it will be hard to exaggerate the trouble, complexities, and expense of time, money, and spirit that will be entailed, if he chooses, as he almost certainly will, to exploit the procedures of due process, with its hierarchy of appeals, and final resort to the courts. And if any such incident becomes a *cause célèbre* into which students are drawn, one can safely predict that the sufferance of the incompetent tenured faculty member will be regarded by many administrators and some faculty colleagues as by far the lesser evil than the costs of getting rid of him.

At this point it seems to me appropriate to challenge the legitimacy of the comparison, drawn by those critical of the tenure system, between the permanent tenure professors enjoy and the absence of anything equivalent to permanent tenure in other professional fields. After all, no one ever takes analogous action against an incompetent physician or lawyer. If they are barred, it is for a breach of professional ethics that is not necessarily related to strict professional competence. If they are sued for damages and they lose, they still have their professional status. The incompetent physician and incompetent lawyer may lose patients and clients,

211

and earn less than their more competent colleagues, but they are not officially stamped unfit by their peers. A tenured professor, on the other hand, who is dropped as incompetent is *officially* and *publicly* labelled, and no semantic strategem about the reason for his separation can conceal the actual fact very long, especially if he invokes the protection of due process. In the event of hardship cases, as most cases in middle life are likely to be, the evaluating committee of colleagues may well behave like the English juries in the early nineteenth century. Unwilling to bring in a sentence of guilt when defendants were charged with the capital crime of sheep stealing or pickpocketing, out of compassion they raised the standards of judicial proof so high that they could conscientiously give the wretched defendant the benefit of reasonable doubt. May not something analagous occur if after a periodic review of a tenured faculty member's career, an action for dismissal is initiated?

II

Is there nothing, then, that can be done to counteract the evils of the permanent tenure system? I believe there is something that should be done. It is something that requires not a profound institutional change that most faculties are sure to protest but a serious implementation of the present probational period, and a courageous opposition to strong, current tendencies that would in effect place the burden upon faculty committees and administrative authorities to justify failure to grant permanent tenure after the probationary period is over.

The granting of permanent tenure in the academy should be regarded as the final and most important stage in the academic career of the scholar-teacher. It is much more fateful than the marriage tie which these days can be cancelled or severed with greater ease than any tenure contract. "Tenure" unfortunately in too many situations is something that simply "happens" to a person without the preparation, investigation and ritual celebration that are appropriate to a lifelong commitment to him by the university at an average cost of more than a half-million dollars. In most of the instances that have come to my attention of tenured faculty who have lapsed into apparent professional incompetence, I have been able to ascertain that they were marginal cases when their original tenure status was being considered, and reasons other than their proficiency as scholars and teachers were given disproportionate weight.

Let us candidly acknowledge that no system of determining who is entitled to permanent tenure can be failure-proof. Some candidates will come through by luck or bluff. But the more seriously the decision is taken, the stricter the standards of scholarly selection, the greater the convergence of expert professional opinion, if not the consensus, the more likely it is that the bestowal of tenure will not be regretted. To be serious about bestowing tenure means that it must be considered an accolade to be *earned*. It means that when there is doubt, the answer should be "no." It means that the probationary period must be construed not as one in which the teacher's behavior or achievement is to be assessed merely as satisfactory but in terms of whether, at the end of the probationary period, the best interests of the department and of the students require that his affiliation become permanent. It means that the untenured teacher possesses no lien on his post, that the chairman or the faculty committee that originally hires him owes him no explanation, although they may give him one, of the failure to retain him. It means, finally, in contradistinction to the implications of dropping a tenured professor, that failure to bestow permanent tenure does *not* entail a judgment that the untenured teacher is incompetent. A competent teacher may fail to win permanent tenure because at the time when the crucial decision must be taken, a *more* competent teacher, better qualified to serve the interests of the students and department, has become available. However no one who is denied tenure on this ground can be reasonably expected to believe that it was the true ground, which would constitute a good reason for not disclosing it to him. A competent teacher may fail to win tenure because the proportion of tenured teachers to the total number may be too high. Or it may be decided that the area of his study is one that the university has chosen not to support or to close out because a sister institution is specializing adequately in that particular field.

I regard it as extremely unfortunate—indeed dangerous to a healthy tenure system—to blur the distinction between the guarantees given to tenured faculty and non-tenured faculty. It has been suggested that universities furnish all new faculty members starting their careers with a statement of what is expected of them in order to be awarded permanent tenure. One such suggestion spells out the details. Every newly hired faculty member should receive an official statement describing "how long the probationary period will extend, how and when his teaching and research will be evaluated, and how importantly his contributions to the institution and his activities as a citizen will count in the tenure decision."

Except for indicating the length of the probationary period, I believe that this recommendation is an invitation to trouble and possibly disaster. It overlooks the most important criterion of all in determining whether a person should be granted permanent tenure, *viz.*, whether such grant is in the best interest of the department's program of teaching and research, regardless of "how and when" the teaching and research of the untenured faculty member is evaluated. Even a poor to middling teacher may have to be retained because of his seminal research ideas. And even a poor to middling research scholar may have to be retained because he is the only one available to meet the students' educational needs. By referring to the teacher's activities as a citizen as relevant to a tenure decision, it opens the door to all sorts of extraneous considerations. What is a political virtue to one group of citizens may in the eyes of another group be the stigmata of exhibitionism or a deprivation of time and energy on which the academy has first call. It is practically inviting the teacher who does not win tenure to claim that either the nonpolitical criteria are irrelevant or that the political criteria have not been fairly applied.

Further, it is unrealistic and smacks of simplism to claim that the burden of proof that he has been unfairly dropped lies on the untenured teacher whereas in the case of the tenured teacher, charged with incompetence, it rests with the institution. The

214

institution cannot escape the responsibility, moral if not legal, of responding to any grave criticism made of it in an official hearing. Once the untenured teacher makes his charge that he is a victim of political or racial or religious bias, once he claims that his teaching and research is at least on par with that of some tenured teacher of older vintage, who is usually around, a relic of an older, more permissive regime, the institution must join issue, particularly when hearings are public. Hearings for untenured faculty will approach in complexity, time, and publicity the hearings for tenured faculty. And unless tenure becomes automatic, with the expansion of higher educational facilities, the number of hearings will mount very rapidly.

It goes without saying that all colleges and universities should affirm the principle of academic freedom for all teachers, tenured or untenured, but if non-tenured faculty are given the automatic right to contest the decision not to extend tenure, there is a grave danger that this will encourage extremism and offensive expressions of nonconformity in speech and conduct as an *insurance* against denial of tenure. An individual unsure of the weight which his purely professional competence will have in the ultimate decision to grant or withhold tenure, will be sorely tempted to embarrass the university by some particularly outrageous action or statement. Even if the university is courageous enough, despite this quite familiar ploy, to withhold tenure, the natural claim will be that it is his extremism that is the true ground for denying him tenure, and not his incompetence. And it will have a plausible ring to the degree that he *has* successfully embarrassed the university.

Once the fundamental distinction between the conditions of employment for tenured and non-tenured faculty are breached, then the entire tenure system will be irretrievably compromised. There is a natural tendency on the part of anyone who to his own satisfaction has taught for the space of a day at the college or university level to believe that this gives him a lien in perpetuity on the right to teach. To give non-tenured faculty the right to challenge the decision not to renew their contracts by grant of permanent tenure strengthens the presumptive validity of this belief. Once this right of non-tenured teachers to challenge the

215

decision to deny them tenure is incorporated into the official code of procedure, it is a foregone conclusion that most of those who fail to make good will demand hearings, make appeals, and ultimately resort to the courts, despite the fact that most justices from the lowest to the very highest court are no more qualified to pass on delicate matters of academic professional fitness than most teachers are to adjudge complex and delicate constitutional questions. The U.S. Supreme Court has granted *certiori* to a case of a non-tenured college teacher who has alleged that his contract was not renewed because of his political activities. The findings of the Tenth and First Circuit Courts, however, are flatly incompatible on the issue. Having studied previous decisions of the Supreme Court on cases involving educational matters, I am extremely skeptical of the range and depth of insight of most of the justices into questions of professional competence and professional ethics.

Even today the normal gripe of the teacher who fails to win tenure is that he is a victim of gross injustice, of favoritism toward others, bureaucratic manipulation and other indirect violations of his academic freedom. Fortunately, he cannot as yet compel the college or university to justify its action with respect to him. If and when he is able to do so, I repeat, the normal work of the college will be jeopardized by incessant hearings, appeals, and demonstrations.

To be sure there are instances undoubtedly in which tenure is unfairly denied and in which the issue is academic freedom, not academic competence. In such instances we must rely for relief on the *ad hoc* actions of faculty committees who can be empowered to investigate cases of abuse. There are few secrets on campuses with respect to the true grounds for granting or withholding permanent tenure. The best way to destroy the tenure system is to give everybody or almost everybody tenure, and the current tendencies to extend the umbrella of protection and privilege enjoyed by tenured faculty to untenured faculty is a long step in that direction. To me as a firm believer in the tenure system, this is the great danger. It comes from the courts, from administrators and to some extent from the faculties themselves.

In a world of conflicting values and less than infinite resources, one must pay a price for everything desirable. The price of tenure comes high but the costs and undesirable consequences of abandoning it are still higher.

14

Teaching, Research, & Medical Education[1]

(In discussing the impact of expanding research support on the universities, I appeared as a speaker at the 1961 Teaching Institute Association of the American Medical Colleges in the modest role of a social philosopher and educator. I have never administered a government project or a research grant, and have only a distant reading knowledge of the problems of medicine, medical research, and medical education. Whatever temerity my audience found in the fact of my appearance must be laid at the door of the Institute Planning Committee, which overrode my reluctance to speak on this theme. And as I read the completed program, I wondered whether it did not illustrate what Professor Gilbert Ryle, in his *Concept of the Mind*, called a "category mistake." Distinguished speakers at the Institute discussed the impact of research on the faculty, on the students, on the curriculum, and on the administration. To me was assigned the topic, "The Impact of Research on the

[1]From *Research and Medical Education*, a report of the Ninth Teaching Institute (1961). Copyright 1962. Association of American Medical Colleges, Evanston, Ill. The book also appeared as Part 2 of *The Journal of Medical Education*, Vol. 37, No. 12, December 1962.

University," as if the university were something apart from its constituent elements. For a moment I wondered whether the assumption was not very much like that made by an artistically gifted neighbor in Vermont, where I spend my summers. Her husband had carefully pointed out and explained to her the function of the starter, the spark plugs, carburetor, pistons, and other parts of the automobile she was planning to learn to drive. When he was through, she artlessly turned to him and said: "Good. Now show me where the motor is."

Second thought, of course, convinced me that the Planning Committee was much too sophisticated to commit a category mistake, and that the title was merely an invitation to discuss the problem in the larger perspective of my professional interest—which, with some trepidation, I proceeded to do.)

THE INSTITUTIONALIZATION OF RESEARCH

The very formulation of the theme of the Institute, the impact of expanding research on the university, suggests that difficulties exist or can be anticipated because more financial support is available for research in universities than at any time in history; because the source and auspices of this support are rapidly shifting from private philanthropy to government; because the sums involved are so great and the prospective national needs to be met so acute that expanding research implies expanding government support.

There are some who even assert that a plethora of research funds exists, and that the educational function of the university is being subverted by this overwhelming largesse. As an over-all proposition, this is not likely to be accepted by poorly endowed and geographically isolated universities. To them it seems that to those who hath shall be given and from those who hath not shall be taken—their best men by their richer and more influential sister institutions. And invidious differences, resulting in part from the distribution of research funds, are believed to exist between the income, perquisites, status, and prestige of workers in the new vineyards of science and those in the old gardens of the humanities.

Nonetheless whatever the inequities of distribution are—and there *are* inequities—by themselves they are not an argument against the validity of expanding research support by the government; nor are they likely in fact to influence the trend of future appropriations, especially if the private foundations take up the slack in the humanities. Whatever the defects of current research support may be, the reflective scholar and scientist will say what the principled democrat says of the defects of democracy. Just as the remedy of the defects of democracy is more intelligent democracy, the remedy of the defects of research support is more intelligent distribution of research support. The difference here is that whatever the prospects of democracy—unfortunately its future is *not* assured—the prospects of continued and expanded research, despite periodic retrenchments, *are* assured so long as modern civilization continues.

Why? There are many reasons but three will suffice. First, we are living in an age in which it is impossible for a complex society to continue without anticipating and trying, at least in part, to predict and control the problems created by its own growth. The scientific revolution and its technological applications have made the practices of *laissez-faire* in discovery and invention insufficient if not anachronistic. Even if the world were to remain at perpetual peace, these problems of growth would face us. Everyone acknowledges that society is in continual process of flux, but few grasp what this means in the age of modern science. Individuals and groups in pursuit of their own aims are unaware of the unintended social consequences of their own activity, whether this affects the presence of raw materials, the direction of population trends, communication, transportation, even food. Alfred Whitehead, the great Anglo-American philosopher, somewhere said that the greatest single invention in human history was the invention of the organization of invention. In the past, inventions were haphazard by-products of basic discoveries motivated mainly by a desire to know. Today, the continuous, organized, and accelerating quest for new discoveries and inventions in every domain of science and every branch of industry makes it imperative that some agency of the community become aware of its over-all effects upon the nation as a whole, upon its domestic and foreign policies. There must be some agency to support at strategic points, sometimes with massive means, the research required to insure stable growth and to meet expected difficulties. Some things simply cannot be left to the vagaries of individual curiosity and the drive of vested interest. They must be sought in behalf of community interest.

The more extensive our scientific approach to man and society, the more aware we must become of the problems created by our very success in meeting previous problems. It is absurd to call for a moratorium on invention and discovery, as some have done in the past who glimpsed the possible chaos and periodic social breakdowns that may result from failure to anticipate and absorb the shock of the impact of science and technology. The monumental efforts in the natural sciences require recognition of new dimensions in research. Without interfering with individual and group freedom of discovery and invention, what is required is *strategic* invention or discovery in social relations as well as on the frontiers of the natural sciences. Private foundations have done a great deal to encourage this, but I shall argue later that the government should and will underwrite research of this character in ever-increasing measure.

The second reason why, despite all the difficulties in distribution by the government, research support is certain to grow, is the emergence in our time, of a philosophy of health care for the nation. I call it a philosophy because it is based upon the growing belief that the right to adequate medical care, as defined by the *objective* scientific standards set by profession, is as much an inherent right of the individual as his right to police protection or his right to education—and his right has a bite; it is a right to which the individual is entitled independently of his capacity to pay for it. The subject is very complex and I have discussed it elsewhere, but let me say that it seems to be incontrovertible that, despite the opposition of certain professional medical associations, the government will ultimately underwrite directly or indirectly the costs of medical care for most of its citizens. Given the remarkable nature of cumulative medical discovery, whose triumphs, in virtue of the fact that they prolong life, create more medical problems, an ever-increasing part of support of basic and categorical medical research will come from the government. If the health of our people is our basic national asset, it must become a national responsibility.

The third reason why research will continue to expand is the most obvious and immediately relevant of all—the need for defense of a free culture, including the existence of the free university.

A generation or two ago, the availability of research funds in such large amounts would have been regarded both by the administrators and faculty of most universities and colleges as an unmixed blessing. For although the advancement of knowledge does not depend upon money but upon talent, it is easier to attract talent where adequate research facilities and competent supporting staff are present. One may argue that the history of science shows that ample means are neither necessary nor sufficient for the advancement of knowledge, especially for the birth of great seminal ideas. But this can be said about almost any other relevant factor, including leisure. As yet we know little about the nature of intellectual discovery despite what we know about the brain.

We can safely say that, other things being equal, the presence of adequate means of research is more helpful in providing opportunity for discovery and advancement of knowledge than their absence—unless we can show that the very availability of funds prevents other things from ever being equal. Some speak as if plentiful research resources threaten the precious quality of individual creativity, without which instruments are merely shining gadgets and well-equipped laboratories are empty shrines of the spirit. But when men are not coerced, there is no evidence that the quality of creativity withers where ample means of research are at hand. The creative spirit no more thrives necessarily on scarcity than, some Social Darwinians to the contrary notwithstanding, genius thrives on want or poverty. The simple fallacy here is to assume that because the creative spirit sometimes or often over-comes obstacles, these very obstacles are a cause of the presence of the creative spirit.

What is ominous in the availability of massive research support to the educational enterprise of the university? First and most important of all, we must explore the possibility that the use of such funds will subvert the very ideals and purposes of the university as a community of scholars dedicated to the discovery and publication of the truth. Particularly in the United States, where government support seems to many almost synonymous with government control, there is a vague and inchoate feeling that the intellectual freedom of the university is put in jeopardy, and that where the university becomes dependent to any considerable degree upon government support, it is giving hostages to fortune that it may some day be unable to ransom. This feeling is sometimes combined with the view that the primary obligation of the university to discovery of truth may be undermined by a too narrowly instrumental conception of knowledge. Even the expectation that the fruits of knowledge will be practical or useful may clip the wings of free inquiry by foreshortening investigation. The discovery of new knowledge is its own justification. It is an intrinsic delight that gives immediate satisfaction independently of its benefits in human welfare.

It is not necessary to point out to medical educators that the quest for truth is not incompatible with dedication to human welfare. Basic research may lead anywhere. No one knows when apparently useless knowledge will burgeon into practical fruit. When I was young, the recurrent illustrations of pure knowledge that would never have any practical use whatsoever were the theory of numbers and the theory of relativity.

In the long run, society supports basic research not so much for the delight it gives to the knower, but because knowledge is power and can enlarge and enrich the experience of mankind. For the same reason that man was not made for the Sabbath but the Sabbath for man, knowledge can never be completely free of moral control, no matter how often one speaks of it as being self-justified. There are some kinds of knowledge no civilized community will permit a man to acquire. The shabby pretext of those who served the Nazis that they were advancing human knowledge by discovering the limits of human tolerance under torture was not rejected on the grounds that they failed to learn anything—they did learn a lot about this gruesome subject—but it was rejected on ethical grounds. There are many things one can learn that it is better not to know. That is why knowledge for knowledge's sake, like the slogan of art for art's sake, is inadmissible if taken as an *absolute* value.

The real gravamen of the fear of government-supported research lies in the proud jealousy of the integrity of the university's basic purpose. And that this is so is shown by the fact that, whatever may be the criticism of research grants made by private foundations (in the fields I know the only one I have heard is that their grants are not larger), rarely if ever is their research support regarded as a potential threat to the academic and intellectual freedom of the university and to its abiding vocation to preserve and extend the tradition of scholarship. On the other hand, many and eloquent are the warnings that the vocation of the university is endangered by government-supported research.

Is this vocation of the university a record of historical fact or an expression of a desirable ideal? If we are interested in the truth and not in edifying rhetoric, we must recognize that historically the university, from its earliest days in Europe to not-so-long-ago in America, has very rarely functioned as an autonomous community of scholars dedicated solely to inquiry, discovery, publication, and teaching of the truth, subject to no control or authority except the rational methods of winning new truth. Religious, metaphysical, political, racial, and economic dogmas more often than not restricted freedom of inquiry even in esoteric domains not likely to have an effect on public order.

It is not always realized that the ideal of an intellectually free university, free in the interests of the honest quest of the truth, to criticize the assumptions and basic beliefs of the very society that subsidized it, was a slow and uncertain growth. The ideal is honored today only in the open societies of the West. The history of academic freedom is a history of struggle against restrictions upon thought not only in science, but even more so in the humanities and the social disciplines. There have been historical periods in which political dictatorships, although they kept a watchful eye on what was being done in the universities, did not hamper research in the physical and medical sciences. They sometimes encouraged it. Most of Western science, like most of Western art, developed under political conditions that can hardly be recognized as democratic. Compared to modern forms of totalitarianism, these cultures were relatively liberal and humane, which does not, of course, extenuate their repressive features. The totalitarian dictatorships of the twentieth century, particularly those based upon mystical racial or political dogmas, provide the clearest illustration of the fate of pure science in an unfree society.

To be sure, to the extent that science has practical consequences, a certain accommodation takes place, and restrictive doctrinal pressures are eased in the interest of national survival. No such accommodation can be made by dictatorships of any kind to historical and social research. The historical truth about a dictatorship is always dangerous to it; that is why history is continuously being rewritten under such regimes. Impartial investigation of social and political alternatives, and criticism of the existing government on the basis of such investigation are and always will be considered subversive in any dictatorship.

I have dwelt on these historical details to reinforce the assertion that the ideal of a university as a fraternity of free and independent-minded scholars in all disciplines is integrally related to the preservation of the free and open society. To the extent that one is committed to the preservation of academic freedom, moral consistency requires that one be committed to the preservation of the democratic society that makes it possible. If the society that nurtures the free university, and imposes no metaphysical, religious, or political dogma upon it, is under attack, the future of the university is under attack too. If the free society requires defense, the free university is morally obligated to aid in its defense. For, if what I have said is true, in so doing it is defending itself. Needless to say this does not require that the university officially enlist itself as an institution to further the national interest in any war—this falls within the voluntary prerogative of the scholar as an individual citizen—but it justifies corporate institutional action in behalf of academic freedom.

226

This brings us to the very heart of a paradox. The fear is widespread in the university that to accept research support from the government in behalf of defense programs or projects in the national interest is to imperil the academic freedom of the university, to risk betraying its basic ideals. I must confess I do not share this fear, which is exaggerated beyond reasonable warrant. Grant for a moment that there is a risk. Is there not also a risk to free institutions and to the preservation of academic freedom in not accepting the responsibility for the common defense, if there is a genuine need for the research in question? Which risk is greater? The risk to the university's freedom in accepting research connected with the national defense, or the risk to the very survival of the free university if the defense of free culture fails?

What is this risk to the university that ostensibly flows from the acceptance of research in behalf of defense projects? The risk is that if research funds are accepted for projects whose findings must be classified or restricted, then this is a breach of the ethos of university life—discovery and publication of the truth. So long as the free world is in danger of destruction, the knowledge that would help destroy it must be kept out of the hands of its enemies, who are enemies of the free university too. And conversely, the knowledge that would help preserve the free world helps preserve the university too.

The restrictions of secrecy are annoying but not fatal to the functioning of the free univeristy as a whole. Evidence: during the Second World War many universities accepted restricted research projects, but none complained that it essentially affected the exercise of its intellectual freedom. The secrecy restrictions were a small price to pay for the defeat of Hitler, whose triumph would have meant the end of all intellectual freedom. So would have the triumph of Mr. Khrushchev, who was a more formidable, because more intelligent, enemy. In case of war, it may be said, these universities will swallow their scruples. But in case of war, it may be answered, it now looks as if it would be too late. The only point of defense projects today, indeed the very philosophy of defense, is to *prevent* war. Research projects in defense, like the existence of

227

our deterrent weapons, are our best insurance against war. Because of the nature of modern weapons, there will be no time to undertake the research in an emergency.

The entire issue, however, seems to me to be a red herring. First, universities have been requested to undertake few, if any, defense projects because of practical reasons. Most of such projects are channeled to special agencies and institutes. The overwhelming amount of government support to universities in the sciences is in the field of basic research and science education. The experience of universities on the whole is reflected in the report made to the faculties and governing boards at Harvard University:[2] "The image of a coercive government dictating what shall and shall not be done in university laboratories and libraries simply does not fit Harvard's experience with Washington . . . communication and understanding between the University and the Government regarding the conduct of the research are generally satisfactory, and the impact of federal funds on a particular research project does not seem to differ basically from the impact of money in similar amounts from private sources." It is not the source of the grants that is worrisome, but apparently the amount. Why then this hypersensitivity on the score of risk to academic integrity?

The real nature of the red herring is revealed in the fact that not even in the Second World War, and certainly not today, has the government *imposed* any research project on any university. No one has ever been compelled to work for the government. Any university is free to decline any project, the conditions of whose acceptance it finds repugnant to its conception of the educational process. Most of the projects universities initiate themselves. One would imagine that the universities were being threatened in some way for failure to accept research support for severely restricted projects. This is sheer myth. At most, some universities may feel tempted to accept money under conditions that arouse in hypersensitive souls a feeling of guilt at not living up to their extremely fine professions of perfection. But a little courage to say "no" seems a

---

[2] *Harvard and the Federal Government: A Report to the Faculties and Governing Boards at Harvard University* (September 1961), pp. 10-11.

more appropriate response to temptation than the creation of an imaginary threat as spur to one's sense of virtue and excuse for yielding to the lure of easy money.

There is already sufficient distrust of government support of education at a time when education requires government support to meet the unfilled educational needs of the nation. Why add *needlessly* to the suspicion? No one in any responsible position, so far as I can tell, expects the university to be an agency of government. I am confident that the passion for freedom in American universities and their sense of identification with free society will in the present emergency override their fears. Self-interest may be a factor, for if the legitimate defense needs of the nation require that the government recruit research personnel, it has a competitive advantage which few universities can meet. Some departments in universities on the verge of discoveries or breakthroughs have been known to adopt policies of strict secrecy on matters completely unrelated to defense. If and when a scholar decides to undertake a research project related to defense, if it is of a classified nature, the work can easily be pursued off the campus.

The problems created by the availability of expanding research funds upon teaching and upon the morale of the rank-and-file college teacher are much more serious than any risk to academic and intellectual freedom. I believe this for a number of reasons, but before elaborating them, we must recognize a few important distinctions. First, there is the distinction between teaching on the undergraduate level and on the graduate level. On the graduate level, the good teacher operates on the frontiers of knowledge, leading and inspiring co-workers rather than instructing novices. On the graduate level, the university justifies itself primarily by its research. In consequence, even those with pedagogic skills begrudge the time taken from them to give introductory courses or to supervise dissertations when in hot pursuit of a problem or immersed in an experiment. Sometimes an outstanding scientist with an expository flair will give an introductory course, both dazzling and elegant, but he is not likely to repeat it or make a steady practice of it. In those graduate disciplines in which doctoral dissertations must be supervised, the influx of students creates a staggering amount of work for precisely those scholars who are most distinguished. This is an insoluble problem that can never be met to everyone's satisfaction, but on the university level *first* consideration must go to the scientist and scholar. The students are aware of it.

On the college level, however, the liberal arts college level, the role of the teacher is central, for he must introduce the student to the great traditions of learning, the great problems, the great ideas, the great minds, the great books, which constitute so large a part of the heritage of civilization. He must try to develop persons who are intellectually sensitive, emotionally mature, and methodologically sophisticated at the same time as he helps them to find themselves and to make the choices of calling and career that are so decisive in their lives. The good teacher at the college level must be not only a schoolmaster but, as Karl Mannheim puts it, a lifemaster, by which he means not merely a purveyor of knowledge but a directing, inspiring, correcting force in the life of those he teaches.

There is another and allied distinction I want to make. This is between research and scholarship. Scholarship presupposes familiarity with current research but not necessarily the capacity to engage productively in it. It would be absurd to say that no one can be a good teacher who is a poor research worker, but it would not be absurd to say that a good teacher, whenever he goes beyond fundamentals, must be a good scholar. The scholarship necessary for good teaching requires time for reading and thought, and for periods of intellectual refreshening. It does not require publication.

What I fear about the impact of expanding research support, despite the provision it makes for teacher training, is the subtle discounting of the teaching process. There are facts of academic life of which we are all aware, but we shrink from enunciating them. No one sets out to be only or primarily a good college teacher. He resigns himself to it only when he surrenders his hopes to make a distinctive or creative contribution to his field. In the nature of the case, the prizes, the glory, and the acclamation go to the discoverers of new truth and not to those who, so to speak, process and pass them on. And this will be so to the end of time, even if all scholars and scientists were equally rewarded materially. For what a man values above all is the judgment of his peers, which is keener and goes to the quick more surely than the judgment of impressionable students and harried administrators. If he is interested in posterity, he knows that its judgment will be based on the cold record of achievement, not on the well-taught lessons in the classroom.

The teacher's function is indispensable, but alas, like an actor, he is a sculptor in snow. Every bright young physicist I have ever met took as his ideal Faraday or Einstein, depending upon whether he was experimentally or mathematically minded. The name of the most brilliant teacher of introductory courses of physics I have heard about—the teacher of some students who made distinguished careers for themselves—does not appear in any of the literature of the field. This situation has its analogies in all disciplines, especially in a period when there are portents of breakthroughs in basic and applied sciences, and the surging tide of new discoveries and inventions has set men atremble not only in fear of nuclear catastrophe, which may be allayed by more research, but in expectation of mastering weather and outer space and of plumbing the depths of mind.

Scholars know that research is a field in which criteria of achievement are more or less objective, whereas the assessment of teaching is often problematic. It is not difficult to tell what poor teaching is, but the effectiveness of good teaching is hard to establish.

For these and other reasons, the individual who is primarily a good teacher is usually in a defensive relation to the individual who is primarily a creative researcher. In consequence, the availability of expanding research funds intensifies these tensions. It makes it possible for almost all scientists with even a smidgeon of a new idea to get research support or to be enrolled in a team research. It makes the other disciplines desirous of receiving support in order to extend not merely opportunities for scholarship but opportunities for research. Since research in the humanities is far less costly than in the sciences, representatives of the humanities, without denying the necessity of massive government support of scientific research, are beginning to feel neglected. They, too, can think of projects which, if not exactly in the national interest, are certainly in the interest of humanity. At the very least they can make a book out of their unpublished dissertations. Perish the thought! Very few dissertations worth publishing have remained unpublished.

Lest these words may be misunderstood, I wish to say at once that I strongly believe research in the humanities should be encouraged. The private foundations and associations in this area are doing excellent work. As a rule, government should leave *this* province to them. Further, I believe that all teachers should be scholars and that the life of scholarship demands periodic leisure to travel, to read, and to think. But what I fear is a shift in the humanities from the scholarship necessary to keep teaching vigorous, fresh, and well informed in one's own and cognate disciplines, to research as a kind of mass phenomenon—a shift from appreciation, which should be intensively cultivated, to undiscriminating original research. I fear it for many reasons, among them that the end product of expanding research support in the humanities will be a stream of publications in which we may drown.

There are several important differences between research in the sciences and in the humanities. In the first, research is cumulative and often cooperative. Progress can be measured. Problems once solved are succeeded by other problems. They are not reopened except in the light of new data. A hypothesis rejected as inadequate does not reappear in the same guise. In the humanities, the researcher is more of a lone wolf. He doesn't have to solve a problem. He can merely tell the story of something he finds interesting. There is no cumulative development of findings. Insights are illuminating but episodic. There are few definitive solutions of problems. The present can always reinterpret the past.

This difference is associated with another of greater significance. A scientific research worker can get a tremendous lift from his work even if it is not first-rate. There is room for him even if he is third- or fourth-rate. His contribution may be very modest in itself—perhaps a series of measurements—but it may be useful, sometimes essential, to an epoch-making discovery. At any rate there is always a legitimate hope because of the convergence of interest. Even if he repeats an experiment to check the findings reported by a colleague, he feels himself to be a qualified member in the republic of the elect.

But who in the field of the humanities would write a book just to confirm the findings of another book? And what point or intellectual honor if he did? The person who does research in the humanities is more likely to strike out on his own. Since research is not cumulative or convergent on key problems, his contribution to attract attention must be of very high quality. There is nothing damning about mediocre scientific research, for it has a certain usefulness—but mediocre research in the humanities is sheer waste. There is useless research in the sciences, too, work that is needlessly trivial and repetitive. But in the humanities the danger of useless research is so much greater that it justifies, in the very interest of the humanities themselves, the attitude of *fewer but better*.

How, then, to prevent the encouragement of research from eroding interest in teaching? As you know, the scientific professions with the help of government subsidies are making heroic efforts to improve the curriculum of science education in the high schools and colleges by preparing improved textbooks, taping entire course sequences on television and radio by star scientific performers, and sending outstanding scientists in the flesh to visit colleges in outlying areas that cannot draw on the resources of a metropolitan or university community. As supplementary teaching aids, all these activities are excellent. For purposes of recruiting the ablest students, however, so that there will be a sufficient number of talented scientists to exploit properly the available research support, there can be no substitute for the dedicated teacher who meets students face to face over a prolonged period of time and gives them a realizing sense of his discipline.

The relation between research and teaching may be kept in fruitful tension by developing a mutuality of esteem among those whose interests and talents are predominantly in the field of research and those in the field of teaching. If the research scientist can be induced to recognize that some teaching is a part of his

233

normal academic responsibility, this would be immeasurably helpful. And if he performed his task not in the spirit of personal sacrifice but as a service to the professional community, this would go a long way toward meeting the problems of recruitment.

There are some who are pessimistic about the long-term prospects of developing high-caliber research scientists capable of making rewarding use of available research support. In the end, it is said, biology or genetics will defeat all grandiose plans. The returns in discovery will not justify such huge research outlays for which one can suggest alternative uses. Such matters are largely speculative, but I believe that the pessimism is premature. It seems reasonable to believe that if the government is to help colleges and universities to find, keep, and develop individuals of outstanding talent, it will have to do much more than it is now doing to strengthen education on the lower levels. It must go beyond the present and contemplated federal scholarship and loan programs for graduates and undergraduates, for these reach only those gifted students who are already at hand. The geographical disparities in educational opportunity throughout the country are still enormous. At the turn of the century, J. McKeen Catell published a study that purported to show that a gifted child in a southern state had only a very small fraction of the chance of receiving a good scientific education enjoyed by a child of comparable capacity living in New England. This is still true, although in lesser measure. Unless we assume that the dispersion of native intelligence is a function of geographical distribution, this means that we are far from tapping the potential educational talent of our population.

The question of medical teaching I will leave to more competent hands, but I content myself with one observation in my role as an educator and layman. If, in the liberal arts colleges and universities, teaching suffers as a consequence of disproportionate emphasis upon research, the situation there will still be tolerable. For, after all, no one perishes of boredom, and the situation can hardly be very much worse than conditions which obtained in the recent past. Good students can learn from good books even when they have poor teachers. But clinical teaching in medical schools is different. It plays a far greater role. If teaching is neglected or deteriorates because of disproportionate research emphasis, it is a safe statistical bet that some human beings will die in consequence, who need not have died had the instruction and clinical training of their physicians been better.

As is well known, the major grants for research to the universities from all sources, and especially from government sources, are in the fields of science. This is likely to continue to be the case in the future, and uneasiness has been expressed that this will throw out of kilter the balance among the several branches of learning in the university. It is feared that the fine arts and humanities, as well as the social studies, may be neglected, and that the misunderstanding may be accentuated between what has been called the two cultures by Sir Charles Snow in his Rede lectures.[3] This problem is not acute for heavily endowed universities which can raise supporting funds from private sources to preserve the balance of disciplines, but it may become a problem for others.

Imbalance is a problem that can be considered acute only on the assumption that a university should be equally strong in all the major fields of research and scholarship—an ideal assumption for which I see no compelling necessity in a world of finite resources and limited high-grade talent. So long as universities do not become captives of research opportunities, exploiting them in an *ad hoc* fashion for purposes of budget or prestige, and so long as universities keep firmly before them a view of the distinctive role they can play on the basis of their history, location, and the strength of their tenured faculty—and plan accordingly—I see no objection to concentration in some fields rather than others. Not all universities need strong, if any, graduate departments in astronomy or archaeology or area studies. Universities are not, and should not be, competitive business institutions. They can easily pool their educational resources, when they are in the same geographical region, to everybody's benefit. What is educationally essential is not so much to keep all subjects in balance but to keep the students' understanding of the world in balance, to make it possible for them

---

[3]Snow, C. P. *The Two Cultures and the Scientific Revolution* (England, 1959).

to communicate with one another about common human concerns and about predicaments of the common world that have become intensified by specialists' discoveries.

This is not and cannot be the chief task of graduate instruction which, if serious, *must* be specialized. If the avenues of communication have not been laid down before students reach graduate level, they cannot be easily established subsequently. There simply is no opportunity to do so, if student mastery of some subject is to be achieved. The deficiency is not likely to be made up if, by the time they reach the graduate level, students in the humanities have not acquired some basic ideas in physics and biology and a sense of the nature, reach, logic, and adventure of scientific method. And if by that time students in the sciences have not acquired a sense of authentic values in art and literature, have not had their imagination stirred by the great visions of philosophy and the tragic dimensions of history, it is usually too late. And if neither group has been subjected to rigorous study of conflicting social systems and ideologies and taught to face the problems posed by the advance of Communism, the population explosion, and the challenge to world peace, order, and freedom by the multiple revolutions of our time—nationalist, technological, social—then their views on social and political affairs will be no better grounded than that of any other intelligent reader of newspapers.

Balanced research has no direct bearing on the problem of preventing students in humanities from becoming scientific illiterates, and of preventing students in the sciences from becoming cultural barbarians. This is the task that must continue to be solved, as it is increasingly being solved, by the proper organization of undergraduate instruction in the liberal arts colleges through one or another form of general education. It may be true that in England the cleavage between the literary or cultural mind and the scientific or technological mind is as great as Sir Charles Snow reports. If so, it is mainly due to the intense specialization that begins at a much earlier age than in countries like Germany, France, and even the United States, where this cleavage does not exist in such a pronounced form because of the elements of a common curriculum for most students before they reach the threshold of graduate specialization.

The dangers of intellectual parochialism exist even in undergraduate instruction but these are challenges to pedagogical skill that are currently being met. It is of the first importance to teach the required courses in the basic sciences, which all students must take, as *liberal arts* and not as propaedeutics to research or teaching careers in the sciences. Without sacrificing subject matter, the multiple relations between the exciting advance of science and other disciplines can be explored in such fashion that those who later pursue scientific careers carry away an abiding sense of the many spiritual sources that have fed these multiple relations and of their impact on the world views of man.

The other students, the great majority, will recognize that experimental science—which, despite its Greek beginnings, came down from heaven, as Bergson put it, on the inclined plane of Galileo—has produced the greatest of all human revolutions by changing the estate and condition of man. Experimental science now has given man the power of the Olympian gods, but it has left him with no greater wisdom, for the Olympian gods merely personified the motives and vices of the ordinary man of Greek culture. If one thirsted for wisdom, one did not seek it on Mt. Olympus but in the Agora, the Lyceum, and other corners of Athens haunted by Socrates.

Science as everyone reminds us, has given us knowledge and power but not wisdom. What is the difference between knowledge and wisdom? It is not easy to say. We know that a man can be a learned fool and that a wise man need not be erudite. But does this mean that knowledge and wisdom are to be contrasted, as if they were in opposition to each other? I do not believe so. Reflection will show that no man can be wise who is without knowledge of the object of his wisdom. What is the wise man wise about? Wisdom must be a species of knowledge. It is knowledge of the nature and career of human values in experience and of the best means of achieving them. It is knowledge not only of the means necessary to attain ends but of the ends most appropriately chosen in the problematic situations that require choices between conflicting ends.

It is possible, although difficult, for a man to be wise in his personal life in a society that is itself not wisely organized. But there is no direct clue from the nature of the good life, as the individual defines it for himself, to the nature of the good society—although ultimately the test of a good society is in the character of the individual lives it makes possible. Research for a good society or a better society is primarily but not exclusively the province of the social disciplines or social sciences, in the most comprehensive sense of the phrase, which transcends compartmentalization. Part of this research must be directed to the discovery of the most effective means of eliciting *rational assent* for social programs and policies that meet objective and universally recognized needs. There is something thin about values transmitted by the humanistic tradition unless they are embodied in viable social institutions and practices. We must find, so to speak, the social, operational equivalents of their meaning. It is not enough to intone our devotion, as we have been doing for millennia, to the perennial values of the true, the good, the just, and the beautiful. These values have become, all too often, objects contemplated on occasions of withdrawal from the world, rather than guides to social reconstruction in the world. Programs of social change depend upon many different historical variables, so that the values of "human dignity" may wear a fresh face in the twentieth century not easily recognizable by those who identify it with its classical expression.

Only human beings, of course, can be the carriers of values, but the content of value is social, as well as personal. The reason is that not only what we do to achieve a goal but *how* we do it makes a difference to the very quality of our goals. That is why I cannot accept Snow's division of cultures into two—the sciences and the humanities. There are at least *three* great divisions of culture—and the third, as Professor Lloyd Fallers pointed out recently, is the one in which Snow himself is most deficient. For, as Snow's implied reference to Soviet forced industrialization and collectivization of agriculture shows, he seems to believe that social progress consists in applying technical advances vigorously to society, as if society were itself a factory and the myriad of persons within it so much raw material rather than individual centers of feeling, significance, and dignity. Only adequate social and political study can point the way to the extension of scientific power in our time without the sacrifice of the values of individual freedom, diversity, and dissent. Men have paid a heavy price for blueprints drawn up in ignorance of social, historical, and psychological realities.

Here is a field of research the university should claim as preeminently its own. And it must do so in a nonpartisan spirit, in exercise of a stewardship for the community as a whole. A democracy is the only form of society that can learn to live with the truth about itself. That is why the universities in a democracy should be encouraged to examine and test all important social and political policies in the same experimental spirit with which the natural sciences are pursued, although they will not use the same techniques and procedures. The logic of scientific method must not be confused with the particular methods of any special field. Much of this research will be underwritten by private foundation sources, but in principle the government on various levels should be committed, wherever legitimate needs cannot be met privately, to support of sound inquiry—and by "sound" here I am referring not to the character of its conclusions but to its intellectual quality.

Universities are not the only agencies of society that are capable of disinterested inquiry into the public welfare or common good, but they are the best qualified. That our society stands ready to give a hearing to positions hostile or contrary to its own assumptions is a great source of strength—and of justifiable pride. It is to be anticipated that tensions between the university and the community or state will arise not so much from the pursuit of disinterested research in the natural and medical sciences, but inescapably from disinterested research in the social sciences, particularly when the conclusions of such research seem to challenge the accepted mores at vital points.

In the long run, the government and the community stand only to gain from the university's dedication to careful investigation of relevant alternatives of basic social policy. But in the short run, there are sure to be difficulties whenever the first principles of any large or influential section of society appear to be injured or prejudiced by the findings of evidence or the result of analysis. To be able to withstand the reaction of outraged virtue and indignation, which normally follows the shock of recognition that treasured beliefs have been put into question, the university must be guaranteed its independence of passing popular moods. Private support contributes in some measure to this independence. But the educational need is so vast and continuous and the economic outlook so uncertain, if we extrapolate the existing inflationary tendencies, that it would be completely unrealistic to expect higher education in the future to be self-sustaining. Plural short-term grants by the government, which must be periodically renewed, multiply the opportunities for external pressures, and increase the temptation to yield the intangible values of intellectual independence for material benefit.

Personally, I see the best solution—not the ideal solution, for there is none—in the system that today obtains in England, where through the University Grants Committee the government makes lump grants to universities that are not earmarked for specific purposes. This system would give a university the necessary autonomy to meet educational needs as it sees them, and permit the deployment of resources at the key points of its educational enterprise. This would naturally vary from region to region and from institution to institution.

I am aware of the host of objections that can be raised to this proposal or any like it. They can be summarized in the contentions that general grants cannot be allocated with objectivity, that standards of achievement are not uniform, that the habits of intellectual discrimination and the vision of excellence would be lost in consequence. All institutions would be treated with a mechanical equality that insures mediocrity.

I am not at all persuaded by these objections, which are partly inconsistent with each other. To fear that such a method of educational support will usher in a deadening mediocrity is already to assume that we can distinguish between the good and the bad and the good and the better, that standards in education are not arbitrary or subjective. Not only does this system of making grants work successfully in other countries, but in a modified form some of its principles are in use in those individual states of the union whose educational appropriations cover a variety of publicly supported colleges and universities. A federal board of educational regents, consisting of the most eminent scholars and educators of the country, could be relied upon to assess both educational needs and achievements with as much objectivity as can be exercised in human affairs. After all, even today private foundations distribute many millions of dollars for general educational purposes. They do not do so haphazardly. There is a considerable consensus at any time among scholars and scientists on what is what and who is who in education. Anyone who has ever sat as a member of a committee on fellowship awards to scholars knows that there is a surprisingly large amount of agreement among the panel of judges on what constitutes need, merit, and distinction, and on who is eligible for them. Among the many advantages such a scheme would have, would be the elimination of needless research projects designed primarily to improve the university's ability to meet its general overhead costs. This proposal need not supplant all existing practices. It would leave unaffected the private sector of educational grants to supplement its operation.

Whatever the merits of this proposal, we must recognize that we cannot call into question the desirability of expanding research in the interest of both expanding human welfare and expanding intellectual horizons.

As in all large projects, the detailed questions are of timing and relative emphasis—of more or less, here or there, now or then—which are challenges to our intelligence. We must abandon the rhetoric which, even in the academy, stands in the way of coming to grips with problems. To some, unity means uniformity, diversity spells chaos, support entails control, direction is synonymous with dictation. But every well-conducted piece of research and every successful educational enterprise indicate that these inferences are a series of *non sequiturs*.

Not all problems created by expanding research can be solved in advance, and sometimes we must learn to live with problems that

241

cannot be satisfactorily solved. But before we resign ourselves to what cannot be changed, we must make every intelligent effort to determine the limits of the changeable.

So long as man is a finite creature whose chief instrument of survival is his questing intelligence, his need and imagination will be the twin stimuli to research. When he brings these powers to bear upon problems of self-knowledge and self-change, then—without becoming divine—he will change the very meaning of mortality.

15

Practice & Legal Education

(This chapter consists of my contribution to a Symposium on "The Law School of Tomorrow" held at the Law School of Rutgers University. I should have liked to reproduce the contributions of Messrs. Hutchins and Goodman to which my own remarks were largely a reply. This did not prove feasible. Instead of restating my position in more positive terms, I have let the text stand as originally delivered because it focuses on some key differences in the conceptions both of the university and of the professional school. The point of view I have taken with respect to the central role of "clinical experience and training" in professional law schools, I would apply, *mutatis mutandis*, to the curriculum of other graduate professional schools. This was written in 1966.)

Limitations of time impose a hard choice upon me. I must choose between offering an independent analysis of the theme of this morning's discussion or commenting on Dr. Hutchins' contribution. I have decided to do the latter, not so much to gratify his wish for lively debate, although I hope not to disappoint him, but to focus the discussion on key issues. I stress "discussion" because I have found "debaters" more interested in scoring points for antecedently held conclusions than in a common quest for greater clarity and truth. Debaters make good lawyers of a sort, but bad jurists. On the key issues I am no defender of the educational-legal *status quo.* Although we must seek remedies for existing deficiencies, we must make sure they are not worse than the weakness they would cure. My difficulties are both with Dr. Hutchins' diagnosis of the situation and his prescriptions.

I am not going to say very much about Mr. Paul Goodman's paper because it came to me after I had prepared my own remarks. I observe only in passing that I was brought up in an old-fashioned school of thought in which to characterize an argument as absurd was the worst thing one could say about it. When people believe that the expression "an absurdity" is no longer an epithet of disparagement . . . why, argument is difficult.

Mr. Goodman thinks he is a pluralist. He is mistaken. He is not a pluralist as we understand that word politically. He is an anarchist. If one took his words literally and tried to live by them, our courts would encourage civil disobedience; and peaceful discussion, unless conducted on his terms, would break down. This spells anarchy. And even though Goodman doesn't believe in the police, we would have to call them in to protect him from the consequences of his own philosophy.

I won't say more specifically about Mr. Goodman. Although some of his criticisms of Dr. Hutchins parallel mine, he thinks he agrees with Dr. Hutchins in the main. So be it! This, then, will be a criticism of him too.

I propose to raise a few questions about Dr. Hutchins' conception of a law school, his notion of the practical, his theory of law, and his ideas of a university. I shall leave to others, to you who are better informed than I am of the current curricular practices of our standard law schools, the assessment of his indictment of them as anachronistic trade schools.

That there are such trade schools in existence, where law is taught as a set of formulas without discussion or analysis of legal principles, I have no doubt. I repeat: I am *not* a defender of the educational-legal *status quo* and am prepared to criticize such schools as vigorously as anyone. But that our national university law schools fall within Dr. Hutchins' indictment of the how-to-do-it mold, I doubt very much. Suffice it only to say that on the basis of some familiarity with what is being taught, and how, at the law schools of New York University, Columbia, Harvard, California, and the experiences of my students there with whom I stay in touch, Dr. Hutchins' references to these schools seems to me to be scandalously unjust. He calls for an all-out war against them. But as is usually the case in any all-out war, the first casualty tends to be the truth.

I venture the observation that the character of legal education in university law schools during the half-century spanned by my academic life, has shown an impressive improvement in almost every respect. To a considerable extent we owe encouraging developments in the administration of justice in recent years to the legal education, condemned by Hutchins, whose products on Bench and Bar have advanced the cause of civil freedom and social welfare. The few things that Dr. Hutchins has welcomed in recent developments in law would be hard to explain in terms of his characterization of legal education.

Far from being sunk in the narrow parochialism of the trade school, or the arid technicalities of the how-to-do-it school, instruction has shown an enlargement of social consciousness, a greater concern with the nature of legal principles and their ethical bearing, a profounder understanding of the complexities of the judicial process. There has been a more realistic apprehension of the extent to which landmark decisions both express and redetermine social and political policy.

Of special significance is the growing awareness of the biases of existing law, of the ways in which property in things functions as an instrument of power over people, of the moral issues posed by the demands for human rights, and a more equitable share of our social wealth and services, as well as the difficulties of extending the equal protection of the laws in communities where poverty and prejudice exist. All this is clearly reflected in the law reviews and journals of these so-called trade and how-to-do-it schools, and in the role that lawyers and students, educated in these schools, have played in the various civil rights movements of our times.

245

There is still need for further improvement even in the best of our university law schools, and I shall offer some suggestions later, but no guide to improvement can be found by returning to confused metaphysical notions of natural law. I suspect that even the Yale Law School has made progress since the days when Dr. Hutchins graced its faculty, and much more progress than is implied in his reference to it in the past tense as a trade school.

1. My first difficulty with Dr. Hutchins' conception of a law school is that I do not see why in his view there need exist a law school at all, either at the university or elsewhere. According to him, "The object of a law school is to understand the law." But if understanding, as he conceives it, is the goal, the law can be understood by existing studies in various departments of the university. The philosophy department, for example, offers courses that cover the philosophy of law, jurisprudence, and the theory of evidence. Political science gives many courses in the history and nature of constitutional law. Economics presents courses in labor law, tax law, banking, and finance. Sociology gives courses in crime and punishment, and so on.

These courses have range and depth and are often integrated with neighboring disciplines. They are currently exploring, either independently or by interdepartmental seminars, the great issues stressed by Dr. Hutchins. Nor are they overly concerned with practice. Why, then, shouldn't *these* studies suffice for the understanding of law, leaving the acquisition of the skills necessary for the practice of law to what Dr. Hutchins calls on-the-job training—in effect, a return to the old apprentice system?

What has been left out? Precisely what justifies the existence of a law school—the study of the types of legal *problems* which arise in daily life, and the methods of resolving them satisfactorily, with the least amount of injustice and suffering? Law schools are set up not for the sake of the law or lawyers but ultimately to help human beings to solve legally the problems and predicaments encountered in the pursuit of conflicting social ends.

Let me make the point clearer with an analogy. Suppose someone were to define a medical school, along the lines followed by Dr. Hutchins, as one whose subject is *to understand* the nature of the human body and its healthy functioning. Now we know perfectly well that this can be done and is being done by the biological sciences. But the justification of a medical school, as distinct from an institution devoted to the study of the pure, theoretical sciences of biology, is instruction in clinical medicine.

A medical school exists not merely to discover biological truths but to solve problems of human health. If anyone were to recommend that the clinical aspect of medicine be left to the on-the-job training of the medical apprentice, after he has studied only the theory of health, he would be encouraging widespread manslaughter. I doubt that Dr. Hutchins would entrust himself to a fledgling surgeon who understood the theory of human anatomy but who was learning how to operate on the job. Why should anyone with an acute legal problem that might spell great financial loss or even loss of his freedom entrust his fate to someone whose only preparation for the practice of law is the understanding of its theory?

It is this clinical aspect of the law, and its intelligent study in the law school, that Dr. Hutchins totally neglects. Yet this is the aspect of the law that not only has the greatest impact upon the ordinary man, to whom the lawyer owes a moral obligation to help when he has taken his retainer; its upshot constitutes a crucial test of what the law is declared to be.

A far better case can be made for revising the law school curriculum so that students, under the guidance of their teachers, get some first-hand experience of the law in action in the courts, serving in organizations seeking to defend, extend, or change the law in different sectors of social life, or by serving in government and administrative agencies, than for cutting loose altogether the practice of law from its theoretical study.

Dr. Hutchins protests that such clinical study of the law is a waste of time because the law changes so rapidly that any know-how acquired in law school soon becomes obsolete. This I question on several counts.

First, the history of law shows that the continuities of law and legal practice are just as impressive, if not more so, than the

247

discontinuities: that the rates of change in various fields of law differ markedly; that law as a whole lags far behind social change (contrast, for example, changes in family-law and changes in family life); and that the time-lag is usually great enough to permit fruitful application of what is learned.

Second, if that change were as great as Dr. Hutchins believes, this would affect "knowledge-that" as well as "knowledge-how" (to use Gilbert Ryle's distinction). That is, the knowledge of the law as well as the way it was practiced would become obsolete. There would be no point in even studying substantive law but only the theory of law, which is presumably changeless.

Third, and most important on this issue, to recognize and to be prepared for legal change is not incompatible with education for practice. By "practice" I don't mean the knacks and tricks of the trade that may end in what Veblen called "trained incapacity" when new inventions make the trade superfluous. Nor do I mean merely the procedural know-how of where and when to file papers, which can be performed by the legal automaton that Mr. Hutchins speaks about, but rather analytical know-how, the capacity to engage in fruitful research, to view problems from new angles, to look for fresh analogies, especially the ability to apply principles and rules to specific cases, distinguishing between the relevant and irrelevant. *These* are the basic skills. Clinical medicine shows far greater changes than legal practices, but the properly trained physician can master these changes in virtue of the basic skills he has acquired. In law, as in medicine, a good practical education can nourish and strengthen the powers of flexibility.

Finally, Dr. Hutchins' insistence in the paper he originally submitted—also implied in what he said this morning—that a purely theoretical study of the law is the best practical education, makes no sense on his own premises. A pragmatist like Dewey can say, "Of all things, theory is the most practical," because for him ideas are plans of action. But Hutchins' theory of ideas makes practice or experiment emphatically irrelevant both to their meaning and their truth.

If, as he has told us, the practical aspects of the law are just what cannot be learned in a law school, but only on the job, then how can the best practical education be a theoretical education? And since we are assured that students have until now never received a proper theoretical education in law in their trade and technical schools, how can he possibly know that such an education is the best practical one? After all, to make such an assertion is to make a statement of fact, not theory. But facts cannot be established by decree, only by experience. And since by his own admission the experience is missing, Dr. Hutchins cannot really know what he says he knows, namely that the best way to improve the *practice* of law is to cast it out of the law school.

With this approach to fact, it is easy to eat your cake and have it too. You can also eat your neighbor's cake, because facts are established by decree.

2. This brings me to Dr. Hutchins' conception of "understanding" the law. As far as I can make out, he believes that the law has an essential nature than can be grasped by rational insight into its principles, which are rooted in the nature of man. And he makes an invidious comparison between this view and the doctrine that "the law is what the courts will do," which he said he learned when he was at the Yale Law School.

What is taught at the Yale Law School may sometimes be true, or have some element of truth in it. There are obvious difficulties in defining the law as what the courts will do—Holmes' bad-man theory of the law—as every judge knows who is puzzled about the proper rule to apply to a case. But, however we define law, I submit that a study of what the courts will do, on the basis of the relevant social, political, and economic forces in society and on the basis of relevant studies of the judges' intellectual biographies and value commitments, together with what Holmes himself recommended—the critical reading of "reports, treatises, and statutes"—a study of all this is not incompatible with intelligent understanding of the law. Indeed, if knowledge of the behavior and operation of any institution is relevant to its understanding, as common sense and science affirm, the study of these complex extralegal factors, like economic doctrines and religious dogmas that influence what the courts decide, pruned of the exaggerations of the legal realists, is an integral part of the understanding of the

249

law. No one can deny this unless he denies the multiple facts of judicial legislation or asserts that such legislation is only a logical explication of what is merely implicit in the text of statutes or in the Constitution.

For example, I challenge anyone on the basis of legal principles alone or even of plain logic to make sense of the checkered pattern of the courts' decisions on state-church relations, and of some other important subjects, independently of whether one approves of these decisions or not. This is especially true wherever the doctrine of *stare decisis* is abandoned. In commenting on some recent court opinions in this field, I have been grateful that there is no such thing as logical contempt of courts. Otherwise I would have run the danger of spending the rest of my life in jail. However we define the law, one sensible test of whether we understand it—not of course whether we morally approve of it—is whether we can reasonably predict which rules, commands, or social interests, whose conflicts generate legal problems, the courts will sustain.

It is a commonplace that merely successful prediction is not a sufficient condition for understanding or explanation. I can predict that every time it rains my rural telephone will go dead. No one seems to know why. But if anyone has a true explanation, he must be able to indicate the conditions under which it will or will not work and, if the specific data are known, make conditional predictions. What is predicted is not thereby understood, but what cannot under any conditions and any amount of relevant data be predicted is not truly understood. Mr. Hutchins confuses necessary and sufficient conditions for true understanding of law. He is like the man who says he understands the new mathematics perfectly well but he can never get the correct answer when he uses it. The behavioral and social sciences, properly developed, can help us to explain—as well as predict—the law.

3. If we seek the source of Dr. Hutchins' defective understanding of "understanding" law, I believe we can find it in his theory of law. According to him: "Law is an ordinance of reason directed to the common good." I will say something about the source of this later. But surely there is a difference between saying that law *is* "an

ordinance of reason directed to the common good," and saying that law *should be* "an ordinance of reason directed to the common good." The difference between the descriptive sense and the prescriptive or normative sense of these expressions is crucial to any mode of thinking worthy of being called understanding.

If we make an inventory of the laws under which we live, whether statutory or common law, who will have the hardihood to claim that they are all ordinances of reason directed to the common good? Who is prepared to argue that our marriage and divorce laws, our laws on sex behavior, therapeutic abortion, attempted suicide, voluntary euthanasia, our bankruptcy laws, our laws of real property, negligence, the whole corpus of administrative law, not to mention our laws of evidence—which in some respects haven't even caught up with Bentham and which strike Continental jurists as so odd—are all of them "ordinances of reason directed to the common good"?

If Dr. Hutchins holds to this theory of law and is prepared to accept the implications of his words, if he really means what he says or has written, then he must also hold that the vast reaches of the positive law, which are certainly not ordinances of reason and which, far from being directed to the common good, further class and professional interests and a complex variety of entrenched powers, are really not part of the law. A law school that exists to understand the law as Dr. Hutchins understands the law cannot understand the law in action, the law as it is lived and suffered, its burden of tradition and its legacy of ambiguity and contingency. No wonder such a school turns its back on the quest for understanding the operative sanctions that may not be altogether rational and/or moral, for it rules them out *a priori* as law. Such a school can have no room in its curriculum for the law as practiced. Presumably, the ordinances of reason for marriage, divorce, and abortion are to be laid down independently of the findings of scientific and social inquiry into the effects of current laws and practice of human behavior.

I regard this as a *reductio ad absurdum* of the position. Let's call it a position of high-minded error brought on by excessive moralizing. It is excessive not because it wants to make morality central to the law—that should be the continuing concern of all of us—but because it overlooks the centrality of intelligence to morality. For the task of an intelligent morality, among other things, is to determine what the law is, how it actually works in practice, and how it affects human behavior, in order to be in a better position to improve it. As Professor H. L. A. Hart has argued in his critique of Professor Don Fuller's Augustinian notion that an unjust law is not a law, any position that fudges or obscures the distinction between what is legally valid and morally valid, as does Dr. Hutchins' view, tends to bestow "an aura of mystery and authority" on whatever official system of law exists. It facilitates a semantic slide from "the customary" to the "natural," from the "natural" to the "normal," from the "normal" to the "reasonable," and from the "reasonable" to the "desirable." The road to legal absurdity is often paved with moral tautology and logical ambiguity.

4. I turn now to Dr. Hutchins' idea of a university. This is even more difficult to accept than the bizarre conception of a law school unconcerned with the practice of law. I could write a book challenging his contentions on the main points. Indeed, I already have. But here, too, I must content myself with only a few questions, leaving to others the detailed correction of his exaggerations of the state of the American university. What he says doesn't square with my own lifelong experience within it. It doesn't square with the fact that with all its limitations, and they are many, the American university today on the whole is a freer, more scholarly, and more creative institution than it has been in its entire history. Like the law school, it has still far to go to become an embodiment of all our educational ideals, but we can improve it more effectively if we realize how far we have come from what it used to be.

Dr. Hutchins would have us believe that the university has supinely yielded to every pressure group, that it is willing to offer "every conceivable kind of training" and undertake "every conceivable kind of investigation." But he is a hard man to please because he also condemns President Perkins of Cornell for saying that in order to maintain excellence, Cornell may have to concentrate in certain fields—a preeminently common-sense point of view

because no university can achieve excellence in everything. There
are some things all universities should study, but not all universities
can study all things or concentrate in all areas. Why should the
University of Nebraska develop a department of oceanography, or
why should Rutgers University establish another astronomical
observatory when there is one across the Hudson River at Columbia? Even if we had unlimited material resources, biology might
defeat us. We may not have enough talent to do everything well at
all places.

Dr. Hutchins also taxes the university with incoherence
because it does opposite things. And a university presumably
cannot do opposite things and be a university. But why not? Can't a
university have a program to explore the skies and an opposite one
to plumb the earth, sponsor a study on the causes of war and
another on the conditions of a stable peace? Even university
departments do opposite things—and properly. In some universities the sociology department gives a course in social organization,
and it gives another, a much more popular one, in social dis-
organization. My own department at N.Y.U. gives a course on
rationalism and another on irrationalism. English departments give
courses in tragedy and its opposite, comedy. Nor do these courses
necessarily have to be related to each other; that is the function of
the subject matter. There is no incoherence here if we do not
confuse—I hesitate to attribute such a lapse to an Aristotelian—a
contrary with a contradictory.

It is simply not the case that our university faculties are
uninterested in general questions of academic freedom and tenure.
Nor is it true that they have lost their autonomy with respect to the
content and organization of their curricula. And no one should
know better than the former president of the University of
Chicago![1] To me university faculties seem to be almost continuously concerned with these questions—to a point where I am
sometimes tempted to define academic freedom as freedom from

---

[1] I am referring to the resolution of the Academic Senate of January 1944 in which the
faculty challenged the view of the President of the University of Chicago that the function of
the university was to revolutionize the values of society.

curriculum committee meetings. What *is* true is that the universities of this country have rejected Dr. Hutchins' views of the nature of university education. Unfortunately, they have not always taken to heart my criticisms either. But it would be presumptuous on my part to assert that they have therefore abandoned university education.

The nature of the university has changed with the times. If you want to know whether these changes are progressive, the answer must lie not in what a university *can* do or *can* be, but what it *should* be. A university, to be sure, should serve society without being subservient to society. But how can it best serve society? Mainly by becoming a center of intellectual adventure and discovery, a birthplace of fresh insight and vision, an arena where fundamental ideas are propounded, challenged, clarified, and where students of a subject are prepared by competent teachers to become its masters. The university adds new knowledge to the store of the past as it sifts and tests the legacies of the past.

In the nature of the case, therefore, where the university functions properly, it must concern itself with the identification and imaginative study of the great problems of the present and emerging future. The problems enumerated by Dr. Hutchins, and other problems as weighty, have been discussed in American universities for years. Here he is banging on an open door! Long before Hutchins discovered the importance of technology, long before Jaspers discoursed about it, American universities were discussing different facets of the technological revolution in connection with the work of thinkers like Marx, Dewey, Whitehead, Norbert Wiener, von Neumann, and others. University scholars, long before Hutchins discovered the social problem, proclaimed the necessity of social invention to cope with the accelerating output of the technological revolution. This is no new thing. Go back thirty-three years and turn the pages of the Hoover Commission volumes on *Recent Social Trends in the United States*. You will find them concerned with the issues that have just been discussed in the recent reports of the *National Commission on Technology, Automation, and Economic Progress*. The reports of both commissions are largely the work of university professors. One need only read them to realize how unjust and irresponsible are the charges against the university on this score.

For the university to function most effectively, in my view, at least two preconditions are involved. First, the university must presuppose that its students have had an adequate liberal arts college education. It cannot offer a substitute for it, since the forging of new perspectives and the winning of new truths require a study in depth, some specialization. Without specialization we cannot have a university; we can have only a college. The college has its own virtues. They are not those of a university.

Secondly, and more important, the university requires freedom from restraints by state, church, business, labor—these days from students too—and freedom from any religious or metaphysical dogma, in order that its faculties pursue and publish the truth as they see it, subject only to the ethics and logic of rational inquiry. This makes the university an open society in which there are no official orthodoxies or heresies, in which scholars work singly or together, but in any case voluntarily, on their own problems.

Consequently, the university as an institution, the university *as such*, cannot take the responsibility for the uses to which knowledge is put. It cannot set out to remake society by reform, revolution, or counterrevolution. It cannot organize crusades or raids against the community. It must critically consider all such proposals without becoming the partisan of any. Its members, of course, remain free as individual citizens to engage themselves in social action. Personally, I regard such action as their social duty, but that is not the function of the university.

This conception of a university contrasts sharply with that of Dr. Hutchins', except on one point—my only point of agreement with him—namely, the importance of clarifying the great problems of our time. This the universities are already doing. But the university is not the home of *a* or *the* community of scholars in quest of a hypothetical and largely mythical unity of knowledge. It is the home of *communities* of scholars and also of those lonely and gifted pioneers of the mind, like Willard Gibbs, Charles Peirce, and Gottfried Frege, who do not work in communities but prefer, with a few students, to work alone. It recognizes that some disciplines are related to others; that no discipline is completely isolated from some other; but it rejects the metaphysical extravaganza that all disciplines are necessarily related to each other. Not even all problems are related to each other! And it denies—and I congratulate Mr. Goodman on his insight on this point—it denies that the "circle of knowledge" exists.

When Dr. Hutchins speaks of "the corporate illumination that can be expected from an intellectual community each of whose members and each of whose subjects enlightens and is enlightened by the rest," he is not describing the existing worlds of knowledge. He is making a speculative assumption which in somewhat different form has been made not only by Hegelian idealism, as Goodman points out, but by dialectical materialism, and some types of Christian metaphysics, whose dogmas of unity have blocked the path of scientific inquiry.

We live in a world in which pluralities are as manifest as unities. Everything is related to something else but not to everything else. The truth or falsity of the theories of relativity, of genetics, of philology have nothing to do with questions of socialism or capitalism or social planning or when promises should be considered binding contracts. They are not in one circle at all. As William James once wrote in a letter to F. H. Bradley: "A Universe concatenated from next to next, and thereupon connected more or less in various degrees, has all the UNI in it that the facts require."

There is no "circle of knowledge" because, despite Dr. Hutchins, there is no center—or rather for each scholar the center of his "circle of knowledge" is his own set of problems. It is an open question whether even in the special disciplines, in which some fields are related to others, it makes sense to speak of the "circle of knowledge." What is the center of the "circle of knowledge" in physics or mathematics?

The conflict between Dr. Hutchins' conception of the university and the current conception comes to a head in his approving quotation from Jaspers, and his comment on it. "The university," says Jaspers, "must face the great problem of modern man:

how out of technology there can arise the metaphysical foundations of a new way of life that technology makes possible." Jaspers believes that Reality is the Incomprehensible, and his writing sometimes reflects it. But leaving aside his violation of logical grammar, his drift is clear. The university must strive to create a new way of life. And Dr. Hutchins comments: "I take this passage to mean that the university must fashion the mind of the technological age."

Why must it? Why cannot the age fashion its own mind or minds on the basis of whatever truths the university discovers about man, nature and society? Technology may unify the world sooner than ideology, but by itself it cannot solve problems of value. To fashion anything means to have a goal or end. Benjamin Franklin and Karl Marx long ago defined man as a tool-making animal, but the ends for which a tool are used, although limited by the nature of the tool, are not uniquely determined thereby.

Who, then, sets the goals or ends in behalf of which the university is to fashion and refashion the mind and life of man? Let the university declare that its essential function is to fashion the mind of the age, and I predict that some other institution will fashion the mind of the university.

In a free society there is no one institution to which can be entrusted alone the refashioning of the mind of the age. This is what we all do, if we are interested in doing it, as individuals or groups. Ultimately, this is determined by the political life of the free society in which the scholar has the same rights, duties, and responsibilities as all other citizens, but into which the university as such cannot enter without becoming a creature of partisan interest.

The source of Dr. Hutchins' views about the organization of the university and its function of redirecting the mind and life of our society by law is not hard to find. I quoted him as defining the law as an ordinance of reason directed toward the common good. It now turns out that the ordinances of reason determine not only the law but the university and the shape and mind of our whole society. This statement about the law is a partial quotation of a sentence in Aquinas, in *Summa Theologica*, which Dr. Hutchins unaccountably abbreviates. In Aquinas the sentence reads: "Law is an ordinance of reason for the common good, promulgated and emanating from him who has the care of the community."

The proximate source of the law is the ruler; the ultimate source is Divine Reason. But no matter who has the care of the community in this view, its good is allegedly grounded in metaphysics or natural theology, which is the true center of the circle of knowledge of man and nature. I do not know whether Dr. Hutchins believes this. He once did. In any case, the proposition is demonstrably false. Neither the good nor the common good can be derived from any metaphysical statement without palpable question-begging, introducing value terms into the definitions of being.

Just as objectionable is the implication that the university is the agency for the promulgation of the common good. The premise of a free society is that the common good does not emanate from the university or church or court or any institution that pretends to expertness in wisdom. Its hope is that out of the clash of conflicting public opinions and interests a rational public policy will develop through the multiple mechanisms of the democratic process.

At most, the university can provide the relevant knowledge and insights for rational choice. At best, it influences social change by indirection. If it strives deliberately to reshape the mind and life of the age, instead of leaving the citizens of a free society to make up their own minds about the uses of knowledge and goals of social action, it usurps a political responsibility not its own.

In conclusion: My advice to the founding fathers of the Rutgers Law School of Tomorrow is based on a different conception of utopia from that of Dr. Hutchins. Oscar Wilde, anticipating a society in which the slavery of machines has banished the slavery of men, declared: "A map of the world that does not include Utopia is not worth glancing at, for it excludes the one country at which humanity is always landing." But utopia must be on the map, with some lines showing how to reach it from this place and this time.

The recommendation that the law school of the future study chiefly jurisprudence seems to me very dubious advice because, in one sense, Dr. Hutchins' sense, it means studying everything, and in another sense, the more usual sense, not enough.

Intelligent study of the conflicting schools of jurisprudence presupposes some familiarity with substantive law. Otherwise, it is an exercise in verbalism. Without such antecedent knowledge, the advice to study jurisprudence is on all fours with advice to a scientist to concentrate not on the subject matter or practice of science, the know-how of experiment and the techniques of mathematical analysis, but to study the philosophy of science instead.

Someone who knows only or mainly the philosophy of science is not a practicing scientist; nor can he be said to have knowledge of science. Similarly, someone who studies only or mainly metalegal theory and the miscellaneous doctrines and conflicting definitions that constitute so large a part of the literature of jurisprudence, is not studying law or preparing for its practice. Jurisprudence and the philosophy of law have their uses, but they are most fruitfully pursued in the context of the positive law, its problems and challenges. That is the way it is being taught in the best law schools of the country.

My advice is quite different from Dr. Hutchins'. My advice is to do better what the best university law schools of our time are already doing. Staff your law schools with scholars who are great teachers, including successful practitioners who are also scholars. And of special importance is it to increase, not decrease, the place of the relevant social and behavorial sciences and interdisciplinary studies in the law school curriculum. Even if law is regarded as the empire of reason, which unfortunately it is not, we need to know more about the factors that interfere with its exercise. Law students will become not only lawyers but judges and government officials. The law should be so taught as to facilitate their functioning in these roles. A great teacher is one who fires the imagination even when he deals with humdrum detail. At the same time, although he does not talk about reason, he thinks clearly and logically and can inspire others to do so too. And it is logical thinking that seems to me to be currently in shortest supply in the law. This is especially true for recent Supreme Court decisions.

Holmes's aphorism about logic and the law has been much misunderstood. Experience, of course, remains the source of the law, but without the capacity to learn from it, to formulate principles and check them by their consequences in practice, men become the victims of change and not the masters of it.

It is not illiberal to teach the craft of the law, if only the result is an honest and competent craftsman. The honest craftsman of the law does not think of himself primarily as a corporation lawyer or labor lawyer, or criminal lawyer, but as a journeyman in the workshops of justice.

Law students should have a touch of dedication as well as being intellectually gifted. Select them, therefore, from among those who have a calling or vocation for the law, a sense of it not only as a way of earning a living but as a way of living one's life, who want to succeed but who also want to be "moral men in a moral society."

Were there a legal equivalent to the Hippocratic oath, your students, upon the completion of their studies, would not swear allegiance to any creed. Their pledge would be to the service of man—to all men—in the never-ending task of resolving human conflicts in order to maximize human freedom under law.

16

Teaching as a Profession

Teaching is not the oldest profession because for millennia the practices of those who taught were not regarded as defining a profession. Teaching in ancient times was so obviously an extension of mothering and later of parental guiding that it seemed somewhat incongruous, and inappropriate to the intimacies of the teacher-pupil relation, to consider it as an activity upon which a price could be set. It was something done in the family or among friends or as part of the initiation into a clan or a priestly cult. Even as late as Plato there seems to have been among the traditional-minded a marked hostility to those who set themselves up as teachers for hire, especially to free men, and who instead of dispensing wisdom offered to give instruction in it for a price.

This suggests there is a certain ambiguity in the term "teacher" that it is necessary to clarify in order to do justice to teaching as a profession. We sometimes speak of the "prophets" as the great teachers of the human race, those who supply the visions without which the people perish. These are the moral geniuses or leaders and most of them have not been teachers by profession. Vision and leadership cannot be a profession. Anyone who proclaimed himself a professional prophet would in the eyes of others be proclaiming himself a fraud.

Sometimes we use the word "teacher" to mean not a prophet but a great critic who, like Voltaire, satirizes the foibles, stupidities, and barbarities of his time. A professional critic has a place in society but except in rare instances he must be more than a mere critic to have a place in the classroom. Every professional teacher worth his salt must also be a critic of the evils of his society wherever they bear upon the content of his instruction. But whereas the professional critic may be a specialist in *exposing* sin and ignorance, the professional teacher has the harder task of *removing* the ignorance, making students aware of the *meaning* of good and evil, and developing their capacity to make balanced judgments.

Finally the term "teacher" is used to mean the "discoverer" or the "researcher." In this sense he need not have students or be active in a classroom. It is in this sense primarily that those associated with the university rather than the liberal arts college, are teachers. In this sense—as inquirers—it makes little difference to their professional competence whether they are halt, dumb, or blind.

All the foregoing senses of the term "teacher" are irrelevant to the sense with which I shall be concerned in the rest of this chapter, *viz.*, the classroom teacher. The classroom teacher *per se* is not a prophet or critic or scientific researcher or pioneer. If he is, he is not likely to remain in the classroom for long. His function is not so much to discover truths but to transmit them and to help develop the skills, attitudes, and values that will enable his students to live with these truths and perhaps find some themselves. As one educator has felicitously put it, he adds to "the sum of human knowers rather than to the sum of human knowledge." He is not a teacher like the historic Socrates, although he uses the Socratic method, who taught those who were confident that they were already learned, that they are really ignorant. In the main he begins with those who are unformed and ignorant. And if he is wise, he teaches them in such a way that although they are less ignorant they know that neither he nor they are ever wholly wise or infallible. The classroom teacher is the professional teacher *par excellence* and he is unable to exist without students and, except where he himself is a private tutor, without schools. I have strongly distinguished this sense of teacher from all the other senses because despite the flattery to the professional teacher resulting from the interchange of meanings, in the last analysis he suffers from it. Too much is expected of him and too little is awarded him.

The paradox of the situation is that although much is expected of the teacher, his profession on the whole has been held in small regard independently of his individual achievements. The low estate in which teaching was and is held is reflected in the comparative evaluation of the professions. It used to be focally expressed in the index of their comparative earnings. Although their economic lot has been appreciably improved in recent years compared to lawyers, physicians, architects, journalists, and other professionals their earnings are still quite modest. The only lavish rewards the teacher gets is not in coin but in compliments. But teachers like scholars could easily resign themselves to a life of genteel poverty, if they were sustained by a sense of the importance of their work. Their own private judgment of the importance of their work, like the judgment most people make of themselves, depends largely upon the judgments of others. And what the others think is that by and large professional teachers are recruited from the men and women who are not good enough to succeed in worthier pursuits which require more brains, more toughness, and greater risk and courage. Mencken, a professional critic whose vogue in this country during the twenties and thirties is hard to explain except on the hypothesis that professional teachers did not do their work properly, exaggerated when he said: "The truth is that the average school-teacher, on all the lower levels, is and always must be essentially an ass, for how can one imagine an intelligent man engaging in so puerile an avocation?"[1] Nonetheless, Mencken was expressing a widespread if not dominant mood. When he called teaching "an avocation" rather than a vocation, and an unmanly one at that, he was really implying that it was not part of the serious

[1] *Prejudices*, 3rd series, p. 244.

263

business of life. How many Americans today regard teaching, especially for men, as a major calling in the same rank as commerce, banking, engineering, soldiering, law, or medicine? How many children whose ambitions accurately reflect what the community honors say that they want to grow up to be a teacher?

The causes of the low estate in which the professional teacher has been held in the past are many and complex. But undoubtedly one of the most influential factors in generating a low esteem of teachers has been the easy assumption that almost anybody can teach. In the past it was true that almost anybody could teach. Little if any professional preparation was called for. It was sufficient if the teacher knew more, and was physically stronger, than his students.

Teaching differs from most other professions like medicine in that poor teaching bores but does not kill. In most other fields the consequences of professional practice for good or evil are swift, palpable, and capable of objective evaluation without much difficulty. The effects of poor teaching, however, especially in the past, were not evident and so long as the teacher was a good disciplinarian, it was easy to believe that what the student didn't learn one year under one teacher he might learn another year under a different teacher. Further, the exceptional student, with capacity and drive could survive many poor teachers and learn despite them. For of the very best students it might be said that they educate themselves.

In recent years dissatisfaction with teachers has become widespread because of the growing belief that teachers are failing to teach properly in consequence of incompetence or disinterest. This belief has been encouraged not by scientific evidence but by the unremitting propaganda of influential critics, administrators, and spokesmen of minority groups.

In the early days of public education only a small percentage of the educable youth went to high school and a still smaller percentage to college. A certain natural selection operated so that although very many naturally gifted youths did not go to high school and college, it is probable that a larger proportion of those who did attend were naturally more gifted than those who did not attend.

Today, however, in the era of mass education when more than 80% of our youth attend high school, when no matter what their natural gifts, the demands of intelligent citizenship require that we educate practically the entire population, the role of the teacher in the educational process has become more crucial than ever before. His professional training as a teacher is of transcendent importance since it must equip him with the skills necessary to give the best education that *any* child can assimilate. The teacher today must be better prepared than in the past because the advance of knowledge shows that the major problems of our times involve whole areas and not special subject matters. He must be better prepared because he can no longer rely upon traditional values and certitudes but must help develop a living faith in democratic values. He must be better prepared because he must compete with more and more powerful distracting influences in the field of popular culture than in the past. Never was it so false to believe that almost any knowledgeable person of good will can teach well after a little cramming in pedagogical methods. Nonetheless, as we shall see, there seems to be a revival of the notion that teaching is not a profession but an avocation acquired *after* one has been properly educated in some major field of knowledge.

Every profession is defined by its function and the proper performance of function depends on knowledge. But the knowledge the teacher must have differs from the knowledge possessed by other professions in its generality. Like other professions, teaching, too, rests on specialized knowledge. But it cannot be only specialized, for there is hardly any subject that, when properly taught, does not have its interrelationships with other subjects, its intertwining roots, and complex problems that often require for their analysis data from different fields. Every teacher therefore must have a sound liberal arts education not merely as a foundation upon which to build—and which is forgotten, as is the case with most professions, once something is built upon it—but as something to be used, added to, and enriched throughout his teaching experience. The engineer and physician may have some excuse for regarding a liberal education as *preparatory* to their specialty which is progressively becoming more specialized. For a teacher a liberal arts education is a *continuing* process necessary to keep his mind alert and his capacities for significant cultural experience alive. This is necessary not only in the interest of continued mastery of the subject matters to be taught but to prevent the deterioration which invariably sets in when teaching becomes a standard routine of teaching the same things the same way day in and day out.

Knowledge of subject matter is necessary but not sufficient. For teaching as a profession is not only a matter of knowing *what* but of knowing *how*—knowing how to communicate in such a way that the student acquires the knowledge, skills, and intellectual habits which make it possible for him to continue his education and ultimately his self-education. This would be a commonplace were it not seemingly so often denied. Some of the most vehement and vitriolic critics of modern education are convinced that our children are ignorant and slovenly in their intellectual ways, because their teachers are literally only superficially trained in the subjects they are teaching, hardly better-informed about what they teach than their more intelligent students. No evidence has been offered for this astonishing charge except alleged attempts by principals and superintendents to discourage teachers from continuing graduate studies in their subject matter—and a peculiar interpretation placed on one of the ambiguous dicta of modern education: "We do not teach history (or geometry) but children."

Literal minded critics are the bane of fruitful discussion. The alleged attempts to discourage teachers from adding to their knowledge turn out on further inquiry to be not at all an expression of anti-intellectualism but only a reminder that good teaching is knowing-how and not merely knowing-that. Not all the knowledge in the *Encyclopedia Britannica* carried in a man's head is of any use in the classroom if an individual is deficient or uninterested in the skills of teaching. Interest in knowledge for its own sake is a wonderful thing and it may open up a desirable career as a research specialist. But it is not the same thing as interest or capacity in teaching as a profession. The teacher must learn as long as he lives but if he is deficient in communicating knowledge it is perfectly legitimate to request either that he learn the skills and techniques of teaching before he adds to his knowledge of fact or that he change his vocation.

The plain meaning of the statement "We do not teach history we teach children" is *not* the absurd implication that those who teach history teach it to no one but that unless the teacher is continuously aware of *whom* he is teaching, he will teach history or any other subject poorly, and often in such a way as to develop a profound aversion to it for life. The profession of teaching is preeminently the art of developing the power of thinking, the habit of intelligent observation, the sense of discriminating taste, the capacities of appreciation, expression, and effective communication. In the classroom that is what knowledge imparted or acquired is relevant to. There are occasions when a physician is called upon to remind a colleague that "We do not merely practice medicine: we attempt to cure our patients." This is a reminder that *qua* physician he is concerned primarily with the health of his patient. This is not true for the experimental biologist who is concerned only with knowledge and truth. However, it no more means that the physician should ignore, or dispense with, the findings of the experimental biologist than that the teacher can succeed in teaching most children without the ordered presentation of subject matters.

The hidden assumption behind the views we have been criticizing is not the traditional one that anyone can teach but that anyone who has knowledge—who has technical competence in a specific subject matter—can teach. This is the view widely prevalent, despite vehement avowals to the contrary, among the liberal arts colleges. But if we would judge institutions by their practices not by their professions, it will be apparent that most colleges appoint as teachers individuals who have never been trained to teach, who rarely are evaluated from the point of view of their capacity to teach, and whose performance as teachers is *not* tested by those who know what good teaching is or even checked against the evaluations of those they have taught. If bad educational practices in the classroom constituted a bar to college teaching, most colleges would lose a considerable portion of their faculty.

Nonetheless, since all things may be questioned, one might very well ask whether teaching skills can be taught. Even among teachers—though not on the lower levels—one hears: Teachers are born, not made. Teaching is a knack—either one has it or one hasn't, and nothing much can be done about it.

If teaching skills could not be taught then teaching as an art would differ from all the other arts we know. After all, some proficiency even in the arts that seem most clearly dependent upon native capacities, like painting and music, can be acquired by almost anyone not deaf or color blind. Teaching—good teaching—is certainly a difficult art. It can be acquired by experience, which is admitted by many who are proud that they never took professional courses in teaching. It can be more readily acquired, however, if one's own experience is preceded by intelligent observation and analysis of others' experience. No matter how excellent one's native capacities are, professional courses in teaching together with inspiring models of classroom procedure, will improve them. What one brings to the actual experience determines what one makes of it. Professional training in teaching enables the teacher to bring a vast amount of tested techniques and insights to the living occasions of classroom instruction. This is especially true in inducing the fruitful participation of students and the self-activity which provides the best basis for self-education at a later time. Without give and take between teacher and student, without an answering response of the student to a problem, there is no genuine teaching. Lecturing is not teaching; it is usually enforced listening. And even lecturing is an art which with a little trouble may be acquired to a point where one's lecturing is at least interesting.

In a certain sense we may say that great teachers like genius in any field are born. But *good* teachers are made, and when teachers have become good they can always become better. And what we need are good teachers—hundreds of thousands of them.

Ideally every child or student should have his own teacher just as every patient has his own doctor. The difficulty with teaching as a profession is that the teacher in one and the same class and usually at the same time must motivate, interest, and instruct students of varying capacities, varied backgrounds, and varied personal histories. He must not be too slow for the quick-minded or too fast for the dull-witted. So long as they are his charges, he has a responsibility to help each one of them to get as much as he possibly can from the educational experience. It is in this equality of concern for all individuals no matter how unequal their capacities that democratic education consists.

That is why neither mastery of subject matter nor of the techniques of instruction, or both, is enough. There must be something else present which Pestalozzi calls love and which seems more accurately to be described by the phrase "imaginative sympathy." Sympathetic understanding is the one quality, if any, which seems underived in the set of traits necessary for good teaching, and even it may be deepened and expanded by thought and training. But whether innate or acquired, its place in teaching can hardly be exaggerated. Some philosophers have gone so far as to suggest that sympathetic feelings are the only direct source of knowledge we have of the inner experience of other human beings. Although it is questionable whether this is epistemologically valid—sympathy like pity and love may blind as well as reveal—it is indisputable that it provides the warm hunches and sensitive leads about other people's feelings, their possibilities of growth, and their character which behavioral tests ultimately verify. That is why the personality traits of the prospective teacher are so important. He must not only be intellectually aware of the possibility of wide variation in the emotional patterns of his students, he must have the power of discovering them and of assessing their bearing upon the way students learn and develop. Whether he is teaching the child or the adolescent, he should know his student better than the student knows himself. Every good teacher must be something of an actor in respect to techniques of instruction and something of a psychiatrist in recognizing the blockages and difficulties which stand in the way of the fullest liberation of the intellectual powers of the individual student. We sometimes say that he must stand in the place of the parent but his task is much more arduous not only because he plays the role of multiple parents but because he actually attempts to carry out in a small portion of the day what parents presumably achieve without explicit effort but only by indirection and force of example over a long period of years. How many parents can teach their own children even when they explicitly seek to do so?

We are not through with the professional qualifications of the teacher. Today, more than ever in the history of our country and our culture, the teacher must have an abiding sense of his responsibility as a molder of values, as the chief if not the only custodian of the values of freedom, of intellectual courage and independence threatened by periodic fanaticism, lawlessness, and mindless political reaction. The dimensions of the contemporary crisis of Western civilization can hardly be exaggerated. It is so grave that we do not know whether we can count on more than a few decades before the issue will be finally determined. Until then every teacher must regard himself as the guardian of the life of the free spirit which is the most glorious aspect of the heritage of Western civilization. He must develop and keep alive a passion for freedom in those who some day may be called upon to defend freedom with their very lives. He must do this not as a warrior, not as a crusader against the infidels, not as a propagandist for nationalism, but as an educator. This means that his faith in freedom, and of those he instructs, should be the outcome of inquiry, of a clarity born of knowledge, of an assurance that has withstood examination of all relevant alternatives. This means that the professional preparations of every teacher must be more thorough than in the days when we could rely on the comfortable securities of distance and tradition. Among the paradoxes of our time is the fact that although the material character of our lives depends more and more upon technological advances, it is men's ideas and ideals, what they believe, that are decisive in determining the future. We can no longer rely on the home, the church, the voluntary associations of town, street, and guilds to do the main job, to develop the ideas and ideals, the readiness, the habits of work, and uncoerced discipline necessary not only for the survival of democracy but its proper functioning. It may no longer be possible to achieve this goal but if it can be done the schools can do it best, not alone but in the vanguard of social effort. William James somewhere refers to democracy as a kind of religion. If democracy is a religion, the public schools are its churches and the teachers its dedicated servants, who serve the community. Democracy, the public schools, the morale of the teaching profession, to continue the metaphor—all are in need of continuous Reformation.

At this point some one is sure to suggest that we abandon this exalted conception of the profession of teaching for a look at the sober realities. These realities disclose a state of intense dissatisfaction with the teaching profession at a time when technically the pedagogic training of teachers probably is more thorough, and certainly no worse, than their training in the past. Why, then, the mounting criticism? Primarily because of social changes, especially in large cities, which have resulted in decentralized Boards of Education and an increased role for spokesmen of militant minority groups who feel that their children's educational needs have been neglected even when active discrimination is not practiced. Other factors enter into the situation, which are beyond the power of the schools directly to affect. Whatever the causes of dissatisfaction with teaching are, to the extent that they can be traced to poor teaching, the only response can be improved methods of selecting and educating teachers.

The liberal arts colleges are legitimately concerned with the academic preparation of the teacher. They believe, and I think rightly, that the academic background of the teacher should be at least as broad and as thorough as that of other professions, that the teacher must feel at home in the sciences, the social studies, and humanities which constitute the minimum indispensables of the liberally educated man and woman. But unfortunately they go on from here to make invidious distinctions between teaching as a profession and other professions. More and more the sentiment is being expressed that after the A.B. is awarded either a few courses in pedagogy or practical apprenticeship of very limited duration or both is a *sufficient* preparation for a life career as a teacher. It is one thing to recognize that in a period of emergency men and women may be licensed after a hurried special course of study under forced draft. It is quite another thing to assume that this normally fulfills the requirement for preparation.

Teachers recruited this way are not likely to remain in the profession. To most of them it is a *pis aller*, a steppingstone to something more profitable and less wearing, or a stop-gap to marriage and the serious business of life. Think of the gamut of professions and vocations from clergyman to a junior accountant that no one would dream of filling with untrained or hastily trained individuals. Is the role of teacher less significant, less needful of special qualification and preparation? On the contrary, if we remember that the student's character as well as mind, indeed, his entire personality must be an object of concern whenever it is relevant to what he learns or fails to learn, then we cannot be content with anything less than a comprehensive preparation which will be adequate to a calling in which an individual expects to spend his life.

Adequate preparation must begin at least where the preparation for the other leading professions must begin. The desire to become teachers must be awakened in students *before* they are enrolled in education courses just as the desire to become physicians, lawyers, engineers exists in students before they attend the professional schools of medicine, law, and engineering. All too many students become teachers only because they do not know what they want to do or because they are not good enough to qualify for what they planned to do. It is here that the liberal arts college can begin to render distinctive service to professional education. Its outstanding members must capture the imagination of the best youth so that they see in teaching not a surrogate or consolation career but an opportunity to do a difficult, honorable, and honored life-work with the community's most precious resources.

The practical difficulties in realizing this conception are enormous. They must be faced even if when recognized they indicate that the position sketched here can only be a directing guide in long-time planning.

First of all, in relation to the natural distribution of talents we may be asking too much. There may not be enough highly qualified men and women, intellectually and emotionally, to serve as teachers. If the supply of available talent falls far short of the demand, and the demand is growing annually, it may be very difficult to raise the standards of admission to the profession, improve the character of the professional education of teachers, and therewith elevate the levels of performance in the classrooms. The medical schools and the law schools succeeded in lifting themselves by their boot-straps into their present excellent professional position only because the supply of applicants exceeded by far the available places. Medical and law schools (and to a lesser extent the engineering schools) can select the pick of the crop and still be full to capacity. Were schools of education to follow suit they would not fill their classrooms, and even if they did they would be unable to meet the growing need. Even if there were no difference in the intellectual capacities of the candidates for different professions, there would always be a numerical disparity among them for the simple reason that every child normally needs a teacher but needs a physician only occasionally, which remains true when he becomes an adult. In the nature of the case, then, either some individuals will be certified as teachers who in the light of the most adequate standards are not qualified intellectually or emotionally to pursue the calling or those who are already teaching will have to instruct more students under conditions which make their teaching less effective. In short the present emergency may be chronic.

Secondly, no matter how urgent the appeals, no matter how persuasive the call for teachers, it is not likely to be heeded unless the economic rewards of the profession of teaching are sharply increased. The teaching profession, it cannot be repeated too often, must not be staffed by those for whom teaching is a residual choice. It must attract those for whom it is a primary choice and who are intellectually at least equipped to do something else. But the individual who is capable of doing something else, especially of preparing himself for some other profession, must feel that the rewards are somewhat commensurate. He must feel some assurance that a day will not come when contrasting his standard of living and what he might have had or comparing the opportunities open to his children and those of his confreres in other professional groups, that he will not regret his choice and become embittered thereby; or what is almost as bad, scurry desperately around in a quest for extra income by night work, week-end work, summer work. The dedicated souls who choose the life of genteel poverty sooner or later realize that they have chosen it for their wives and children, too, who may not be so dedicated or so philosophical about poverty which is always a relative conception. The church was wise in its day when it provided that those who chose poverty must also choose celibacy. In a secular culture however such provisions for teachers are unwise as well as impracticable.

The difficulty is that if teachers are to be paid on a scale to attract the ablest persons to the profession, taxpayers, unless properly educated by a new generation of professionally qualified teachers, may revolt. This is another illustration of the Platonic paradox of the philosopher-ruler and the ideal Republic. One cannot come into existence without the other and they cannot come into existence simultaneously. If many communities today find the tax-burden onerous and look with jaundiced eyes at the appropriations for schools, it does not require much imagination to anticipate the reaction to a school budget that will make teaching a comparatively well-paid profession.

Thirdly, if local communities cannot secure the services of able and well qualified teachers, it is practically inevitable that they will set their own standards of qualification. When they do so, among the criteria of selection may be capacities and beliefs that are incompatible both with professional capacity and integrity. And yet the need for good teachers is no less in communities that cannot afford them than in communities that can. Perhaps their need is even greater. However this may be, the morale of the profession and the public respect for it require uniform standards of certification as far as possible. Special circumstances and special regions may require special qualifications but these should be over and above, not a substitute for, a common minimum of professional training.

None of these practical difficulties, it seems to me, can be overcome throughout the country unless the certification of teachers and their remuneration become a matter of federal concern. Federal support and federal administration of education do not necessarily entail federal control of education in any objectionable sense. So long as the Federal Government does not attempt to lay down doctrine or impose curricula upon the schools, so long as the goals, and methods of the educational process are developed by local Boards of Education with the cooperation of professional educators and concerned parents, there need be no fears for the traditions of freedom. On the contrary by liberating schools from the burden of material care, a new era of educational freedom and experiment may set in. On educational and ethical grounds an excellent case can be made for underwriting the educational budget of the country as a whole by the resources of the country as a whole.

The day may be far off before all this comes about. It is not necessary, however, to wait supinely for it. The members of a profession that numbers more than two million can do something as teachers, as parents, as citizens to improve the status of the teaching profession and thereby raise the quality of the day by day teaching woven into the texture of every child's life. No work is more needful. No work is more useful even when not completely successful. No work so clearly benefits ourselves, our children, our nation, and the cause of universal freedom.

Part III:
Appendix

For their historical interest I reproduce in the following two chapters most of the text of two papers—one originally written in the mid-thirties and the other in the mid-fifties. They throw some light on the continuities and differences in the educational climate of those decades as compared with the seventies.

17

A Challenge to
the Liberal Arts College
of the Thirties

Whether by accident of training or personal inclination, the overwhelming majority of teachers in American liberal arts colleges are little interested in philosophy of education. The phrase itself suggests to them loose palaver and amorphous subject matter that had better be left to specialists in such things in schools of education. Yet it would be comparatively simple to show that the solution of most of the professional and special problems which have a concrete impact upon the life of the individual teacher involves the larger issues of educational policy and philosophy. Questions of academic freedom, salary, tenure, faculty participation, departmental growth, or retrenchment—even the very continuance of subjects in the curriculum require, at some point, reflection upon the nature, future, objectives, and justification of the liberal arts college. When such reflection takes place only in years of declining enrollment and shrinking endowment income, it suffers the disadvantage of all belated thinking. It is apt to be content with *ad hoc* proposals, to be nearsighted and opportunistic, and to cease when "things pick up."

Even if it were possible, teachers would find it undesirable to let administrators think for them on fundamental questions of

277

educational philosophy. Nor would enlightened administrators themselves desire it, for in the last analysis it is the teaching corps that must implement all educational reform. What is carried out in the spirit of cooperative understanding is more likely to be fruitful than the mechanical fulfillment of an administrative decree. The real difficulty as far as faculty opinion is concerned is that it usually knows better what it does not want than what it does. And, as a rule, what it does not want is any change that may affect the relative position of departments to one another or modify teaching procedures which habit and tradition have made easy and natural. Perhaps the most important single reason for the lack of a positive educational philosophy among liberal arts college faculties is that in the past they have not been encouraged to think of such matters, and that no effective mechanism has existed to transmit whatever thinking has been done to those in a position to act on it.

The effects of social changes outside the liberal arts college have brought into focus problems that cannot be met without fundamental revaluation of the objectives and curricular organization of the liberal arts college. The overcrowding of the professions, the growth of unemployment, the decline in endowment gifts, the decrease of student enrollment in many institutions, the sharpening of ideological issues—in short, the manifold consequences of periodic economic depression—have resulted in a general challenge to the liberal arts colleges to justify their educational procedures. The colleges generally have not been insensitive to this challenge. From one end of the country to another, experiment and discussion are rife.

The present paper is a contribution to this discussion. It attempts to formulate a set of objectives for the liberal arts college in the modern world, and to indicate briefly the general curricular changes which follow as corollaries.

Before proceeding with the argument, it is necessary to look at the phrase "liberal arts" a little more closely. For unfortunately, many proposals for revision of current educational practices are ruled out as incompatible with the meaning of "liberal arts," as if there were a clear unambiguous meaning attached to the phrase that strictly determines what its content should be. If it is freed of historical associations and derivations, and examined in terms of its actual function in use, what does the educational concept *liberal arts* mean? What is its opposite? The useful arts? But who among the defenders of the liberal arts will admit that they are useless? Sometimes the liberal arts curriculum is contrasted with the vocational curriculum. This, as we shall see, has some interesting implications, but as a matter of fact the liberal arts college used to train for vocations too. The teachers, ministers, and better-paid public servants have largely been drawn from the ranks of the college-educated, and even today a liberal arts education is a sufficient preparation for many kinds of careers. Flatly to contrast the liberal arts with the vocational arts is merely to express the invidious distinctions that one set of vocations—those which regard themselves as the primary banner bearers of culture—draws in relation to others.

Sometimes the goals of the liberal arts college are defined in more exalted terms, but they never serve as criteria of differentiation. For example, not infrequently we hear that the objective of the liberal arts college is "the discovery and achievement of the values and significance of life, through the organization of knowledge, the development of discipline, and the conservation of the common good." This is fearfully vague, and on occasion nothing more than a platitudinous evasion of thought. The vagueness becomes apparent just as soon as we ask, What values? What knowledge? and What is meant by common good? But whatever is meant, such a characterization does not distinguish the liberal arts college from other institutions. It requires considerable hardihood to maintain that a typical product of a vocational scientific school, say an electrical engineer, is less concerned with the common good, less disciplined, and less inspired by the spiritual values of life—whatever these are taken to be—than a superior product of the liberal arts college, say one of those much-lauded students who complete their studies with an undying interest in Virgil or Proust.

From almost any point of view the distinction between the liberal and vocational is a difficult and shifting one. It is almost universally recognized that courses called cultural can play a helpful and liberalizing role in vocational curriculums by providing a sense of the social context within which technical knowledge can be applied. Moreover, I do not believe that any harm would be done if certain courses, called vocational, particularly those which demand the use of one's hands and eyes in aesthetically satisfying activity, were to be introduced into the liberal arts curriculum.

We can describe what liberal arts colleges do, but we cannot at the outset define what they are; for no definition will be adequate to what all colleges which call themselves liberal arts colleges are doing. Consequently, no proposal for reform of the liberal arts college can be ruled out on the ground that it is not in keeping with the meaning of liberal arts. Since there are many kinds of liberal arts colleges and many ways of conceiving their meanings, intelligent discussion can revolve only around the question: What *should* be the meaning of a liberal arts education? When this question is raised, nothing can be ruled out by definition.

Although it is impossible to discover a common purpose in all existing liberal arts colleges, it is easy to point out common weaknesses. These weaknesses are reflected in two types of criticism that may be leveled against the liberal arts college. Out of these criticisms, some suggestions for the objectives and curriculum of the liberal arts college will emerge.

The first type of criticism flows from the fact that students of liberal arts colleges, thrust out into the world after their formal education is over, rarely know what they are qualified to do. When they do know, they are often unable to find appropriate opportunities for putting their talents, interests, and educational accomplishments to socially profitable use. Few are the college teachers who have not heard their students ask at the end of their four years: What am I fitted to do? What can I do? How can I find work which will permit me to deepen the interests I have already acquired? Granted that the student has increased his mental stature and emotional maturity, has a liberal arts education no further function to perform? Is the further significance of the liberal arts training to be found only in the differential economic value a college degree has in the marketplace?

A Challenge to the Liberal-Arts College of the Thirties

There is a considerable number of educators, some active in colleges which are more like country clubs than institutions of learning, who would promptly respond that this is no concern of the liberal arts college. They would assert that the circumstances which make it unlikely that the majority of liberal arts college graduates will be absorbed in socially useful and remunerative work, are beyond the control of the college; that the graduates of vocational schools face the same situation. They believe that students who study for any other reason than sheer love of it are introducing base material considerations, and therewith prove themselves to be no true students at all.

These answers, now grown quite fashionable in some authoritarian educational quarters, which seek to divorce the liberal arts college from any of the vocational liaisons it has contracted in the years of the so-called prosperity era, express under present social conditions a dangerous class conception of education. They presuppose that a liberal arts education is to be the exclusive concern of that class which need not face the pressing concerns of combining educational interests with an active career. In short, they form a leisure-class conception of liberal arts education no matter what educational rationalizations are offered in its support.

Despite the tissue of cloudy verbiage which covers the concrete proposals for the "pure" liberal arts college, we must recognize this policy for what it is—a break with the democratic conception of American education and a conscious stratification of the educational potential of the country in terms of income levels. Whether the theoretical formulations of this position call for training in leadership, or for a curriculum which is classical and conservative, or for a student body which is aristocratic in social outlook is of subsidiary importance. Nor does the fact that—despite its avowed social independence—a body of students so circumspectly selected is sure to serve, politically and socially, certain tendencies in government and business, gainsay the dangerous implications of this sharp separation in principle between the cultural and the vocational.

It is true that colleges cannot appreciably affect or control the

281

social conditions which frustrate the careers of so many of their graduates and jeopardize the integration of work, personality, and status in the community. But the conclusions which should be drawn from this are not that vocational ties with the outside world should be broken—How indeed could this remedy the situation?—but that efforts be intensified by the college, in co-operation with other social agencies, to study, explore, and suggest the possibilities of vocational activity which the changing social order opens to culturally and technically trained men and women. More educational institutions believe in individualization of punishment than they do in individualization of guidance and educational experience; but individualization of guidance—sadly neglected as it is in most liberal arts colleges—is not enough. Students cannot be helped to find themselves *in abstracto*. They must find themselves in relation to the concrete social situations of which they sooner or later become a part. This has import for the question of curriculum, but it also has bearings upon the attitude of the liberal arts college to the future of its students. The future of its students must be as legitimate a concern as their past. College instruction and guidance in the present must reflect that future just as they now, in some ideal cases, reflect the students' past. In a rationally conceived plan of education at least as much attention would be given to "disposing" of students as to "getting" them. Were the college to recognize this as its responsibility—a responsibility that in most cases might not extend further than weighty advice—far-reaching changes, whose detailed character cannot be elaborated here, would ensue.

There are many problems which must be met by this assumption of new responsibility. Such problems do not exist for those who subscribe to a leisure-class conception of liberal arts. But they may in consequence have to face others. From any point of view it seems a hazardous thing for the liberal arts colleges, which are public or, through remission of taxation, semi-public institutions, and therefore ultimately dependent upon community support, to pretend that what goes on within their walls is one thing, and what goes on beyond them, another. No matter how pure its pursuit of truth and scholarship may be, once the vital connections between curriculum interests and the larger social interests of the community are lost, the college is imperiling its own future.

There is an even more important criticism, however, which may be directed against the typical liberal arts college curriculum. It is addressed ofttimes by the student to his erstwhile teachers when asked to review and assess his schooling. He finds the world in a state of political ferment and the social order in transition, but his knowledge and training are largely irrelevant to both. At no time, with the possible exception of the first century of the Christian era, has the individual been confronted with so many conflicting paths to social salvation and damnation as today. The average student graduates from college chronologically qualified as a citizen of the political community, endowed by virtue of his youth and idealism with more energy for good or evil than any other age-group, conscious of the limitations of existing leadership, and yet tragically unprepared to orient himself to the stormy winds of doctrine blowing from all points of the compass. He may be in possession of oddly assorted items of information of varying degrees of accuracy, but he has little understanding of the actual functioning of the social order—its tensions, trends, and basic problems. He may be in the grip of a political religion, and unequipped to examine critically the enthusiasm to which he is captive. He may be indifferent, bewildered, or a victim of sloganized thought. Finding that the classroom, his teachers, his textbooks, do not make the world intelligible to him, he is apt to pick up a universal formula or a panacea from the pamphlet of a zealot. He probably knows more about the eighteenth and nineteenth centuries than about the twentieth—since he lives in the present, he apparently does not have to study it. He probably thinks that science is "great stuff" but has little knowledge of the elements of scientific method, and applies it to problems of current life and society even less.

The extent to which this attitude prevails even in the cures offered for American college education is illustrated in the curriculum of a recent college whose basic course of study consists of the world's hundred greatest books. At the end of the third year, the students have reached as the furthest point in their study, a book published in 1739. In the remaining year of their education everything from 1739 to the present is covered, with only two books considered in the twentieth century, both in higher mathematics. Not a single work published since the First World War, a not unimportant event in history and culture, is even on the list. Aside from the violation of sound pedagogical principles involved in the whole conception, this is social snobbism in reverse. Apparently the social problems of all times are worthy of study but not our own. The problems of unemployment are a legitimate subject of investigation if only they bear on the decline of the Roman Empire. Modern architecture, housing, and politics would warrant attention in the curriculum if only they could be shown to be continuous with the problems of the Greek city-state. The critical study of the speeches of politicians is vulgar unless the politicians have been dead at least two thousand years when they have acquired the dignity of statesman.

In his well-known *Idea of a University* Cardinal Newman defined the purpose of a university to be primarily the discovery and publication of the truth. In this sense the liberal arts college is obviously quite different from a university, for only few can be pathfinders in the search for truth. He assigned, however, a practical function to the university that can with greater plausibility be applied to our liberal arts college. He said: "If then a practical end must be assigned to a University Course, I say it is that of training good members of society." An inescapable ambiguity lurks behind the undefined concept of the good, but however it be defined, it is possible to discover what the necessary elements are in the preparation of good members of society. The challenge of the social order to the liberal arts college is a challenge to abandon the policy of cultural dilettantism and to prepare its students, by appropriate educational experience in the present, to make intelligent choices among the fateful alternatives being shaped for them by the development of new social forces and problems. This in turn represents a challenge both to the present curriculum of the liberal arts college and its methods of instruction.

284

A Challenge to the Liberal-Arts College of the Thirties

The time is passing, fortunately, when an eminent educator could publicly proclaim that it was preferable that students confine themselves to the mysteries of the forward pass than concern themselves with the mysteries of politics. The forward pass has its place on the college campus, but more important is the organization of a curriculum that will make every student aware of how the society in which he lives functions, of the forces molding his civilization, and of the crucial problems of his day which await decision. This knowledge is necessary for every student because no matter what his specialized pursuit may be, the extent to which he can follow it and the contextual developments within his own field depend upon social situations outside it. An engineer today whose knowledge is restricted only to technical matters of engineering, or a physician whose competence is limited by traditional medical training, is ill-prepared to understand the basic problems which face his profession or even to plan intelligently for a life career. The conditions of effective functioning in any vocation depend upon those pervasive social tendencies which set the occasions for the application of knowledge, provide employment, and not seldom determine even the direction of research. The social factors which influence the individual as a person and a citizen sooner or later affect him as a specialist. The first corollary then of our discussion is that a prescribed social science curriculum, properly integrated into problem and survey courses, must be basic in a modern liberal arts education.

To assert this in the present departmentalized setup is almost like a deliberate invitation to misunderstanding. A social science-oriented curriculum, however, does not mean that the courses which are now given by the social science departments—courses that only too often justify students' references to them as "snap" courses—are to constitute the core of the curriculum. What is intended is that courses be organized around *focal social problems* and given not by a particular department but by competent individuals from any or all departments. Courses of this kind are not something which already exist; they are something to be achieved. Their content is definite but not fixed. They do not

285

exclude the study of historical background and origin but apply simple principles of relevance to direct the selection of material from out of the unlimited past. They do not exclude great books of the past and present but only arbitrary lists of books that indicate what the teacher has read or would like to be able to read. They do not exclude tool courses where these fit in with individual needs discovered by the type of guidance discussed here, nor courses which foster appreciation of the arts that enrich and enlarge the student mind; but these are to supplement education in those social realities which affect every kind of personal and vocational activity the student will subsequently engage in.

The disciplined intelligence, the relevant knowledge, and the capacity for cultural appreciation, associated with the liberal arts college in the minds of traditionalists, are not thereby ignored. Indeed, a good case can be established for the likelihood that these qualities will be more significantly achieved by a curriculum that makes the major social problems central than by the majority of contemporary liberal arts curriculums which are neither classical nor modern but a sweet-sour mixture of credit courses leading to a degree but not to an education. There is not a single value claimed for the traditional liberal arts curriculum that cannot be more widely, adequately, and interestingly realized by a curriculum integrated around the basic social problems of our times. Certainly, if we judge the success of the liberal arts colleges by the findings of Mr. Learned acting for the Joint Commission of the Association of Pennsylvania College Presidents and the State Department of Public Instruction as well as the Carnegie Foundation, it would be hard to imagine any reform which will lead to a more scandalous situation.

Knowledge of the social and technological scene is necessary, but knowledge alone does not determine policy. Policy is the use of knowledge in behalf of certain aims or ideals. Knowing the nature of the social world, the question arises: What should be done about it? Every social philosophy is a proposal that something be done in the world, a plan of action to conserve or change aspects of social life. A glance around him is sufficient for the intelligent student to see that the community is arrayed under different banners, that conflicts rage not so much about what is but about what should be. Knowledge is sterile unless fructified by ideals and values. In the press of controversy, however, these ideals and values are usually affirmed as acts of faith. They are partisan commitments justified only by the emotional security they give to believers. They spread by contagion, unchecked by critical safeguards; yet the future of civilization depends upon the character of these faiths. It is therefore requisite that their study be made an integral part of the liberal arts curriculum. Systematic and critical instruction by competent teachers should be given in the great maps of life—the ways to heaven or hell—which are being unrolled in the world today. Ideals and philosophies of life are not parts of the world of nature, but it is a pernicious illusion to imagine that they cannot be studied scientifically. Their historical origins, their concatenation of doctrine, their controlling assumptions, their means, methods, and consequences in practice can and should be investigated in a scientific spirit. There are certain social philosophies which would not dare to undertake such an investigation for fear of not being able to survive it, but it is one of the great merits of the democratic way of life and one of its strongest claims for acceptance that it can withstand analysis of this sort. It is incumbent upon the liberal arts college to provide opportunities for close study of all the dominant social and political philosophies, ranging from one end of the color spectrum to the other.

Instruction in the social and technological forces shaping the world, and in the dominant conflicting ideals in behalf of which these forces are to be controlled, goes a long way. But more important than knowledge, is the method by which it is reached, and the ability to recognize when knowledge constitutes evidence and when not; and even more important than any particular ideal, is the way in which it is held, and the capacity to evaluate it in relation to other ideals. From first to last, in season and out, the liberal arts college must emphasize methods of analysis. It must build up in its students a critical sense of evidence, relevance, and validity against which the multitudinous seas of propaganda will wash in vain.   It must enable its students, through their own independent thinking, to confront the claims of ideals and values with their alternatives and the relative costs of achieving them.

The present-day liberal arts college is conspicuously weak in developing critical intelligence. Judged by its curricular efforts to teach students how to think, how to read intelligently, how to approach problems, how to formulate relevant and searching questions, the liberal arts college must be pronounced a dismal failure.   This failure is not only intellectually scandalous, it is socially dangerous.   For the natural susceptibility of youth to enthusiasms, its tendency to glorify action, and its limited experience, make easy recruiting material for all sorts of demogogic movements which flatter its strength and impatience.   Recent history furnishes many illustrations of how, in the absence of strong critical sense, youthful strength can lead to insensate cruelty and youthful impatience to extraordinary folly.   It is true that people who are incapable of thinking cannot be taught how to think, and that incapacity for thought is a failing not restricted to the young. Most students can, however, and should be so taught that at the very least they are made aware of whether they are thinking, of what they are thinking, and the evidence one way or the other for conclusions heard or advanced.   The specific instrumentalities by which this is to be achieved, whether through special courses or special methods in all courses, cannot be discussed here, but there is one guiding principle that must be observed; the critically minded teacher *may* fail in developing logical thought patterns in his students; the uncritically minded teacher *must* fail.   Any revision of the curriculum of the liberal arts college is doomed to futility unless it involves a revision of the haphazard character of selecting teachers in the liberal arts college.   The education of the college student is at least as important to the community as the education of the young child.   Should not as much thought and concern be devoted to the qualifications and criteria of good college teachers as to good kindergartners?   But this is a theme for another occasion.

The proposed reorganization of the curriculum of the liberal arts college revolves, then, around three fundamental principles:

first, making the student aware of the major social problems of the world in which he lives and is going to live, and providing the relevant knowledge from any field necessary to understanding them; second, critically orienting the student to the philosophies of life, society, and history in behalf of which such knowledge is used; and third, emphasis upon method in evaluating both facts and values. Is this all? many are sure to ask. Are not the colleges to teach specific social doctrines—conservative or liberal or radical? Are they to be—can they be—neutral in the great social struggles of the day? Vocational considerations and courses in the area of free election aside, I am prepared to assert that the fulfillment of the objectives just listed exhausts the genuinely educational function of the *required* curriculum in the liberal arts college. The college as such is not called upon to formulate, or impose, or indoctrinate its students with either a philosophy of life or a philosophy of society. Neither money nor metaphysics should serve as principles of organization although the sources of money and the varieties of metaphysics may constitute legitimate objects of inquiry. Its bias, if a conclusion reached by analysis and argument can be called that, extends only to the selection of the subject matter which it considers educationally relevant, that is, to the social science-centered curriculum, and its reliance upon the methods of scientific inference. But it must not tie its teaching of that curriculum to a political or class view. This does not mean that teachers are to be prevented from presenting their own opinions or solutions of problems, after a critical examination has been undertaken of available relevant alternatives. *Officially*, however, the college must not identify itself with one partisan group rather than another. Its aim must be the objective study of social conflicts, not their resolution. The practical function which Cardinal Newman assigned to the university is to train good members of society, not members of the good society. I would modify this, in a way which Newman's theological commitments would not allow, to say that it is to train "better" members of society, that is, individuals who can make their own discoveries and decisions about the nature of the good society.

Does this not run counter to the widespread and legitimate

assumption that the colleges must serve society? No, unless by serving society is meant being a servant of society—Fascist under Fascism, Communist under Communism, and happily confused under democracy. In building the curriculum just described, the liberal arts college is meeting its obligations to the community—obligations conceived in the spirit of loyalty not merely to present social needs but to the great traditions of the past and the still greater possibilities of the future.

There remain several questions concerning the relationship between the required liberal arts curriculum and the problem of intelligent guidance. The former is general; the latter, necessarily individualized. The most practical arrangement would be to begin with the first but not to end it when the period of specialization commences. Required courses that precede electives tend to become conventionalized, and since they are taken when the students are relatively immature have little effect upon later habits of thought, particularly if two years of study intervene between the end of the required curriculum and graduation. It would be foolhardy, however, to attempt to deduce details of organization from the basic principles discussed here. They are offered as principles to guide the liberal arts program, not as blueprints to be put into effect everywhere at once. Each liberal arts college must begin with its own problems and community relations. Further experiment is not precluded but a frame of reference is necessary to prevent experiment from being blind.

18

Education
& Creative Intelligence[1]

It is related of William James that he began a course of lectures by reading to his class large extracts from Henry Sidgewick's "Lecture against Lecturing." I must confess that whenever I discourse about education I feel like discoursing about the futility of discourse about education—particularly the ends of education. How multiple, encompassing, and vague are the recommended ends of education! Education for citizenship, education for maturity and health, education for world and intercultural understanding, education for self-understanding, education for freedom, or loyalty, or peace, or vocation. Despite this plethora of apparently diverse principles, educational practices at any period, barring professional schools, do not exhibit a commensurate diversity. Most schools and colleges until recently have done pretty much the same thing after a while, despite what they said. The history of education, especially American education, leads one to the generalization that educational institutions respond more to social

---

[1]Read in part at the 27th annual meeting, Eastern Association of College Deans, Atlantic City, N. J., Nov. 26, 1955 and at the biennial conference, Association of Wisconsin State College Faculties, Eau Claire, Wis., April 27, 1956.

needs and pressures than to first principles. It would be extremely hazardous to guess *what* a college is teaching or *how* a college is teaching on the basis of knowledge of its declared objectives alone. This tempts us to the conclusions that the formulations of ends and principles represent obeisances colleges make to the traditional ways of talking about education or, when news of change or innovation is in the wind, to the current jargon of reform. They are not reliable guides to what actually goes on in the classroom.

Although we are tempted to such conclusions, we should resist them, for it would follow that educational ideas and principles are of slight importance because of no immediately perceptible effect. If this were so, it would be hard to explain the fear in which so many people stand of educational ideas, or at least of some ideas. It would be hard, for example, to explain the prolonged, organized, and systematic vendetta waged against the educational philosophy of John Dewey, among the molders of American public opinion—newspapers, mass periodicals, and some of the churches.

This fear of ideas may be exaggerated. It certainly exaggerated the extent to which Dewey's ideas made headway in higher education. But it is testimony to the fact that ideas *do* count and that when they do not, they *can* count, not perhaps immediately but in time. Ideas count not because needs and interests, impulse and passion, cease to operate when we think, but because, as visions of possibilities and plans of realizing them, ideas gradually affect our own conceptions of our needs and interests. In this way, they acquire the motor power to change the world. The difficulty is to know when we have ideas and when we are merely repeating catchwords that trigger not thought but only emotion. The difficulty is to know when our words make significant assertions or proposals of a kind that are relevant and testable and when they are vacuous abstractions functioning as slogans.

At first blush it seems as if all this is provided for in contemporary education. If one reads, or listens to, discussions about the purpose of education, he will find there is not lacking in the enumerated objectives reference to the importance of "critical thinking," "the cultivation of reason," and "the use of intelligence." But there is a number of puzzling things to account

292

for. Is there any indisputable evidence that the college-bred or educated are more thoughtful about general social and human issues—about precisely those concerns which are crucial for the survival of democratic society—than those who are not college educated? How in fact do we *know* that we are educating for thinking? There are to be sure, some technical subjects like mathematics and physics which cannot be done at all except by thinking—and hard thinking. But these are just the disciplines from which there is no automatic transfer of thinking skills and habits to the field of social policy. The pronouncements of some of our greatest scientists on social issues, especially foreign policy, are certainly no more distinguished than those of lesser mortals, and are occasionally just as irresponsible.

Sometimes it is assumed that education in any academic discipline of an intellectually rigorous character necessarily makes for enlightened, *i.e.*, liberal and humane, attitudes in social affairs. Education for intellectual training, in this view, is *ipso facto* education for freedom. Before assenting, we would do well to reflect upon the historical fact that the great milestones in the achievement of Western freedom and the recognition of the rights of man were not primarily the result of movements born in the great universities of Europe whose vocation was scholarship. In the Wilhelmine era, the universities of the German Empire were the Mecca of scholars everywhere. Yet they were hardly notorious for being either centers of social enlightenment or democratic infec-tion. We owe the growth of freedom far more to the dissident churches and the labor and trade union movements than to the citadels of European learning. Indeed, to the extent that students and teachers were active in social affairs, aside from movements of national liberation, they gave leadership and support more often to reactionary causes than to liberal and democratic ones. European social-democracy was not born in the university.

In the United States, especially since World War I, the situation has been different. On the whole, the colleges and universities of this country, to the degree that they have had an influence on social affairs, have spoken for the *public* interest rather than a class interest. Nonetheless, that influence has been slight, mainly because of the absence of feudal traditions and of fixed physical and social frontiers and partly because of the role of demagogues in American political life, the distrust of ideas, "anti-intellectualism," and the absence of great ideas in the academies themselves.

With the emergence of the cold war, there developed a split in the attitudes of large sections of the general population on the one hand and, on the other, of members of colleges and universities and those associated with them in kindred pursuits. This split in attitudes was provoked by a whole cluster of issues posed by the conflict between the democratic and Communist worlds. Whatever differences in attitudes existed did not flow in the slightest from any sympathy toward Communism on the part of either group. It reflected different conceptions of the degree of danger and of the relevance and adequacy of different methods of combating Communism, particularly as the cumulative consequences of defeat and retreat made themselves manifest. Popular emphasis has been on what we may call security in its multiple forms; academic emphasis has rightfully been on freedom, especially the freedoms that are imperiled in the quest for security. Both elements are integral to the question, for, although at points they conflict, it is also true that the exercise of certain freedoms contributes to security, while the conditions of freedom must themselves be properly secured. At first glance, it is hard to understand why this was not realized. Nonetheless, it is undeniable that suspicion, distrust, and vague resentment were stirred up against colleges and universities leading to such foolishness as special loyalty oaths, while in turn a counter-sentiment of being distrusted, harried, and even persecuted was voiced on occasion among some of the faculties of the country.

The fact that our education has not immunized our citizens against waves of irrationalism should be a cause of great concern to us as educators. To a considerable extent, the trouble has been that our thinking about social and political matters, not only popular thinking but our own academic thinking, has become sloganized. Attitudes crystallize around expressions like "the American way of life," "national security," "freedom," "loyalty," "progressive education," and "free enterprise," which then become semantic fetishes that short-circuit genuine thinking. Genuine, fruitful thinking presupposes an awareness of problems and, where they are urgent, concrete proposals to meet them. A problem in human affairs is more than a mere difficulty or obstacle which can be forced or hurdled by effort. It involves the recognition of the presence of incompatible or conflicting value elements in a situation. It requires analysis of means, of concrete programs that strive to do justice to both value-elements, even though both cannot be realized in an unqualified form. It involves readiness to modify the specific ends-in-view with which we approach the problem in the light of the consequences of the means used. And whatever the solution, if there is a solution, it must involve reliance upon knowledge of relevant fact and, therefore, a willingness to inquire into the facts.

How much of our discussion of the multiple problems connected with freedom and security, at home and abroad, proceeds this way? The market place crying for security applauds any declaration and any measure designed to achieve it, independently of whether the declarations are followed up and whether the costs of the security measures in individual hardship and injustice are actually necessary. The academy, in the name of freedom, is eloquently and justifiably indignant about the abuses, hardships, and injustices of hastily contrived measures of security and of declarations which mislead us and others. Yet, it often gives the impression that there is no problem of security at all, only a synthetically concocted excitement about it; that the cold war is the result of bungling by Western statesmen, instead of a deliberately initiated move in the Communist strategy of expansion. But serious problems, like serious wounds left unattended, fester. Korea was a problem long before the U.S. withdrew her troops from it, and it is still a problem 150,000 casualties and 24 billion dollars later. But when thinking about it might have done some good, who thought about it? If those who are professionally concerned with ideas do not think about problems—problems that are sensed by ordinary citizens only as vague difficulties—then demagogues are sure to capitalize on public ignorance and frustrations. Happily, McCarthy was defeated, but not by the academy, not by the aroused intelligence of the country, but—by overreaching himself.

If in the abstract we define thinking as an affair of problem-solving, then in the concrete a great deal of our social and political discussion cannot be regarded as thinking, for it does not even reach the level of problem-facing but takes the form of the counterposition of slogans. Let us ask ourselves frankly: To what extent are the actual problems connected with the causes, spread, strategy, and threats of international Communism, and the defense of the free world against it, seriously studied as problems in our schools? The ironical truth is that far from being too much concerned with Communism, as the detractors of our schools charge, our institutions of learning concern themselves too little with its intelligent problematic study. The American Citizenship Committee of the American Bar Association once proposed that the study of the theory and practice of Communism be required in all secondary schools of the country. The recommendation was promptly voted down. This is significant; first, because the proposal came from educational laymen to professional educators who should have been the first to have given the subject curricular emphasis; second, because of some of the grounds offered for rejecting it. It was said that some students might be infected with what they study—a fear which no one took seriously—and, what was apparently the decisive point, that some teachers might have difficulties in their communities with local cultural vigilantes bitterly opposed to Communism.

What a commentary upon the educational scene! Communism is rightfully declared to be one of the most formidable enemies of free institutions, and yet in many quarters there is reluctance to study *how* formidable it is, *what* makes it formidable, and *how* the formidable danger can be reduced. How often have we heard Jefferson quoted to the effect that if a people expected to remain free and at the same time ignorant in the modern world, it was expecting what never was or will be? Denunciations of Communism which are uniformed, even when uttered by those who love freedom, are merely virtuous slogans and as ineffective as incantations.

Even more disturbing is to observe evidences of sloganized thinking in educational circles. This expresses itself in fantastic exaggerations of the forces of intellectual repression outside the academy, underassessment of the realities of freedom within it, and a neglect of manifold opportunities to do the necessary work of thinking without asking anybody's permission. We hear slogans like "the black shadow of fear" and "the reign of terror" which are supposed to exist in our colleges. Robert Hutchins with his characteristic flair for exaggerated inaccuracy claims that "everywhere in the U.S. university professors, whether or not they have tenure, are silenced by the general atmosphere of repression." Mr. Hutchins apparently can only hear the sound of his own voice.

It may be that we educators do not talk as much as we should, but we have talked more than we ever have in the past. The question is: What have we to say? My point is that we do not talk enough about problems, and the way we tend to talk seems ineffectual. As a kind of compensation for this ineffectuality, there is often heard in educational quarters a new slogan—the importance of nonconformism. It requires only a moment's reflection to see that the terms "conformity" and "nonconformity" are relational and that, unless one knows the what, why, and how of conformity or nonconformity, the terms are meaningless, more accurately emotive symbols communicating at best a mood.

On the other hand, if we define conformity merely as agreement of belief, we should have to say that scientific method is the most reliable method of achieving conformity, since it is the most reliable method of reaching agreement of belief. Who ever heard of a nonconformist mathematician as distinct from a meta-mathematician? If our language is silly enough, short-change artists and swindlers may soon call themselves arithmetical nonconformists. A man who professes a doctrine he does not believe may be called a conformist. Is he also a conformist if he sincerely believes it? Is he still a conformist if he has a good and sufficient reason for believing it? If you call such a person a conformist, too,

297

the term has no intelligible opposite that can be fruitfully applied in making necessary distinctions.

The life of intelligence consists not in the mouthing of slogans, no matter how traditional or liberal, but in analysis, in Socratic questioning, in uncovering presuppositions, drawing implications, defining fields of relevance, and elaborating hypotheses which are testable and which promise to lead to fruitful conclusions. Men thinking never make a slogan of "nonconformism." Those who do make a slogan of it tend to defy larger groups in which they have no roots or intimate associations in order to keep favor or status in some smaller group to whose prejudices they themselves conform with far greater "fear and trembling" of intellectual deviation than the philistines they condemn. This is particularly true of the psychology not only of left-wing political sectarians, but of ritualistic liberals. Nonconformism with the democratic outlook of the majority of the community is *de rigueur*, but is compensated for by an intense desire to conform with the canonical orthodoxy of the left-wing or ritualistic group.

Unfortunately, sloganized thinking breaks out in places where we have a right to expect some intellectual sophistication. A few years ago, the New York City Regional Meeting for the White House Conference on Education recommended, as part of its very first point, that our schools "should help develop the art of dissent." What is commendable in dissent as such? Gerald L. K. Smith and William Z. Foster were both dissenters. What we require is neither assent nor dissent but independent judgment. It is just as idiotic to make a fetish of dissent as of assent.

The task of education is not to produce conformists or nonconformists, but intelligent men and women who will see through slogans and who will take responsible positions on current problems of importance, unafraid to agree or disagree with anybody. But a position is never responsibly taken, whether of agreement or disagreement, of conformity or nonconformity unless it is based on knowledge of the relevant evidence in the case and on reflection of the consequences of alternative policies with respect to the evidence.

No society which seeks to meet the domestic or foreign problems with which it is beset can be indifferent to the intellectual character and level of the instruction given and received in its educational institutions. This is particularly true in a democracy like ours where each vote counts for one and no more than one and where the qualification for casting it, short of feeblemindedness or insanity, is not an intelligence test but a settled domicile and a minimum age. It is all the more true in a world of ever-growing technological, social, and economic complexity, where issues are rarely clear and never simple and on which experts frequently offer divided counsel.

Any pressure or threat, therefore, no matter what its source, no matter how sacred or patriotic its inspiration, which seeks to limit the free play of inquiry or exploration of possible alternatives and solutions to problems is, in the first instance, a grave blow to democratic society. In the most literal sense, it is a subversion of the assumption on which our society professedly rests. It abridges not a personal or selfish vested right of the teacher as a member of a professional guild but the civic right of all citizens to improve their chances of leading freer and more prosperous lives. It abridges it in much the same way as external interference with freedom of medical research is not merely an invasion of the physicians' sphere of competence but a deprivation of our chances to enjoy better health. This must be stressed, because, although it is obvious that where the health of the community is at stake the community must stand behind the physician, unfortunately it is far from obvious to many that where the wisdom of community decision is involved it is no less a community matter. That is why academic freedom is everybody's business and not only the professor's business.

In the natural sciences the lesson has been learned and the right of untrammeled inquiry largely won. It was not always thus, particularly when the physical cosmos was considered a moral cosmos. Even today when certain inquiries into problems of genetics seem to bear on social issues about which some persons feel strongly, we will hear hysterical outcries demanding the suppression of inquiry. On the whole, in democratic countries there is no political party-line or officially enforced church dogma which arrests the march of creative intelligence as it mounts from the earth and sea to the skies leaving behind awesome feats of engineering as its monuments. In social affairs, however, although it has some important technical achievements to its credit, like the institutions which make the life of a great modern city possible, creative intelligence lags far behind. It has not solved the social and human problems generated by the very triumphs it has won in bending material forces to human will. It has mastered the problems of production but not of full employment and equitable distribution, won our wars but not our peace, calculated to a nicety the logistics of human energy at work but failed as yet to make the work of most of mankind a significant and rewarding experience.

It is in the field of social problems and social conflict, broadly conceived, that our most pressing tasks lie. Not only must our creative intelligence devise the institutional patterns and procedures, the schemes and programs, to meet our own troubles, but it must also cope with the challenges of ancient cultures and peoples wakened to modernity by a touch of science and made feverish by a nationalism all the more virulent for being so long delayed. And, most difficult of all, we must work out techniques of persuasion to win the consent and cooperation of those affected by what we propose. Intelligence in human affairs, without infringing on the dignity of human beings or forgetting that persons are not raw materials, must show something of the same creative imagination and inventiveness in reconciling apparently incompatible ends, the same patience and willingness to experiment, which primitive man showed in solving the problems of how to get across a river without getting wet and his modern descendants, in learning to fly without breaking their necks.

The social and political problems of our age cannot be wished or prayed out of the world. They must be met somehow. The effect of scientific technology is to create new needs everywhere. Even in India where Gandhi's spirit is venerated, his way of life is not. Renunciation goes out of fashion among the masses when there really is something to renounce. Sooner or later institutions have to accustom themselves to the pressure of new needs which are historical variables and grow with the possibilities of their fulfillment. The question is not whether social changes will take place, but in what direction and by what means. Some of the groups that seek to curb or inhibit freedom of social inquiry are motivated by a professed fear of violent change or revolution. And yet the logic or illogic of suppression is that it tends to bring about the very things it fears. For, when habit or customary use and wont fail, as they do when social crises arise, only two alternatives of social control remain. The first is the method of creative intelligence whose life consists not in a quest for total solutions but in a series of measures of piecemeal change. The second is the violent method of reaction or revolution. If the scientific and experimental attitude in social studies is impugned or discouraged, if teachers are made to feel that the power relationships of society, which are in uneasy equilibrium anyhow, are beyond criticism, then the more successful the intimidation, the less likely are the chances for orderly and peaceful change. Those responsible for the change are failing, to adapt Erskine's phrase, in the moral obligation to be politically intelligent.

This assumes that morals and politics cannot be dissociated. Today our greatest moral problems are political problems. It also assumes that we can be intelligent about morals. *i.e.*, intelligent in our judgment of values, as well as in our judgments of fact. These are large assumptions. Let us examine them.

2

To some readers the argument so far, may appear as an elaborate exercise in question-begging. Am I not taking too much for granted in assuming that intelligence, whether of the creative or garden variety, can do justice to complex social affairs, especially value-conflicts? Am I not underestimating the strength of the irrational in men? Is it not, to start with, an illusion that human beings, especially in the mass, are willing to be guided by their intelligence in human affairs, even if it is available? And is it available? Does not modern science itself show that intelligence is merely an instrument of the power drives, class interests, ego, and idiomaniacal strivings of the subconscious? Have not even rational philosophers, like Bertrand Russell, proclaimed that "reason has nothing whatever to do with the choice of ends"?

These raise very large issues which can only be touched upon briefly. Let us begin with anti-intellectualism. This is a very ambiguous expression. If one is opposed to anti-intellectualism, must one be in favor of intellectualism? Intellectualism, in scientific philosophic circles, is usually prefaced with the adjective "vicious." "Vicious" intellectualism, as Peirce and James and Dewey criticize it, is a mistaken theory of the way in which intelligence operates. And they recognize that there are vicious anti-intellectualisms too. The issue among most philosophers is not whether we should use our intelligence or reason, but, rather, what is the proper analysis of intelligence or reason.

Anti-intellectualism as an issue which concerns the citizen is not a philosophical doctrine about modes of reason but a question of the causes and consequences of the attitude of distrust toward rational, scientific inquiry whenever a momentous practical or political decision is in the offing. This is not the same as a distrust of intellectuals. For very often in the past, especially in labor groups, this distrust has been of the social status of the intellectual, not of his intellectual function. The history of human culture does not show that professional intellectuals have been overly sympathetic to the needs and aspirations of the common people. In the literature of social apologetics the people have been portrayed as beasts of burden and, when aroused, beasts of prey. There is, therefore, a healthy kernel in the popular distrust of the social position of the intellectual which reflects the time when, as a priest or lawyer, clerk or tax collector, he was on the periphery of the ruling group but not a member of it. Significantly enough, such distrust was never strong against the physician whose function usually took precedence to his status. Some of that latent distrust is revived whenever it is proposed that human affairs be administered by experts or a "brain trust," with its connotation that a favored few have a monopoly of intelligence, if not of virtue.

To the extent that anti-intellectualism, by a process of transference, is directed from the past position of intellectuals as poet laureates of the *status quo* to the function of free intelligence in social or political affairs, it is largely the result of the activity of "bad" intellectuals. The demagogue is usually an intellectual manqué or frustrated, sometimes an "armed Bohemian," but always power hungry, who exploits the fears and grievances of the community—fears and grievances which the community, including those whose professional function it is to think, have failed to resolve.

But can they be resolved by intelligence? Let us look at some of the considerations urged against the possibility of its use. And by intelligence in this context I mean reliance upon the rationale or pattern of scientific inquiry to reach a warranted conclusion about fact and policy, which is emphatically not the same thing as the use of scientific techniques varying from field to field. A neurosis, which cannot be put in a test tube, can still be studied scientifically.

A common objection today calls attention to the complexity, unmanageability, and unpredictability of the world, especially of the social scene. It speaks contemptuously of "the optimistically drawn blueprints" and "plans" which seek to box humanly uncontrollable forces into their simple geometrical designs.

This objection can be put much more eloquently. But even if everything said about the limitations of intelligence were true, the conclusions would be a *non sequitur*. Granted that man is a finite, limited creature, temptable and fallible, what follows? How limited, how finite, how fallible is he—and how can we tell in advance of effort? How often has failure been redeemed by success? And, further, problems approached in a scientific spirit are not approached with blueprints but with hypotheses. Blueprints and detailed, definite plans mark a termination of a phase of inquiry and are scientifically subject to modification in the course of investigation and construction. To impose blueprints where the conditions of their application are absent, to force conclusions on facts, to insist on a plan irrespective of its consequences is precisely the opposite of the scientific attitude.

It is one thing to recommend intellectual humility, ten-tativeness, and a certain resignation to failure before the stubborn intractabilities of men and events. But it is quite another thing to speak with a Jove-like dogmatism about necessary limits of inquiry, thus making a claim that is belied by the profession of cosmic piety which prefaces such speech. We cannot be certain, this criticism tells us—a lesson scientific intelligence long since learned. We are then told of at least one thing that is certain—that we will fail.

There is not a single argument or consideration directed from this standpoint against the proposal to use scientific intelligence which does not, *mutatis mutandis*, hold for the field of medicine. The suffering we relieve today is no guarantee that we shall not suffer tomorrow from other, and perhaps, worse, diseases. Nor have we a guarantee that we will ever find a cure for cancer. But who, therefore, would stop the unremitting search for one? Of course, the social world is more complex than the biological and physical world, but this is no sure criterion of what exists within or without human power. Although we cannot plan the weather, we can plan to meet the social effects of the weather. If we can plan to defend ourselves in the eventuality of war, why are we foredoomed to failure in planning to meet changes in population, employment, migration, and price levels?

Another type of argument directed against the adequacy of creative intelligence to cope with the problems of men and society comes to the fore when we ask: "Very well, what should we put in its stead?" What is the third viable alternative to the methods of force and the methods of scientific intelligence? The answer comes in a thousand variations: tradition and history. The advocacy of scientific intelligence in social affairs is regarded as a continuation of that terrorism of Reason which in the past put the ax of criticism to the trees of tradition and threatened to transform the shady woods of human culture with its self-regulating ecology into an area of sandy desolation.

What is true in this charge is the insight, always relevant, that human beings cannot escape history when confronted by their problems. Indeed, in no area does intelligence start from scratch and, least of all, in social affairs. But history and tradition are taken as data when we are confronted by problems, not as solutions. Wise decisions take note of them not as the direct source of principles or ends, but as conditions which affect methods and means of carrying them out. The traditions and history of the South did not lead to the decision against segregation. If they spoke, they spoke for segregation. But its traditions and history are certainly relevant to the wise implementation of the decision. The very existence of acute social problems testifies to the fact that history and tradition are no longer sufficient to give the contentment and ordered satisfactions men require for their lives.

Those who invoke history as sacred usually do so to resist change. But since there never is one tradition—the American way of life, like the Greek way of life, is woven of many conflicting strands of thought and practice—and since history itself is a pattern of complex plural changes, anybody can read out of them ancestral blessings for any current venture. All history, including our own, is a record of revolution and civil war, as well as of evolution and peaceful cooperation. Logically, therefore, history cannot determine what we select from it as our guide. In addition, it should be apparent that some of the most difficult problems we face today arise from the conflict between cultures with different traditions and histories. We can recommend to each decent respect for the opinions and beliefs of the other. But we still must come to grips with the facts of objective conflict. To leave it to history alone is to leave it to war. There is no substitute for history but it is never sufficient.

There is also the view that any conception of creative intelligence which leaves God or the Creative Source of all intelligence out of our reckoning cannot provide a firm basis for social reconstruction and political wisdom. Any human plans not sanctioned by reference to the Divine Plan, it is said, invite disaster. It is unquestionable that there have been great religious revivals in our country, whose bearings on American education and culture have been marked. But what problems did they help solve? True, some years ago, Congress established for the use of its members a new prayer room. Who will contend that it had any effect on

305

legislation? I shall not discuss here the substantive assertions according to which the foundations of a good society rest upon religious principles. It is a very complex problem. My only question in this connection is the relevance of theological belief to creative social intelligence. It seems to me demonstrable that the "truths" of theology are compatible with any social system. God can never be left out of account, because by definition He is everywhere. The pertinent observation here is that from the same religious premises diverse recommendations have been drawn in domestic as well as foreign policy. For example, one group is inspired by its religious affirmations to call for a moral crusade against Communist aggression. Another group, on the basis of the same religious affirmation, urges a counsel of accommodation, caution, and unilateral disarmament, emphasizing almost as much the shortcomings and imperfections of the victims of Communist aggression as the crime of the aggressor. Now moral crusades, as well as policies of appeasement (which do not, of course, exhaust the alternatives), have been justified on other and purely secular grounds. Therefore, irrespective of the truth or falsity of religious or theological assumptions, they are neither necessary nor sufficient conditions for the solution of any social or political problem whatsoever.

This brings us to the view that the processes of creative intelligence can operate only where ends are antecedently given. The role of intelligence, we are told, is merely to fashion means to achieve ends about which we cannot be wise. This flies in the face of a long philosophical tradition, from Socrates to John Dewey, which has taught that virtue consists precisely in being intelligent or wise about one's ends. Now, if no one can be reasonable about ends, if intelligence is mere cunning in the use of means, virtue as well as wisdom is a superfluous word. On this position, ends are wishes or preferences or commands. As expressions of desire they are all on the same moral level. They are neither desirable nor undesirable, because, presumably, one can be intelligent about how to kill and about how to avoid getting killed. But the decision whether to kill or not to kill is outside the province of intelligence.

If this theory were valid, the prospects both for education and democracy would be grim indeed. The whole position is based on a faulty psychology and a failure to note that, far from our ends (whether conceived as wishes, preferences, or desires) being fixed, our moral problem actually arises when ends conflict. Most people in difficulty do not know what their ends are. We commit ourselves to our ends often blindly or on the basis of authority, but sometimes on the basis of verifiable fact, more particularly on the basis of what it costs us to realize them. The more we are trained to assess evidence in any field in which we make a choice, the stronger become our habits of evaluation and the more often do we modify the ends chosen or substitute other ends for them.

Sometimes, those who deny that intelligence can modify ends stress the extent to which human beings are swayed in their choice of ends by sophisms, propaganda, and brass bands. This is only too true, but the significant admission here is that ends can be and are changed. If they are modifiable by bad and irrelevant argument, there is nothing that prevents them from being modifiable by good or relevant argument, providing the capacity for intelligent inquiry exists and provided there is a disposition to use that capacity. And it is precisely here that the educational agencies of a democracy have an enormous responsibility. They must teach not merely the facts, but how to test them, how to relate them to problems, and how they bear upon relevant alternatives. They must also stir imagination and sensibility in envisaging the effects of proposed modes of conduct on the human situation. In other words, they must develop the habits of intelligent choice and decision in personal and social affairs, in the relation of person to person and persons to groups. Passion and emotion, as such, are not the enemies of intelligence. But prejudice is. And prejudice is passion or emotion expressed or formed outside the context of inquiry. Hume and his modern followers to the contrary notwithstanding, reason or intelligence is not necessarily the slave of the passions, even though the passions are always present. For intelligence can govern, modify, frustrate, and find substitute equivalents for passion, and this role, when it is exercised, is more like that of master than slave.

I do not pretend to have established my position here but only the intellectually grounded right to hold the view that we can and do intelligently reflect on ends or goals. For the healthy functioning of a democracy depends upon the emergence of an informed public opinion, one capable of appraising conflicting policies and choosing wisely among them, *i.e.*, being intelligent about ends although the means of execution may be entrusted to experts. If it were true that intelligence is incompetent or has no jurisdiction here, there is no way of distinguishing between the demagogue and the responsible leader. Every difference could become a provocation to a struggle, every struggle an incipient civil war. That social conflicts and class struggles are sometimes resolved by honest inquiry into their causes and consequences, and not by chicanery or physical force, suggests that we are dealing with a question involving not the *possibility* of using creative intelligence in human affairs, but with the question of its diffusion and degree.

This often gives rise to a shift of position. Granted, it is said, that ends are modifiable by intelligence. However, the capacity to use intelligence for that purpose is limited by nature. As society grows in complexity, the availability of intelligences able to settle difficult questions becomes less and less, leaving only an elite in a position truly to know what is for the best interests of society. But the assumption of democracy is that the majority of the electorate is sufficiently intelligent to determine what its best interests are and what are the best policies of furthering them. This is a fiction, so the allegation goes. Where the masses have power without knowledge, and without the intelligence requisite to acquiring and applying knowledge, they are a potential mob. Characteristically, emphasis is placed not on democratic process and participation, but on a type of constitutionality which keeps in check the unintelligent demands and desires of the masses, protecting them as much as the elite from the consequences of their own ignorance. The fear of the tyranny of the majority, about which we are hearing more and more, follows from the distrust of the intellectual capacities of the masses and the counterposition of the mob to the elite.

This tendency to think of the majority in a democracy as if it were a constant threat to the minority runs through the entire history of our country. In the main, this concern in the past with what a majority could do revolved around the fear for the safety of the institution of property. It was assumed that men's intelligence would be roughly measured by the amount of property they possessed, so that if those without property ever acquired the right of suffrage, they would immediately expropriate the propertied minority. This dread eventuality never occurred. The small property-holder used his suffrage in an attempt to prevent the large property-holder—Big Business—from expropriating him. But the fear of the majority remained. It often took the form of a desire to respect the civil rights of minorities. As a matter of fact, the legitimate rights of minorities have been more crassly abridged by other minorities than by majorities. But if it were true that the majority of men, in affairs of their common concern, were inherently and irremediably devoid of sufficient powers of intelligence to determine their interests and choose wisely from among ends, the basic assumption of democratic government would be rendered untenable. For that basic assumption, without denying differences in intellectual power among men, is committed to a belief in their educability. This was the source of the American faith in universal education, in the education of the masses at a time when, elsewhere in the world, education was a leisure-class privilege. No one put this faith more clearly than Thomas Jefferson, who wrote: "I know of no safe depository of the ultimate powers of the society but the people themselves, and if we think them not enlightened enough to exercise their control with a wholesome discretion, the remedy is not to take it from them, but to inform their discretion by education."

This does not mean that majorities are always right. Neither are minorities. It means, as Justice Frankfurter once put it, that the appeal from unenlightened majorities in a democracy must ultimately be made to enlightened majorities. It means that our reliance must ultimately rest not on vetoes or courts or any other mechanism which can be used just as well as an instrument of oppression as of defense of freedom, but on the liberal temper and rational spirit. This temper and spirit cannot be forged overnight to meet an emergency. It must develop in the course of the entire educational career of the student.

The essential proposition of the democratic faith is that men are sufficiently reasonable to discover, in the light of the evidence and the give-and-take of free discussion, a better way of solving their common problems than they can either through anarchy, on the one hand, or despotism, on the other. This proposition asserts a matter of fact. Is it true? It cannot be established as true by faith, but only by the same generic method of reasonable inquiry present wherever we seek to discover in any field which of two conflicting hypotheses is truer or more adequate. The evidence is not all in. Until the character of our education changes so that greater emphasis is placed upon the habits of reasonableness and creative intelligence, we may not be able to tell. Some evidence we have from our past history, but it is a mixed bag. Some evidence we have from social psychology, which suggests that, despite variations in native intelligence, in some fields consultation, discussion, mutual criticism, and committee thinking give better results than the pooled conclusions of individuals working independently of one another.

Not irrelevant to the argument is the evidence provided by the history of governments based upon elites, whether despotic or totalitarian. It may confirm Winston Churchill's observation that democracy is the worst possible form of government except all the others which have been tried.

Despite all the favorable evidence, our belief in democracy, which at bottom is a belief in the educability and reasonableness of man, involves a risk that in the future our creative intelligence may not rise to new occasions rapidly and effectively enough. We can fulfill our own responsibilities—by avoiding slogans, focusing on problems, keeping open the channels of free communication, putting our thoughts in order, and courageously defending them.